THE TRAMWAYS OF BIRKENHEAD AND WALLASEY

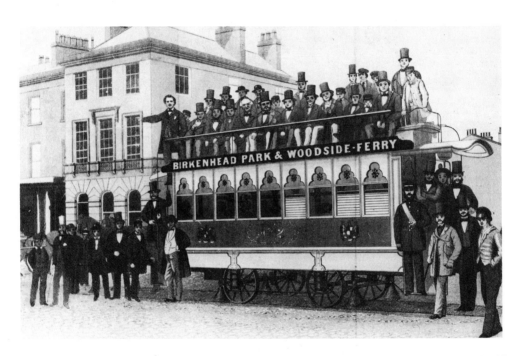

Birkenhead was always very conscious of its pioneer role in the history of tramways. This engraving was made from a photograph taken on 30 August 1860 (reproduced on page 33) showing the opening of Birkenhead's street railway. George Francis Train stands on the upper deck with arm outstretched, below him at street level is Robert Main, who assembled the American-built cars. The boy at the other end of the upper deck is James Clifton Robinson, later chairman of the London United Tramways. The photograph was taken in Hamilton Square at the junction of Argyle Street and Price Street. *(The Birkenhead News, 26 May 1900)*

THE TRAMWAYS OF BIRKENHEAD AND WALLASEY

T. B. MAUND, FCIT and MARTIN JENKINS, B.A.

First published 1987
ISBN 0 948106 03 4

Published in Great Britain by
The Light Rail Transit Association
Albany House, Petty France, London SW1H 9EA

Printed in Great Britain by
Netherwood Dalton & Co Ltd, Bradley Mills, Huddersfield, West Yorkshire

Contents

Introduction

The Wirral peninsula, sandwiched between the Rivers Mersey and Dee, possesses even today after several decades of urban sprawl and motorway development one of the most diverse landscapes in the United Kingdom. Seascape and river, docks and industry, slum and opulent suburb, unspoilt village and rolling farmland, all nestle together in an area twelve miles long by eight miles wide. The two largest and most important towns, Birkenhead and Wallasey, lie at the north-west tip of the peninsula.

In early times the Roman city of Deva (Chester) was the port and commercial centre of the region and the forest of Wirral was a desolate and thinly populated district lying to the north-west. The Dee was then the principal river, its numerous small ports providing the trading links to Ireland and the rest of England and Wales. As the Dee gradually silted up, trade moved to the Mersey and the fledgling port of Liverpool founded by King John in 1207. Liverpool had virtually no road links into the Lancashire hinterland until 1776 so most traffic crossed the river by ferry and continued by road towards Chester. Birkenhead and Wallasey owed their prodigious growth in the late nineteenth century to their close links with Liverpool and the development of their ferry services.

The origin of the name Birkenhead is believed to be Norse 'Byrkehaved' indicating a harbour, the 'Birk' stem appearing also in the name of the River Birket, one of the twin streams which fed the Wallasey Pool, a natural creek, later developed as docks which formerly separated Birkenhead from Wallasey. The latter name is said to be Celtic in origin, Wealas-ey meaning Island of Strangers or Welshmen. Surrounded by water on three sides and marshy bog on the fourth, it was an inhospitable place inhabited by smugglers and wreckers — "a place to be avoided" where even the clergy would exhort their parishioners to wait until the end of a sermon once a wreck had been reported so that all "could start fair" in the race for the spoils.

Before the Industrial Revolution the Wirral was largely agricultural with some fishing, the principal townships being Neston and Tranmere. Industrialisation of Birkenhead began in earnest in 1824 when William Laird built a boiler works on the south shore of Wallasey Pool. Later he transformed the Tranmere Pool into a shipbuilding complex, still occupied today by Cammell Laird's. He also supported plans to convert the adjacent Wallasey Pool into a port to rival Liverpool where dock dues were considered excessive. To avoid the congested Mersey approa- ches, a canal was considered which would have linked the Pool to the Dee. The engineers involved were no less a trio than Thomas Telford, Robert Stephenson and Alexander Nimmo. The scheme foundered but was later revived without the canal. The first docks in Birkenhead were opened in 1847 as part of a grand design to turn the whole Pool into a dock system — the Great Float. The last dock was opened at Bidston in 1933. From 1858 the docks on both sides of the Mersey were administered by the Mersey Docks and Harbour Board (MDHB) who were responsible for roads, bridges and railways within the dock estate.

Laird envisaged 'a magnificent city' at Birkenhead with elegant squares and long, wide streets laid out on a grid pattern. These grandiose plans were only partially realised as immigrant labour, largely from impoverished Ireland, flooded into the region especially after the potato famine of 1847 when over 300,000 arrived on Merseyside in the space of a year. Hundreds of small terraced houses were hastily erected, the town developing in a haphazard fashion with only Hamilton Square and a few splendid Georgian mansions surviving as reminders of Laird's original dream. Birkenhead thus became an industrial town with shipyards, docks and associated manufacturing activities. Hundreds lived within walking distance of their place of work but the wealthier middle classes, many of whom worked in Liverpool, lived in the town's Victorian suburbs.

Before 1830 Wallasey comprised a number of scattered settlements along the north bank of the Pool, the main village being Poulton a thriving little port with regular sailings to Ireland. Never supporting a real industrial base, small factories were established during the nineteenth century including a brickworks at Egremont and shipbuilding and pottery at Seacombe. Later the largest flour mills in the world were built on the Wallasey side of the Great Float. Modern Wallasey is an amalgam of the older hamlets with the newer areas such as Egremont and New Brighton both of which owed their growth to the expansion of the ferry network. The latter was conceived as a superior dormitory town for people working in Liverpool. There were to be tiered rows of villas each commanding an uninterrupted view of the Mersey estuary. However it developed primarily as a holiday resort with a catchment area extending to the Potteries, the Midlands and most of South Lancashire. Wallasey's population grew prodigiously and by 1920 42% of the working population was employed outside the town boundaries.

The ferry boats provided a life-line for both Birkenhead and Wallasey and the principal crossings at Woodside and Seacombe represented a journey of only ¾ mile. Ancient 'rights of passage' had existed across the Mersey since the Domesday survey. In 1330 the Benedictine monks of Birkenhead Priory were granted a Royal Charter to operate the Woodside ferry and levy tolls for the conveyance of both goods and passengers. The Seacombe right of passage gave the farmers of Wallasey access to the market in Liverpool.

From 1817 steam gradually replaced sail on the ferries of which there were ultimately ten — from north to south, New Brighton, Egremont, Seacombe, Woodside, Monks, Birkenhead, Tranmere, Rock, New Ferry and Eastham — those further up stream at Ellesmere Port, Ince and Runcorn falling outside the scope of this work. The advent of steam increased the reliability and regularity of the ferries encouraging a migration from Liverpool to the Wirral and this, coupled with improved landing facilities and vessels, led to the growth of considerable cross-river commuter traffic. This in turn prompted demands for internal transportation to convey passengers to and from the main ferry terminals.

The tramway history of Birkenhead and Wallasey is sharply contrasted. Birkenhead occupies a unique place for the tramway historian with its pioneer street railway opened in 1860 and its tramcar "manufactory". Many of the most famous early names in British tramway history either lived or worked in Birkenhead — G. F. Train, George Starbuck, G. F. Milnes, G. C. Milnes and Thomas Voss. The Birkenhead tramways were electrified and most of its fleet of electric cars delivered within the space of two years. Wallasey had only one horse car route and continued to expand its electric system until 1911. Birkenhead's last trams were delivered in 1913 and Wallasey's in 1920. Birkenhead's fleet of 65 passenger cars included some knife-board doubledeckers of a highly original design whilst Wallasey's 77 cars all bore a marked family resemblance.

Both undertakings suffered from railway competition especially after the electrification of the Mersey Railway in 1903 but Birkenhead was more seriously affected as passengers could choose between the train and the ferry. This forced the tramways and ferries departments to forge close commercial links and although such ties were hardly acknowledged at Wallasey, connections between tram and boat at Seacombe were meticulously observed. Both tramways lost traffic to self-inflicted motor bus competition in the 1920s and the extension of the Crosville bus routes to Woodside and Park Station further damaged Birkenhead. The trams in both towns were improved after the War but the retention of cars of Edwardian design hastened their demise. Abandonment in Wallasey spread from 1929 to 1933 and in Birkenhead from 1925 to 1937.

Abbreviations in the Text

AEC	The Associated Equipment Co Ltd		M&G	Mountain & Gibson Ltd, Bury
BTH	The British Thomson-Houston Co Ltd		P	Poulton (tram route)
Brush	The Brush Electrical Engineering Co Ltd		RE	Royal Engineers
cwt	hundredweight (20 cwt equals 1 ton)		RL	Rake Lane (tram route)
ER&TCW	The Electric Railway & Tramway Carriage Works Ltd, Preston		S	Seabank Road (tram route)
			sq ft	square feet
GE	The General Electric Company, USA		sq in	square inches
£sd	pounds, shillings, pence (UK currency to 1971)		UDC	Urban District Council
			UEC	The United Electric Car Co Ltd
McGuire	The McGuire Manufacturing Co, USA		WD	Warren Drive (tram route)

A brass token used as a prepaid fare on the Birkenhead Street Railway. The design on the reverse could represent either London's Marble Arch or the Birkenhead Park entrance. *(Williamson Art Gallery and Museum)*

1 The Birkenhead Street Railway

Early Transport in Birkenhead

In the early 1830s the population of Birkenhead was about 4,000 and growing rapidly. Town Improvement Commissioners were appointed in 1833 and they included such famous names as Laird and Brassey. The stone slipway at which the tiny ferry boats of the time landed and embarked their passengers was overlooked by the Woodside Hotel and at low water the ferry had to stand off, passengers being taken to and from the slip in landing boats or bodily carried by burly seamen. As traffic increased Hugh Williams, who ran both the hotel and the ferry, found it increasingly difficult to maintain an adequate service. He lacked the capital to expand and in July 1835, 18 prominent residents formed a company, the North Birkenhead, Woodside and Liverpool Steam Ferry Co., to take over the ferry lease. The new company built a substantial stone jetty and lighthouse which still exists as part of the ferry approach. Following the acquisition of new boats, a much safer and more reliable ferry service was provided and the town was set for a new period of expansion.

In 1837 the Chester and Birkenhead Railway Act was passed. The promoters viewed their line as a potential new route to Liverpool and the ferry interests correctly foresaw that whichever ferry secured the railway traffic would have a tremendous advantage over its competitors. The railway wanted to use Woodside but a clause in the Act precluded any extension to Woodside before branches were laid to serve Tranmere and Birkenhead ferries. The authorised terminus of the railway was at Grange Lane, approximately on the site of the later Birkenhead Town station near the present day Mersey Tunnel (Queensway) entrance.

A new ferry known as Monks Ferry was opened in 1838 as a rival to Woodside. Its claim to be the true successor of the Benedictine ferry was successfully contested by the hereditary owner of the ferry rights, F. R. Price and by the Woodside company as lessees, and Monks Ferry was closed down by an order of the court in 1840. Having established that there would be no legal objection to reopening the ferry purely for the use of railway passengers, the railway company purchased the assets of the Monks Ferry Company and proposed to link its station with its ferry by constructing a tramroad "on the surface of Ivy Street and the crossings of other streets". Plans were placed before the Birkenhead Commissioners on 7 April 1840, almost six months before the railway was opened to traffic but a Town's Meeting was distinctly

hostile and on 5 August 1840 the tramroad proposal was withdrawn. In due course the railway was extended in tunnel to Monks Ferry and Ivy Street had to wait another 37 years for its tramway. However it is of interest to note that the first proposal for a street tramway in Birkenhead came 20 years before the much publicised activities of G. F. Train.

In 1847 the railway was extended into the Dock Estate and over the years its tentacles reached every quay and warehouse. There were eventually three road crossings over the docks between Birkenhead and Wallasey and all eventually carried grooved railway tracks in the road surface. This complex network of railways, swing and lift bridges was to become a serious obstacle to the linking of the tramways of Birkenhead and Wallasey.

Gore's Directory for 1849 lists a number of omnibus services for the first time and it is unlikely that they originated much earlier than this date. They were of two kinds — the purely local routes performed by the Birkenhead men and the country routes, really a development of the stage coaches, performed by people based in the outlying villages. The horse-drawn omnibus was essentially a middle-class conveyance and remained so throughout its existence as its fares were too high to attract the patronage of the working classes on a regular basis. The early services were planned to provide facilities for business people to travel to and from Liverpool and the vehicles stood idle for the greater part of the day. The principal local service was run by Henry Gough of the Woodside Hotel from Woodside to Oxton and Claughton six to seven times daily; he also ran from Hoylake via Moreton at 8.00am and 3pm returning from Woodside on arrival of the 10am and 4.30pm boats and from West Kirby via Grange, Upton and Claughton at 8am returning at 4pm. On Sundays his vehicle left Woodside at 10am and returned from Hoylake at 6.30pm. Other country routes ran from Hoylake and Parkgate.

In 1851 Gough's service was running only between 4.00 and 8.00pm, an hourly service throughout the day being provided by Bretherton's (presumably the former stage coach operators) and a less frequent service by George Stacey of Village Road, Oxton. By 1854 Gough's business had been sold to Thomas Evans, a carriage proprietor of 14 Grange Mount. The Goughs are commemorated by "Gough's Landing", one of the bars in the present day Woodside Hotel.

The Evans family were among the many Welsh immigrants to Merseyside and Thomas, born on 5

December 1819, was destined to be the most influential in the transport affairs of Birkenhead. He and his relative James were both omnibus proprietors in their own right but worked closely together. In the early 1860s James was running a Woodside-Oxton service and occasional day excursions to Parkgate; carriages were hired out for weddings etc. He seems to have faded from the scene about 1865. In later years Thomas brought his sons into the business. He became a Town Commissioner in 1864 and was Chairman in 1871-2. After incorporation he became an Alderman of the new borough and was chairman of the Watch Committee for several years until 1892. In 1876 he was one of the subscribers to the Liverpool United Tramways and Omnibus Co. Ltd.

By February 1860 the principal omnibus service ran half-hourly between Woodside and the Talbot Hotel via Chester Street, Grange Lane, Devonshire Road, Slatey Road and Oxton Village from 8am to about 9.30pm. There were also five trips from Claughton (Balls Road) to Woodside via Palm Grove, Claughton Road and Argyle Street. During summer, four trips daily were run to the Green Lodge Hotel, Little Meolse and a Hoylake operator, Hornby, came into Woodside once a day from West Kirby. There was also a bus each morning from Lower Bebington at 8.45am returning from Woodside at 6pm. The proprietor is unknown and it seems to have succumbed to railway competition.

As the Evans' business expanded more premises were acquired and by 1864 business was being carried on from 2-4 Devonshire Road, 4 Chester Street and 44-46 Balls Road; there was also a forge at 1a Camperdown Street. Their vehicles ran under the fleet names "Atlas" and "Hero" which were well known in London horse bus circles and it is possible that some if not all of their vehicles were obtained second-hand from London and retained their original names. Another was named "The Spider" a fact which brought forth an uncomplimentary press comment in 1866. "Mr Evans' bus is well named the Spider. It only comes out in fine weather and a shower of rain sends it scampering back into its hole again. It would suck the traffic dry if it could but its web is only flimsy and its company more select than numerous. Not a desirable animal at all".

A Rock Ferry omnibus service, described as the 'Atlas' omnibus with six trips a day between Egerton Park and Woodside was started by Thomas Evans in 1862. It did not last long; the removal of Rock Ferry Station from Rock Lane to Bedford Road on 1 January 1863 may have affected it adversely as the new station was much closer to the middle class residential areas.

Reflecting Evans' lack of enterprise, an hourly Line of Docks omnibus service was introduced by a new proprietor, F. W. Theobald, as from 8 February 1864. Theobald was in a substantial way of business and his initiative was lauded in the local press. He was cartage agent to the Birkenhead Railway Co. and the Electric and International Telegraph Co., auctioneer and general commission agent with premises at Monks Ferry Railway Livery Stables and Theobald's Repository, Ivy Street. The service caught on and earlier journeys were introduced after only a week's operation; by late May, the addition of a second vehicle permitted a half-hourly service to be run. The terminus was nominally the Halfway House Hotel, Corporation Road but advertisements grandiloquently described the route as serving "Dukes Bridge, Halfway House, Canada Works and the New Graving Docks" and, in 1866, with the opening of the railway to Hoylake it most likely gained additional traffic as a railway feeder service.

Enter G. F. Train

George Francis Train had come to Liverpool from America as a young man in 1850 in connection with his family's shipping interests. The White Diamond line had been founded by Enoch Train by 1839 and had almost 20 sailing ships in the Liverpool-Boston trade by the late 1850s. In 1858 G. F. Train joined forces with Mr. James Samuel C.E. to promote a Bill in Parliament to authorise the construction of tramways in London and elsewhere.

Train was probably acting on behalf of Robert Morris, a Philadelphia merchant banker who had financed several American street railway schemes. James McHenry of Birkenhead appears also to have financed some of Train's English schemes and certainly rescued the Birkenhead line from extinction after Train had left the town. Street railways had become established in the United States and offered considerable advantages over the horsedrawn omnibus where there was sufficient traffic to justify the high initial capital expenditure, as the same horses could pull a much greater load and, if the track were properly maintained, the passenger enjoyed a much smoother and quieter ride. Train's Bill was thrown out, to a great extent because of the tenacious opposition of Sir Benjamin Hall, First Commissioner of Works, whose carriage had been involved in an accident whilst crossing a mineral tramroad in Wales.

Train was well known in Dock Board and other commercial circles. He watched with interest the experiments with omnibuses adapted to run either on the roads or the Dock Board railways, originated in Liverpool by W. J. Curtis in 1859. When, in January 1860, following the Dock Board's demand for a toll of one shilling per return journey for the use of their rails, the omnibus proprietors withdrew their vehicles, Train accepted the terms. His approach to the Dock Board apparently made the omnibus owners think again as the service was resumed and continued for several years. (See *Liverpool Transport Vol. I* by J. B. Horne and T. B. Maund, LRTA 1976). Train undoubtedly knew John Laird who was a member of the Dock Board and the most influential man in Birkenhead, and in February 1860 he approached him with a view to constructing a street railway in the town. On Laird's advice he wrote to the Birkenhead Town Commissioners on 9 March 1860 as follows:—

> Liverpool,
> 9th March 1860
>
> The Chairman of the Road &
> Improvement Committee,
> Birkenhead
>
> Sir,
> Being desirous of introducing Horse Railways into the leading thoroughfares of Birkenhead, as expressed in my letter to John Laird, Esq., of 21st February I hereby apply to you and the Commissioners for permission to lay down lines along the following routes:—
> > From Woodside Ferry up Hamilton Street and Grange Lane to Oxton and Claughton, returning by way of Claughton Street, Argyle Street, etc., and also from Hamilton Square to Birkenhead Park as a branch line.
>
> I should be quite disposed to adopt any other desirable route that your Engineers might suggest. If after 6 months' trial the Committee should desire the rails to be removed, I hereby agree, upon 3 months' notice, to take them up and put the road in good order again. As the rails will be laid level with the streets and roads, they will not offer the slightest obstruction to ordinary vehicles. On the contrary, the car track will rather invite carriages, carts and omnibuses.
> I am prepared to prove to you that the Horse Railway cars recommended themselves to the public as the greatest improvement yet known for street and road traffic.
> Their advantage may thus be summed up in contrast with the present omnibus. They are much more roomy and comfortable, are safer, more convenient of ingress and egress, especially for ladies, children and elderly people, run without jolting, noise, dust, mud and are more regular and punctual.
> The only privilege I request in consideration of the expenditure of money, time and labour, is the sole right to run on the rails a car with flanged wheels. With this conceded to me, I will undertake to keep the track in repair free of expense to the Town, thus saving to the ratepayers a great part of the paving rates, or if you cannot grant this exclusive right I will contract to keep the entire routes in repair at 10 per cent less than is now paid.
> I have a model at 5 Temple Place, which shows at a glance the working of this system of locomotion, and which I shall be happy to exhibit to any of the Commissioners who will favour me with a call.
>
> I am, Sir,
> Your most obedient Servant,
> Geo. Francis Train.

There was, as usual, opposition from the omnibus proprietors and others, but the Commissioners were impressed with Train, who had a dynamic personality and a persuasive manner. A contemporary described him thus:—

> "He has a strong Yankee twang about his speech which would at once stamp him as from across the herring pond. But apart from this he was a fine orator, had a great gift of language and was in every respect a cute and clever business man. He had a persuasive, unctious manner about him and, strange to say, whatever might be one's opinion on a matter George Francis Train could soon make him take a directly opposite view. He was most excitable yet a strict teetotaller. He was looked upon as an extraordinary man and was respected and popularised for being so. Most people trusted him whilst many idolised him . . ."

After taking legal advice, the Commissioners advised Train that they had no power to grant him exclusive rights to a part of the highway. Train's letter of 9 March has often been quoted but his second letter, repeated below, in reply to the Commissioners first decision was to have far-reaching consequences.

> To the Chairman, Roads and Improvement
> Committee, Birkenhead   29th March 1860
>
> Dear Sir,
>   Referring to my application of 9th inst. for permission to lay down Horse Railways in Birkenhead and to the remarks and explanations made by your Committee this morning, I now beg somewhat to modify my proposal so as to meet the views of your Law Clerk and Surveyor.
>   As it appears the Commissioners have not the power to grant me any exclusive right or privilege connected with the rails when laid, I withdraw this stipulation and invite all vehicles to use them trusting that I shall be protected from all unnecessary obstruction. The routes desired are:—
>   From Woodside Ferry, up Hamilton Street and Grange Lane to Oxton and Claughton returning by way of Claughton Road, Argyle Street and so on and also from Hamilton Square to Birkenhead Park with leave to extend them towards Bidston when desirable.
>   But I shall be quite disposed to adopt any more preferable routes that may be indicated by your Surveyor. Should the Commissioners, after six months' trial, desire the rails removed, I agree to take them up and restore the Roads to good order, three months' notice being previously given. And I shall consent to any equitable arrangement whereby the Commissioners may become possessed of the rails and stock should they wish.
>   Yours etc.
>   George Francis Train.

On 17 April the Commissioners received protests from landowners in Grange Lane and Claughton Road but nevertheless appointed a Special Committee comprising members of the Ferry and Roads and

Improvements Committees to come to terms with Train. This Committee was ultimately named the Street Railway Committee but was dissolved after about a year.

While the Commissioners deliberated Train patented his system and on 7 May 1860 the Birkenhead Street Railway Co. Ltd. was registered with a capital of £10,000 in £10 shares. "The egg", he said "will shortly be chipped in this country under my patent at great cost and labour and I shall endeavour to prevent my chickens (as is too frequently the case with valuable inventions) from becoming somebody else's hen".

On 22 May the Commissioners signed an agreement with Train authorising him to construct a double line from Woodside ferry, along Shore Road, Argyle Street and Conway Street to Park Entrance. The full details have never been made public but it is known that Train had bound himself to lift the rails and reinstate the road if the Commissioners were dissatisfied with the line. Sureties of £3,000 plus the plant and materials were given.

There was considerable opposition and John Laird dissuaded Train from pressing for other routes, believing that if the first line were successful tradespeople in Hamilton Street, Grange Lane, etc. would soon request the Local Board to grant permission for the street railway to be extended to all parts of the town. The Shore Road approach to Woodside was not ideal but the gradient on the lower part of Hamilton Street was too steep for the cars. One Commissioner, Mr. Aspinall confidently predicted that Mr Gough's Woodside Hotel would be demolished to provide a site for a grand "horse railway terminus".

On 4 July the *Liverpool Daily Post* reported that a petition had been organised and placed at the ferry, for the extension of the street railway to Oxton and Claughton. Soon after, construction started at Park Entrance and by 1 August was half way down Argyle Street. 56 labourers were employed and a few worked all night. On Sunday 15 July the works were visited by hundreds of people including many from Liverpool and a few Americans. Tenders were invited for horsing the cars and a few "competent and sober"

drivers were invited to apply at the office, 23 Lord Street, Liverpool on 31 July. The first car ran on the line at 4.00am on Wednesday 22 August driven by the engineer, Mr. Andrew Pallas of Philadelphia.

"The line answered to perfection notwithstanding that some of the curves formed an angle of 30 degrees" *(Daily Post)*. A full trial for Train and his associates took place on Wednesday 29 August and the following day the line opened officially with considerable pomp and ceremony. At 1.30pm all four cars, with a band aboard the first one, assembled at Woodside to meet the principal guests. The horses had bells on their collars and after the inaugural journey the cars went into public service until nightfall, carrying 4,500 passengers in all. Birkenhead, therefore, had the double distinction of having the first purpose-built street railway in Britain leading to the first public park to be established in Britain. The Park had been landscaped by Sir Joseph Paxton and opened by Lord Morpeth on 5 April 1847, the same day as Morpeth and Egerton docks.

As a stunt, Train had sent out invitations to all the crowned heads of Europe except the King of Naples. He also invited Garibaldi whose sons happened to attend school in Wallasey. In the event over 300 people of lesser eminence attended a sumptuous banquet and drank eleven toasts. Train presided and spoke at some length in reply to the toast of his health. The toast to the "Civil Engineers of England" was responded to by Mr. James Samuel of London who had acted in a consultative capacity.

A contemporary report published in the *Daily Telegraph* of 1 September 1860 states:—

"The cost has been from £1,800 to £2,000 a mile, and it would be greater where the roads are regularly paved. The vehicles which Mr. Train has had built will accommodate from 20 to 30 inside passengers and about the same number of outsiders (sic). Before each pair of wheels there is a broom or sweeper to remove stones or other obstacles.

"Two horses are used to each car and it is said that a speed of 7 or 8 miles an hour can be kept up without distress to the animals or real injury to the roadway."

Below: G. F. Train letterhead of July 1860.

GEORGE FRANCIS TRAIN'S PATENT.

G. F. Train stands on the front platform of one of the original Birkenhead Street Railway single deckers (3 and 4) at the junction of Argyle Street and Cleveland Street in 1860. The engraving is reproduced from Birkenhead Corporation Transport's 50-year jubilee brochure issued in 1951.

"The rails laid have a 6 inch surface of flat iron with a broad rim for the flanges of the carriage wheels which nowhere raise more than three quarters of an inch above ground level. Thus no obstruction is offered to vehicles crossing the rails; but always these vehicles have the chance of running at least one wheel upon the smooth metal instead of on the rough ground".

The *Illustrated London News* of 15 September 1860 throws more light on the proceedings:—

"As a mere spectacle, its inauguration possessed no particular attraction. Shortly before ten o'clock two of the new carriages were drawn out from the depot in Canning Street and placed upon the line. At eleven two horses were yoked to each and proceeded on their way well freighted with passengers, gliding along the rails at the rate of about four miles an hour — a rate of speed which might without difficulty be increased to six or seven miles an hour — smoothly and uninterruptedly. They continued throughout the day to ply for hire with a success which must have gladdened the hearts of the proprietors. To those who witnessed the actual working of the scheme none of its features appeared so prominent as the improvement, so far as increased accommodation is concerned which it has introduced. Travelling by one of Mr. Train's carriages, as contrasted with one of our ordinary omnibuses, is like quitting a narrow and confined room for a commodious and well-ventilated apartment"

The cars were built to the design of Andrew Pallas and imported in sections by Prentiss and Co., American oil merchants, who had premises in Birkenhead and whose principal, Elijah T. Prentiss, was a shareholder in the Street Railway Co. They were assembled by Robert Main, a Woodside coach-builder who moved from Woodside Hotel yard in June 1860 to 26 Canning Street. His new premises were near the north-east corner of the junction of Canning Street and Argyle Street, a site which some years later was destined to be obliterated by the Cheshire Lines goods yard. It was this yard which served as a depot for a year or two; here too was the banquet held in what has been described as an impromptu hall but was almost certainly a marquee. A letter of July 1860 survives requesting permission to lay a short connecting line in Canning Street. Main continued to trade for many more years and after his premises had been acquired, he moved to Parkfield Avenue. Another American, Mr. Bryan, was the manager of the line; he later became cashier at Mills Hotel in New York.

There were originally four cars, two double-deckers and two single-deckers — the latter being intended for winter service. They were 24ft long and 7ft wide with an inside height of 7ft. There were inside

11

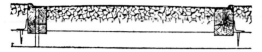
A section of the step rail used on Train's original line, and the method of laying the track. *(D. K. Clark)*

seats for 24 passengers and room for another 24 standing. This provision for straphangers was a new development in public transport in England as standing was not encouraged on omnibuses.

Upper deck seating was also for 24 on a long back-to-back "knifeboard" seat with a protective handrail round the outside. The cars were finished in an attractive light green livery outside and finely lined vermillion inside. Crimson plush cushions, carpets, sliding windows and slatted blinds completed the fittings. The double-deck cars (Nos. 1-2) carried the royal arms and those of Birkenhead whilst the single-deck cars (Nos. 3-4) bore a representation of the British lion and the American eagle with the motto "Unity is the strength of nations".

There is no doubt that they were far superior to the omnibuses of the time. In a very favourable editorial the *Daily Post* of 26 March 1861 remarked "You may actually walk about in them .... There is no danger of hats being knocked off". Another four cars were apparently imported from America in 1861; at least one of these was a one-horse car which the *Post* described as "light and elegant", advising its readers to take a ride to Birkenhead Park in it. Young drivers were employed on one-horse cars as a 16-year old youth, Thomas Mahoney, was killed in June 1861 when his car ran over him. Some, if not all, of the cars had names, like many omnibuses of the period.

Contemporary reports clearly state that the original line was built to a track gauge of 5ft 2in (or 5ft 2½in). This has been disputed by Klapper *(The Golden Age of Tramways, David and Charles 1974)* but correspondence between the company and the Commissioners in 1865 makes it clear that the gauge was, in fact, 5ft 2in. This was a common measure used in Philadelphia to describe standard gauge track of 4ft 8½in, the dimension being taken between the outside edges of the rails instead of the outside edges of the grooves. Train is known to have based all his English lines on plans of the lines in Philadelphia and the New York Third Avenue line.

Contemporary drawings show standard gauge and one can speculate that instructions were misinterpreted and the track was originally laid to the wrong gauge. The track was rolled wrought iron

step-rails weighing only 50lb per yard, six inches wide and nine-sixteenths of an inch thick in the sole with a step rising three quarters of an inch above the sole and a fillet at each side of the lower edge. The rails were bedded on and spiked to longitudinal timber sleepers 6in wide and 8in deep which were let into and rested upon transverse sleepers being spiked to each with an iron knee. The most objectionable feature was the step, which caused difficulties for other vehicles crossing the track.

The line was originally laid at the kerbside and in Conway Street there were two tracks, one at each side of the wide carriageway so that other traffic had to move into the centre of the road to allow the cars to pass. On the Argyle Street side of Hamilton Square where some of Birkenhead's most influential residents had houses, the line obstructed the carriages of the wealthy. By the end of 1860 the company had agreed to remove one track in Conway Street provided that two passing loops were permitted and by early March 1861 it is apparent that this had been done but with no loops, thus causing delays. The Commissioners relented and permitted one loop at Park Street. The removal seems to have been agreed on the understanding that the Commissioners would approve certain extensions.

Opposition to the street railway came from three sources. Many shopkeepers held the view that the swift, smooth ride given by the cars, in conjunction with the ferry improvements, persuaded residents to ride through to Woodside and cross to Liverpool to do their shopping but the line's supporters countered with the argument that the cars were just as likely to be used for more frequent journeys to Birkenhead town centre shops. Secondly the omnibus and hackney carriage interests were understandably hostile as their businesses were threatened. Cab drivers were especially bitter as many people who had used their services now patronised the new cars and there were several incidents when cabbies obstructed the cars at walking pace all the way from the Park to Woodside. These culminated in prosecutions for obstruction and there was a violent incident in January 1861 when some street railway passengers pelted two cabmen with lumps of frozen snow and eventually severely thrashed one of them with his own horse-whip. Some cab-drivers who obstructed the cars were dismissed by their employers.

Thomas Evans wrote to the Commissioners on 30 August 1860, the first day of operation, claiming for damage to his vehicle and James Evans submitted two claims in the first month. There were several others but the Commissioners denied all liability.

The third category of opponent was the influential property and landowning class. Sometimes they objected to the cars passing their properties and in other cases they merely disliked the railbound vehicles obstructing their carriages in the streets. So, despite its popularity with the travelling public, the line very nearly shared the fate of the pioneer line in Liverpool from Fairfield to Old Swan, which was removed after only three months, following condemnation as a public nuisance. The Birkenhead Street Railway owed its survival to the strange love-hate relationship which developed between the proprietors and the Commissioners. The line's clientele consisted largely of middle class, enfranchised people; the working classes could not afford the fares on a regular basis.

Train had always intended moving to London. At the opening of the Street Railway he had invited leading writers and journalists having in view "my intended invasion of the Metropolis". During the celebrations he floated the idea of a literary club from which grew the Savage Club of London. Exhilarated by the success of his Birkenhead venture, Train was anxious to move on and promote further lines elsewhere and at the end of 1860 he sold his interest to his co-investors for £600. However it was later revealed that he had already received a gratuity of £5,000 from the original capital. In London he proposed a number of schemes with varying degrees of success but all of which were short-lived because of official opposition. In March 1861 he was charged in a London court with obstruction and unlawfully breaking up the roadway in Uxbridge Road and it is of interest that a witness on his behalf testified that property values in Birkenhead had increased by 25 per cent along the line of the street railway.

Meanwhile talks about extensions continued. Early in November 1860 the Commissioners had asked the Street Railway Company what extensions it proposed to build and were told:—
(1) A single track up Claughton Road from Conway Street to Palm Grove, up Charlesville, along Water Street and across Mr. Ravenscroft's field to Claughton Road.
(2) Connecting line along Park Road East.
(3) Connecting line along Bridge Street from Hamilton Street to Argyle Street.
(4) Siding into Church Street and one in Chester Street at the ferry.
These proposals were approved though there was further discussion as to the pros and cons of using Oliver Street instead of Claughton Road. It was also stipulated that the section of line from the bottom of Chester Street to the start of Shore Road be removed.

However the company was much more interested in extending the line along Park Roads East and South and up Palm Grove to Oxton which was commercially much more attractive that a route to the, as yet relatively sparsely populated Claughton district. In February 1861 a draft agreement was drawn up between the Commissioners and the Company for this extension and in the following month permission was granted, subject to the landowners widening Palm Grove to 17 yards. It seems that the company persuaded the Royal Bank of Liverpool to finance this. In April the Commissioners were insisting on a Claughton Village extension but on 9 July, following further assurances from the Bank, it was resolved "that the Street Railway Co. be not required to make the extension to Claughton Village prior to making the line up Palm Grove to Balls Road. The company to make the extension to Claughton Village on six months' notice".

From late 1860 the condition of the hastily laid track gave rise to complaints and on 10 January 1861 the company agreed to the Commissioners Surveyor making repairs at cost plus 2½% for administration. Nevertheless the Commissioners did nothing except threaten, complain and criticise the standard of the work done by the company. There were constant demands for the Argyle Street line to be moved to the centre of the road which were resisted by the company simply because it could not afford to do so.

In October 1861 the company proposed a lengthy cross-docks extension to Seacombe and New Brighton but it was successfully opposed by the Wallasey Local Board, as described later.

Work on the Oxton extension was put in hand during the summer of 1861 and a new car shed and stables were erected in Palm Grove near the terminus. The exact date when the line came into use has escaped the record but it was apparently in late August 1861 as on 3 September the seven year old son of a local resident was killed when he jumped from a moving car. At about the same time a new line was built from Woodside ferry approach along Chester Street and Bridge Street to Argyle Street, the track in Shore Road and the lower part of Argyle Street being lifted. In retrospect it is surprising that the line was allowed to be built in Shore Road as an Act of 1858 had empowered the Dock Board to reconstruct it in connection with other major works. The Evans family viewed developments with some alarm and Thomas Evans acquired a powerful ally in the person of William Jackson, M.P. for Newcastle-under-Lyme who lived at the Manor House, Claughton and was reputed to be the biggest landowner in Birkenhead. Jackson claimed that Palm Grove belonged to him and in November 1861 he instituted legal proceedings to prevent the Street Railway Company from using the line along Palm Grove. As access to the depot was at stake, the implications for the company were serious. At the initial trial the proceedings were adjourned and the court did not require the company to cease using the line.

After a few uneventful weeks the Evanses took matters into their own hands. The first hint of trouble came on 31 January 1862 when an omnibus driven by James Evans obstructed a street railway car in Bridge Street by refusing to move off the metals. Then two cars fitted with flanged wheels, the property of Thomas Evans, began running on the company's

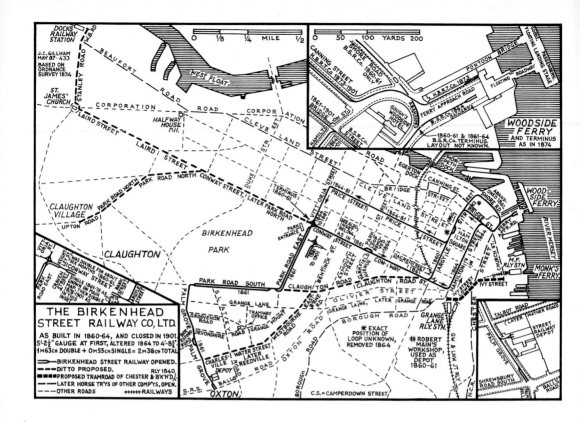

Track plan of the Birkenhead Street Railway (1860-1877). The lines were originally laid to a gauge of 5 ft 2½ in, using step rail, but were later relaid in grooved rail to the standard gauge of 4 ft 8½ in. During the reconstruction, in 1864, the system was worked in two halves with cars meeting at the park entrance.

rails. These cars were apparently purpose-built as they were described in a letter from the company to the Commissioners as "similar to those in use by our company". Over the next few days there were several instances of obstruction and counter-obstruction, some allegedly lasting from 10.00am to 7.00pm, culminating in a series of summonses which were heard together on 7 February. Neither the company nor Thomas Evans were proceeded against, charges being laid against James Evans and several drivers; some were convicted and others discharged. Contemporary reports suggest that the public generally remained loyal to the company, few passengers being carried in the "pirate" cars. The origin of these cars is a mystery as it seems unlikely that Evans could have afforded to have them built new by Main and the only other cars in the country were those used on one of Train's abortive London schemes which closed down in September 1861. Despite the description above, they may have been converted omnibuses.

Evans' tactics were criticised at a Commissioners' meeting on 4 February 1862 but he made it clear that he was relying on the inability of the Commissioners to give exclusive rights to the use of any part of the

highway and on Train's words in his second letter viz. ". . . invite all vehicles to use them (the rails) . . ." Clearly the company was defenceless and solved its immediate problems by leasing the line to Thomas Evans, presumably on condition that he remove his pirate cars from the rails. Several months later they were reported as still being in store. However, Evans' tenure was a short one. When William Jackson's action came up for hearing at Chester Sessions in late July 1862, the company inexplicably neglected to appear and was fined £500 for contempt of court. As the fine remained unpaid, their cars were seized by the bailiff and the service ceased abruptly early in August. The drivers, conductors and other staff, now presumably employees of Thomas Evans, were summarily dismissed.

Under New Management

The plight of the company evoked considerable public sympathy as there was no doubt that the service was sorely missed. One of the Commissioners, Dr. Bayliss, always an enthusiastic supporter of the street railway, spoke out strongly at a meeting. As the *Daily Post* reported ". . . it had enabled

Claughton to compete with Aigburth . . . for gentlemen's residences; houses had sprung up with marvellous rapidity along the line; the ferry revenue had largely increased and tens of thousands of persons had been able, at a small cost, to enjoy the beautiful scenery of the Park". Whilst the Commissioners did not intervene officially it seems likely that some pressure was exerted on Jackson behind the scenes as that same day there was a meeting in Liverpool of "gentlemen not connected with the street railway company to make a communication to Mr. Jackson as to the stoppage of the line". As a politician, Jackson probably sensed that he had misjudged public opinion and came to terms with the company, though what those terms were was not revealed.

A new lease was arranged with Mr. Charles Castle of Liverpool. This was probably a relative of Richard Castle who is known to have run omnibuses on the West Derby route in 1853-7 and was currently providing an express feeder service between Garston railway station and Liverpool town centre. Service was restarted on 18 August 1862 and at the September Commissioners' meeting, Dr. Bayliss remarked that the Board were all very much pleased to see the cars running again. "During the Sunday that they did not run, cars (carriages) were whirling about the township and it now appears that the Street Railway actually preserves the township in a state of comparative quiet . . . for more than a week the township was lost without it".

Whilst events had turned in favour of the company, the directors realised that they must put their house in order. In September they requested the Commissioners to repair the track, laying down the priorities as they saw them and this was agreed. The following month, a petition of 427 names was presented to the Commissioners urging them to take steps to ensure permanent status for the line. This resulted in the insertion of a clause in the Birkenhead Improvement Act 1863 giving the commissioners powers to lay down rails in streets not less than 60ft wide overall. The root cause of some of the justifiable opposition was the protrusion of the step rail above the level of the roads. With the prospect of statutory security, James McHenry, who had backed several of Train's schemes, was persuaded to inject new capital. Authorised capital was increased three times — by £3,500 in February 1862, £10,000 in January 1864 and £5,000 in December 1864. He offered to widen Palm Grove to 40ft at his own expense and asked for it to be adopted to avoid future problems with Jackson. He made firm proposals for the maintenance of the track by the Surveyor at his (McHenry's) expense and requested a lease of the line for 21 years. The Commissioners felt that they did not have the power to lease something which they did not really own but discussions during the autumn of 1863 ended in broad agreement giving McHenry exclusive rights to use the street railway for three years with one year's notice and on the following conditions:—

1. To remove passing loops in Conway Street and Argyle Street.
2. To lay a new line along Price Street and Vittoria Street (Cleveland Street had been proposed but it was only 30ft wide in places, whereas Price Street was 60ft.)
3. To relay the whole line with rail approved by the Commissioners.
4. To change the gauge from 5ft 2½in to 4ft 8½in.
5. To pave with square setts between the rails and outside to a minimum of 9in and a maximum of 12in.
6. Commissioners to keep track in repair at the expense of the company.
7. Rails to be in the centre of the road where required.
8. To run closed carriages to meet boats at 2d (There was also provision for running open cars between the boat connections at 1d)
9. To provide new cars but old cars could be used where adaptable to the new gauge.
10. To observe the Commissioners' by-laws.

McHenry also wanted a double line in Park Roads East and South. The change of gauge was influenced by McHenry's scheme to build a line between Park Entrance and the proposed Hoylake Railway station in Wallasey Bridge Road, with vague thoughts of through carriages and possibly also by a proposal for a standard gauge line between Woodside and New Ferry. The old lease was terminated and McHenry appointed a manager, T. M. Wiswell, who attended a meeting of the Roads and Improvements Committee to demonstrate a new type of grooved rail which would not protrude above the roadway. It was decided to lay a trial length and an agreement regarding rails was sealed on 3 May, to be followed in June 1864 by a general agreement incorporating the points listed above. This agreement also provided for the lifting of the track in Argyle Street between Conway Street and Price Street and the laying of a new inward line along Hamilton Street. Tracklaying work was put in hand immediately and was complete by late September 1864. Cars from Woodside to the Park travelled by way of Price Street and returned via Conway Street; as the gauge of the line between the Park and Oxton remained unchanged, the service ran in two parts for some time. As the Palm Grove depot remained inaccessible to the standard gauge cars, a temporary depot must have been provided, possibly in Main's yard or in Dacre Street where the company owned premises. At Woodside the line was extended at a cost of £250 about 150 yards to the new ferry terminal which had been reconstructed on reclaimed land. This line belonged to the Commissioners and was leased to the company for £100 per year. It seems likely that this was the first municipally owned tramway in Britain.

Reconstruction of the outer part of the line was delayed by arguments about the paving of the double line and the widening of Palm Grove. The settlement with William Jackson provided for the street to be widened to 40ft 3in but the Commissioners wanted 60ft in order to comply with the 1863 Act. As for the double line, granite setts were expensive and the company felt that as other road traffic was lighter in Park Roads East and South, it would be quite adequate and much cheaper to use macadam between the rails. Work had started on reconstruction before this matter was settled so on 23 February 1865, Mr. Wiswell was summoned to appear before the Roads and Improvement Committee to explain the taking up of the rails and breaking of the road in Park Road East. The bewildered man was then required to write a letter during the Committee lunch break, asking for permission which everyone believed had been granted by the agreement of May 1864. At last, in June, the Commissioners agreed to the use of macadam and to forego the widening of Palm Grove, an agreement being sealed on 1 August 1865 by which time the line was almost complete; through running was soon restored. The grooved rails which replaced the step-rail are said to have been suggested by Mr. W. Langley Hall, an engineer at Laird's who later became manager of one of Chamberlain's works in Birmingham.

The opposition had one last attempt to ruin the street railway. In September 1864 proceedings were brought by Thomas Evans and William Gough to condemn the line in Bridge Street which would have prevented the cars from reaching Woodside. The case was based on the legal status of the line and the width being less than 60ft. As large sums had already been spent on elimination of the step-rail and improving the service, public support was firmly behind the company and Evans and Gough (the interest of the latter in the matter is not clear) came in for much criticism. A public meeting on 20 February 1865 passed the following resolution:—

"That the Birkenhead Street Railway Co affords very superior accommodation and comfort to the inhabitants, this meeting considers it most desirable that there should be no interference with this mode of conveyance. . .
"That this meeting strongly condemns the legal action that is being taken by two ratepayers to remove the Street Railway and resolves to adopt such measures as may be found expedient to stay these proceedings."

A week later, the Commissioners called a special meeting to receive a deputation and, in effect, endorsed the public resolution. At the trial at Chester Assizes on 8 April 1865, the witnesses for the plaintiffs performed very badly and the defence proved to the satisfaction of the court that the line,

having been completely renewed, was not the same line that had been laid in 1860. The jury found in favour of the company without the judge having to sum up. Press comment suggested that Evans and Gough expected to be bought off and might have withdrawn the action if the company had agreed to the purchase of some cars which had been laid up for a long time in Canning Street. These were presumably the pirate cars of 1862 and it is not known what eventually became of them.

The street railway should now have been able to settle down but the events of the previous three years drained it financially. During 1862-63 it seems that some of the Oxton omnibuses had been diverted to compete with the street railway and, despite their inferior appointments some traffic was extracted. The costs of relaying and changing gauge had inflated the capital and legal costs had absorbed large sums. By the end of 1865 the company was barely paying its way and was actively seeking economies. Thomas Evans, too, could scarcely have been unscathed. Not only had he dissipated his energies in opposing the street railway when he could have been developing his business on non-competitive routes but had lost the battle and incurred substantial legal costs. The Oxton buses no longer went round by the Park but a new route was introduced along Oxton Road and Balls Road to the top of Palm Grove. In time, the population increase made up for the loss of traffic to the street railway. The cars now ran every 10 minutes from about 8.30am to 8pm then quarter-hourly to 9pm. In 1865 there was then a half hourly service until midnight but this did not continue for long; it had certainly ceased by 1866. Fares were 2d to Park Entrance and 3d to Oxton with books of 25 3d tickets obtainable for 5s. The announcement of these in the press on 20 May 1865 is the first known reference to the use of tickets on tramways anywhere in the world, though metal tokens were in use at Birkenhead and in USA.

In January 1866 the company sought permission to reduce the frequency of the cars to 20 minutes between 11am and 3pm and this was granted until 25 March. A deputation, including George Starbuck the car manufacturer, whose status with the company at that time is not known, tried to persuade the Commissioners to bear some of the cost of road maintenance because other traffic used the roadway between the rails. This was rejected as being inconsistent with the agreement signed by the two parties. In April the Commissioners were persuaded to resolve that the company be required to run open cars at 1d between Woodside and the Park as agreed in 1864, between 8am and 8pm. Whilst it is interesting to speculate whether this might have brought tramway travel to a less affluent sector of the population, the company simply lacked the money to implement it. There followed a series of meetings and letters in which modification of the 1864 agreement was sought and finally, on 28 June 1866, the company's solicitor wrote to the Commissioners asking if they would purchase the street railway on fair terms. The offer being declined, the company then asked for modification of the agreement as to (1) the upkeep of the centre of the road and (2) the £100 charge for the use of the ferry terminal. An extension along Balls Road was also requested.

In September 1866 there was fighting at the ferry between street railway employees and those of Thomas Evans which brought forth press comment favourable to the company. "The tramway has too strong a hold on public opinion for any open attack to have the slightest chance of success". The inequity of the £100 charge was underlined by a letter from the company to the Commissioners in September 1866 complaining of obstruction at Woodside by Thomas Evans' buses. The allegation was refuted by Evans who said that his men had been instructed to avoid all contact with the street railway people. He had however told his men that when one of the two forks at the ferry was unoccupied they should place his bus the Spider there and ply for hire. The previous evening he had been told by the police that the street railway company had placed one of its cars across the way of his buses and kept it there for four hours. Evans stressed that he paid for his stands at Woodside but did not compare his £1.25 fee with the company's £100.

From 1 September 1866 the company endeavoured to stimulate patronage by introducing a 2d flat fare. "And this without competition too" commented the *Advertiser*. In a further move to evoke public sympathy cars were operated free of charge during polling hours for the local elections on 6 November "even though not many people bothered to get off the cars to vote".

Having received no concessions, the company gave six months' notice in June 1867 of its intention to remove the rails unless its financial problems could be alleviated in some way. This alarmed the Commissioners who appointed a sub-committee to negotiate. The company submitted that as the Commissioners had been reimbursed for all expenses incurred in the repair of roads etc in connection with the railway, the £100 Woodside charge should be cancelled and there should be no further charges for maintenance of the streets. Furthermore it should not be compelled to run penny cars and the timetables should be determined by the company. After several meetings a revised agreement was drafted reducing the Woodside charge to £30, obligating the company to repair "the roadwork and ironwork of the line" and to pay £30 per year towards the repair of the streets. The obligation to run penny cars

should be dropped and the timetable should be 8.30am and every 10 minutes until 11am then every 20 minutes until 3pm; every 10 minutes to 7pm and every 30 minutes to 9pm. The agreement would be for three years from 1 January 1868.

The Commissioners refused to ratify the agreement and resumed discussions at a meeting on 15 October 1867 when arguments for and against were considered. Mr Brattan who supported the tramway reminded the meeting that the company had spent £36,650 on capital works including the relaying of Conway Street track twice to meet the Commissioners' wishes. The shareholders had received no return and time was needed for the company to recover. The Commissioners adopted the agreement except that the charge for the use of the ferry terminal was reduced to £50 not £30 as proposed.

In 1868 a new manager, R. J. Vanderkiste, was appointed. The company's affairs were conducted from McHenry's offices at 3 Inner Temple, Liverpool. There are indications in the early 1870s of both neglect and opportunism. It was alleged that during Whit week 1871 the cars were overcrowded and the service was curtailed at the Park. When a Commissioner spoke to the manager about this "the reply had been one of the repulse". Another Commissioner complained of having earlier waited 40 minutes for a car to Oxton. In July 1872 attention was drawn in the *Advertiser* to the state of the pavement between the rails. The matter was referred to the Surveyor as the company was paying the fixed maintenance charge to the Commissioners.

Careful management together with sustained population growth (43,000 in 1871 to 84,000 in 1881) enabled the line to survive. The 2d flat fare was increased to 3d in September 1875, following increases in the cost of provender and horses.

Although the word 'tramway' was in use for urban transport by 1863, the Birkenhead line was always the "street railway" throughout its separate existence. Its turbulent origins marked the birth of a revolution in social habits and, historically, it is of great importance as the first British street tramway to survive. The birth was a difficult one but the deficiencies of its non-statutory origin clearly pointed to the need for Parliamentary action to smooth the way for other undertakings. The draftsman of the Tramways Act 1870 doubtless examined the events which took place in Birkenhead between 1860 and 1867. One body of pioneers who never profited, however, were the ordinary shareholders of the Birkenhead Street Railway Company who never received a dividend. The undertaking became more profitable in the 1870s but only the preference capital was remunerated and that only at 2¼%.

2 Other Horse Tramways in Birkenhead

When the Hoylake Railway was authorised in 1863 the promoters intended to provide a direct rail link across North Wirral to Seacombe ferry but lack of money and other difficulties resulted in it being built only to a point in Wallasey Bridge Road which had originally been intended as a branch line. If the railway was to be successful some form of road link had to be provided between Docks Station and a ferry and, with construction at an advanced stage, an approach was made to James McHenry who formally asked the Birkenhead Commissioners on 27 March 1866 for permission to lay 'a single line of street railway with the requisite sidings from the Park Entrance along Conway Street (sic), Laird Street, St. James' Road and Stanley Street...' The line was proposed to be paved with stone setts outside the rails and with macadam between them as had been agreed after considerable argument for the Oxton extension of the Street Railway. The Commissioners demanded stone setts between the rails and 12 inches either side and refused to agree to sidings i.e. passing loops, which would have made the line unworkable. Despite further representations no concessions were forthcoming and the scheme was dropped.

The railway opened on 2 July 1866 and Thomas Evans secured the contract to convey railway passengers between Docks Station and Seacombe ferry via Poulton toll bridge. It is not known if Theobald's, who already covered most of the route to Woodside catered for the needs of passengers for Birkenhead town centre but by 1870 the advertised rail connections were to and from Woodside at 8, 9 and 11 am, 4 and 6 pm returning from Docks Station 20 minutes later.

The through buses between Woodside and Hoylake were withdrawn; possibly the Hoylake-based proprietors provided a feeder service between Hoylake and West Kirby until the railway was extended in 1878. However, as a result of the insolvency of the banking house which had backed it, the railway was in serious financial trouble in September 1868 when Mr Robert Vyner obtained a Chancery decree for the sale of certain land and 'everything found upon it' for which the railway company was unable to pay. This led to a suspension of railway services for a time and by July 1870 omnibuses were again plying between Hoylake and Woodside twice a day on Mondays to Fridays, three times on Saturdays and once on Sundays. According to *Bradshaw* for September 1870, trains were running between Hoylake and Leasowe Crossing, the boundary of the Vyner estates, with connecting omnibuses between Leasowe and Seacombe ferry via Poulton. By November 1870 *Bradshaw* announced the resumption of an omnibus connection between the railway and Woodside. On 5 May 1870 the Birkenhead Commissioners considered an application from 'landowners and others interested in the Birkenhead, Hoylake and West Kirby neighbourhood' with reference to laying down a tramway to connect Woodside Ferry with Docks Station and a deputation was received two weeks later. On 19 November 1870 a new company, Hoylake and Birkenhead Tramway Co. was formed with a capital of £70,000

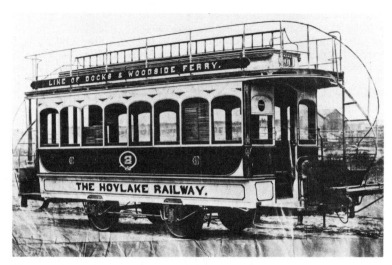

Newly-built Hoylake Railway car 2 of 1873, photographed outside the Starbuck Works in Cleveland Street. Eight cars were required for the service. They were replaced by smaller one-horse double-deckers in 1887. (*Science Museum, Whitcombe Collection*)

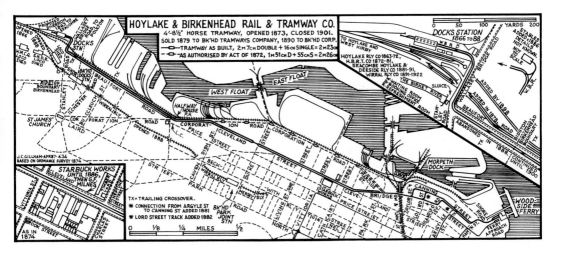

The Hoylake and Birkenhead Rail & Tramway Co's line from Woodside to the Hoylake Railway's Docks Station. The authorised route was along Corporation Street, but the line was built along Cleveland Street, and opened on 6 September 1873.

and it seems possible that the conversion of the railway to a tramway was contemplated as its principal objects were 'to construct, maintain and work tramways in .... Birkenhead, Bidston-cum-Ford and elsewhere in the County Palatine of Chester and to acquire, maintain and work the undertaking of the Hoylake Railway Co.'. The promoters were all London men and included A.C.S. Padeswell Hall M.P., James Walker and F.G.W. Fearon, Secretary of the Trust and Loan Co. of Upper Canada.

The position until 1872 is confused but by late 1871 the through Hoylake-Woodside omnibus service had been reduced to one journey in each direction on weekdays only. Under an Act of 1872 the 1870 company was dissolved and a new company, the Hoylake and Birkenhead Rail and Tramway Co. was formed to take over the railway and build 3.02 miles of street railway between Docks Station and Woodside. There was an obligation to run two workmen's cars each way not later than 7 am and not before 6 pm at not more than ½d per mile with a minimum fare of 1d. The new company paid Mr. Vyner for his land and trains resumed through running on 1 August 1872. A temporary omnibus service was provided between Docks Station and Woodside, perhaps by Theobald's but possibly by Mr. W. W. Townson, a veterinary surgeon, who was destined to play a larger role in local transport affairs at a later date.

The new company lost no time in arranging for the construction of their tramway. As authorised, it consisted of mainly single line with eleven loops. It commenced in two spurs on the north side of Woodside ferry approach, followed the kerb on the north side of Hamilton Street (thereby easing the gradient), into Canning Street which was double

track, then by Sandford Street (returning via Taylor Street), Bridge Street, Marcus Street, Corporation Road, Beaufort Road, a private road belonging to Vyner, (the last few yards of Beaufort Road), Wallasey Bridge Road and into the Docks Station. The Birkenhead Commissioners had the right to veto certain loops and they insisted that the Hamilton Street line be single track. In fact, although authorised to use Corporation Road throughout, the line was constructed along Cleveland Street between Marcus Street and Cavendish Street with the agreement of the Commissioners but without any modification of the powers. It was also built as double track for most of its length. The two sidings at Woodside were the property of the Commissioners and rent of £200 per year was charged.

The contractors were Henry Tabiner and Joseph Perrin and construction commenced on 22 April 1873. Delays were attributed to scarcity of both materials and skilled labour but despite this the Board of Trade inspection took place on 5 September, Maj-Gen Hutchinson walking the full length of the line and riding back to Woodside. Public service commenced on 6 September after an opening ceremony when four cars took 100 invited guests to Docks Station where they boarded a special train for Hoylake, lunch being served in the new carriage shed. The establishment of a rail link with Woodside was celebrated by various special events at Hoylake, a regatta on 13 September, field sports on 15th and a pony meeting at the racecourse on 16th.

Whilst the service was arranged to connect with trains, it catered also for local traffic, supplanting the omnibus service from its inception. The carriage of goods other than passengers' luggage was prohibited. The terminal arrangements at Docks Station were of considerable interest in being probably the

19

first example of a covered interchange between a tramway and a railway. Initially the railway seems to have run the tramway themselves and probably kept the cars in the station and on the line beyond. However, on 2 May 1876 they came to an agreement with Mr. W. W. Townson to work the tramway on their behalf. Certain buildings and stables which were probably built specially, were rented to Mr. Townson for £75 per year and a curve was put in for access (see inset on map). Later there was a triangular layout. The agreement was renewed on 31 August 1878.

Appropriately the cars, of which there were eventually eight, were built by George Starbuck and Co. whose works were situated on the route. They were knifeboard double deckers with eight windows a side with sliding shutters. 'The Hoylake Railway' was painted on the rocker panels and the railway arms appeared twice on each waist panel. Reversed spiral iron ladders gave access to the upper deck. An unconfirmed report states that the cars were painted in the maroon livery of the railway Company's passenger stock.

The Wirral Tramway Company

The New Chester Road leading southwards from the various ferries was the most heavily trafficked road in the district and urban development spread along this artery from the middle of the nineteenth century. The Tranmere Pool, extending a serpentine finger up to the later line of Borough Road was spanned by Brassey's causeway in 1833 and the railway embankment in 1840. The local authority for the area south of the Pool was the Tranmere Local Board who, in their Improvement Act of 1862 obtained powers to lay down tramways or arrange for others to do so and in this way they were a year ahead of Birkenhead.

In October 1862 the North Cheshire Street Railway Co. with a projected capital of £15,000, proposed a line from Woodside ferry to New Ferry Toll Bar with the possibility of a later extension to Bromborough. Applications were made during 1862-63 to the three local authorities, Birkenhead, Tranmere and Higher Bebington. By December 1862 Tranmere was in active negotiation with the promoters and proposed that they should pay half the cost incurred by the Board in altering and widening New Chester Road and metalling and otherwise preparing the road, kerbing, channelling and footwalks, in addition to laying the track at the company's own expense. The Local Board proposed also to reserve the right to give six months' notice to the company who would then have to remove the rails and restore the road.

In February 1863, the Higher Bebington Local Board demanded that the whole road be put in order by the promoters who promptly decided not to cross the boundary and a month later Birkenhead, per-

haps wearied by constant problems with the existing street railway, declined permission on the grounds that they had no powers. They left the door open, however, by inviting a later application if they successfully obtained tramway powers in the Bill which had already been submitted to Parliament. In 1865, negotiations were resumed between the promoters and Tranmere who now required paving to extend to 9 in. either side of the rails instead of 6 in. as stipulated earlier. The cost would have been too high and no more was heard of the North Cheshire Company.

From 1 October 1866 David Edwards, described as a 'beer seller and omnibus proprietor' started a bus service between the Farmer's Arms, New Ferry and the Castle Hotel, Chester Street at 8.45, 10am, 2.30 and 5pm, returning at 9.30, 11.30am, 4 and 5.45pm. The fare was 3d inside, 2d outside or to Limekiln Lane (St. Paul's Road) 2d inside 1d outside. Edwards' premises were on the corner of New Ferry Road (then New Ferry Lane) and Marquis Street. It is not known how long this service endured.

Late in 1873 the Tranmere Local Board was in discussion with promoters of the proposed Wirral Tramway Company who wished to lay a tramway between New Ferry and Woodside. Agreement was reached on fares viz: New Ferry and Woodside 3d; Bedford Road and Fernyhough's Castle Hotel 2d; Fernyhough's corner and Woodside 2d. This Castle Hotel was on the corner of Green Lane and had no connection with the similarly named hostelry in Chester Street. The Tranmere Local Board exacted an undertaking to build a branch to Tranmere Ferry within fifteen (later amended to ten) years but the Board of Trade refused to endorse this and the Local Board decided to wait until the company was incorporated and then make a new agreement. The Wirral Tramway Co. Ltd. was duly formed in 1874 and obtained a Tramway Act authorising it to construct a line from Woodside to New Ferry via Chester Street and New Chester Road with an alternative line along Church Street and Ivy Street. The line was to have been single with passing places at Tranmere Ferry approach, Union Street, Bedford Road and Rock Lane with a double line from Victoria Grove to the terminus where the depot and stables were to be built. The carriage of goods was prohibited and fares were fixed at 1d per mile, minimum 3d, though double fares could be charged between 9pm and 5am. In addition the company was authorised to provide facilities for the 'labouring classes' at ½d per mile before 7am and after 6pm but in fact the Wirral never attempted to run early morning cars.

From 9 November 1875 an omnibus service was run from New Ferry to the Castle Hotel, Chester Street at 10am, 2.30 and 6.30pm returning at 11.30am, 4 and 7.15pm with an extra late bus on

Saturdays. The fare was 3d any distance, inside or outside. The operator is believed to have been John Hart of 49 Holt Hill; his stables were at 3 Church Road, Higher Tranmere. This service is believed to have operated throughout the period of construction.

The contractor, Mr. D. A. Jardine, broke ground at Rock Ferry on 7 September 1876 with promises of completion of the work within three months. Mr. C. H. Beloe was appointed engineer and construction was carried out by his system and under his direct supervision. The 4ft 8½in gauge single line with infrequent passing loops, was laid with Deacon section steel rail weighing 52lb. per yard rolled in 21ft lengths. Side flanges had a total depth of 2 in. The rails were laid on longitudinal sleepers 4in wide and 6in deep bedded in concrete. The sleeper ends lay in 9in long cast-iron chairs tied transversely by two ¾in tie rods. The sleepers were also tied by three intermediate tie-rods passed through and screwed up outside. The ground was excavated to a depth of 7½in and, in addition, two longitudinal trenches 12in wide and 3in deep were excavated under the sleepers. When the rails and sleepers were correctly positioned the bottom of the excavation and the trenches under the sleepers were filled with 3in of concrete thus embedding the sleepers to a depth of 3in and allowing paving with 4in cubic setts laid on a ½in layer of sand. The cost was considerably reduced by using tie-bars instead of cross-sleepers

WIRRAL TRAMWAY:— QUANTITIES AND COSTS FOR ONE MILE, SINGLE WAY, 1877

	£	£
Excavation, 8 feet wide:—		
Macadam, 3 inches deep, 4,693 square yards @ 6d	118	
Below foundations of roads, 668 cubic yards @ 4s	134	
Levelling bottom, 4,693 square yards @ 1d	20	
	--	272
Concrete, 440 cubic yards @ 9s		198
Timber, 2,000 cubic feet @ 2s 6d		250
Iron rails 52lbs. per yard, 84 tons 6cwt. @ £8 10s		717
Staples, 15 cwt. @ £1 2s 6d		17
Chairs, 4 tons 16 cwt. @ £6		29
Fish-plates, 1 ton 11 cwt. @ £9		14
Tie-rods, 5 tons 2 cwt. @ £14		71

		1,568

EXCAVATION AND MATERIALS FOR TRAMWAYS

Paving:—			
Granite sets, 759 tons @ £1 8s 6d		1,082	
Laying, grout and sand, 4,300 square yards @ 1s 8d		372	
		---	1,454
Making good between old and new pavement,			
1,760 yards @ 5d			37
Labour, laying tramway, 1,760 lineal yards @ 2s 6d			220
	Tons.	Cwt.	
CARTING:—			
Rails and fish-plates	85	17	
Chairs	4	16	
Staples		15	
Tie-rods	5	2	
Timber	30	12	
Granite sets	759	0	
	--	--	
Total weight, say 886 tons @ 2s			89
TOTAL			£3,368

but judging by the rapid deterioration of the permanent way this method of construction was unsatisfactory. Beloe later admitted that he regretted not taking out the old pitching and laying a concrete foundation for the whole width of the track. The cost of construction was £3,368 per mile as is set out in the accompanying table reproduced from *Tramways, Their Construction and Working,* 2nd Edition. (D. Kinnear Clark, 1894). Reports that the line was originally built to a gauge of 3ft 6in are incorrect.

The Wirral company had serious problems with their contractor and in October 1876 the Tranmere Local Board took out summonses for not completing road works with due speed and within four weeks as required by the Tramways Act 1870, and also for breaking up the road south of Bedford Road without notice. It was said that the road was left in this state for 7-8 weeks as paviors were taken away to do work in Birkenhead.

It had been hoped that the line would open early in 1877 but failure of the contractor to keep promises led to the inspection being twice postponed. A further complication was the closure of Chester Street and Church Street because of tunnel and bridge works for the extension of the railway line from Grange Lane to Woodside so that 0.43 miles could not be laid at all. When Maj.-Gen. Hutchinson came to carry out the Board of Trade inspection on 22 March, he was not satisfied with the paving and gave only provisional authority for the line to be opened in time for the Easter traffic on Thursday 28 March 1877 on receiving the assurance that matters would be rectified by then. A temporary siding at Ivy Street/Chester Street corner was approved by the Birkenhead Commissioners and this was almost certainly used as the terminus for the first few weeks. The low bridge carrying the Tranmere Pool branch railway line across Chester Street near Waterloo Place dictated the use of single deck cars of which there were originally seven. Demand over the initial novelty ride period exceeded all expectations, 8,706 passengers being carried on the first three days.

On 23 July 1877, Maj.-Gen. Hutchinson re-inspected the whole line, this time including Chester Street and Church Street but, again finding the paving irregular, declined to issue a Certificate. Nevertheless the company started to run cars over the Chester Street lines as soon as the General's back was turned and within two days, probably acting on information supplied by one of the local authorities, the Board of Trade demanded the withdrawal of cars from Chester Street. The directors were obliged to eat humble pie pleading 'mis-apprehension' and a telegram sent on 26 July by the Asst. Secretary for Railways at the Board of Trade, Mr Calcroft, to Maj.-Gen. Hutchinson who was inspecting something in Workington, clearly shows the official attitude.

The Wirral Tramway Company's line ran from Woodside along the New Chester Road to New Ferry, where the cars terminated outside the company's depot. Because of a low bridge, the company used single deck cars. This photograph shows one of the seven original cars bought in 1877.
(Courtesy T. B. Maund)

'Having frightened them, you might let them run holding deposit which they want to withdraw as security repairs being executed.'

The General relented but the line was not properly certified until a further inspection was carried out on 1 November 1877. In addition to the Birkenhead, Tranmere and Bebington local authorities, the Chester and Birkenhead United Turnpike Trust was represented at all these inspections as the road was not freed from tolls until 1883. A line built and owned by the Commissioners on the ferry approach was opened on 19 January 1878. Rent originally agreed at £100 per annum was reduced to £50 from 1 July 1878.

A ten minute service was run, starting from New Ferry at 8.05am and 8.35am from Woodside and continuing until 10.15pm on Mondays to Fridays, 10.45pm on Sundays and 11.15pm on Saturdays. Two additional cars were run on weekdays at 11 and 11.15pm; the finishing times were quite late for those days. In 1879 the fares were as follows:-

Up to 9.00pm weekdays; Woodside and Rock Lane 2d, St. Paul's Road and New Ferry 2d, Woodside and New Ferry 3d.
After 9.00pm weekdays and all day Sundays; any distance 3d.
Special late cars on Mondays to Fridays; any distance 6d.

The traffic proved to be much heavier than anticipated and the small cars and lightly constructed permanent way were unequal to the demand. In 1879 the line was relaid using a heavier section rail at a cost of £2,165 and the seven original cars were sold and replaced by seven new cars of larger capacity. Despite the interruption of traffic during relaying, the company was still able to pay a 6% dividend to ordinary shareholders.

Although authorised to be connected to the lines of the Birkenhead Street Railway Co. at Woodside, the Wirral line was laid separately parallel with and to the north of the earlier line. There was, therefore, a 'double single track' arrangement between Woodside and the corner of Bridge Street where the street railway crossed over the Wirral tracks. No doubt it was felt worth paying a little extra to have undisputed access to Woodside ferry.

The promoters of the Wirral Tramway Co. Ltd. included prominent Liverpool tramway owners, notably William Busby whose family had interests in several undertakings on Merseyside and elsewhere. The company's offices were at South Crescent Chambers, 6 Lord Street, Liverpool from where William Knox, Chartered Accountant, the Secretary carried on business. The firm later became Knox Hassal, Dodd and Co. and was prominent in local transport affairs on Merseyside until municipalisation.

Soon after the tramway opened, an hourly

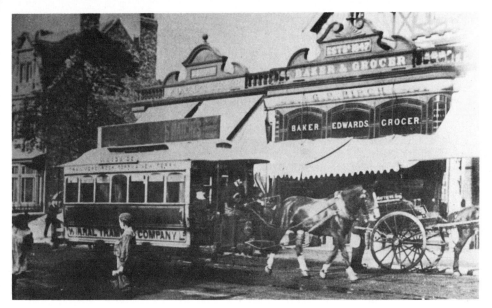

Wirral Tramway Company car No. 6 in New Chester Road in the 1890s. Note the passenger seated on the platform. *(Grosvenor Museum, Chester)*

omnibus service was introduced between Tranmere ferry, Dacre Hill and Woodhey via Old Chester Road in an attempt to bring traffic to the ferry which was losing ground to Woodside. This seems to have run until about May 1886 when the *Advertiser* announced that the Dacre Hill omnibus had been 'done to death by the tunnel railway'. As the Mersey Railway had only reached Green Lane at this time, the inference is that the omnibus had been extended to Woodside in the meantime.

Below: A share certificate issued by the Birkenhead Tramways Company, incorporating a quite accurate drawing of Woodside Ferry in the 1870s, with the Ferry Buildings and the then new Woodside Railway Station. *(Courtesy J. B. Horne)*

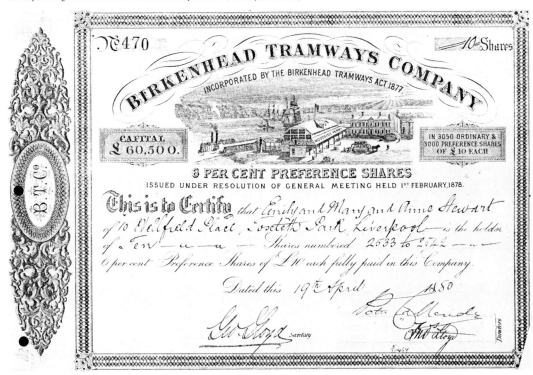

The Birkenhead Tramways Company

There were now three separate tramway routes in Birkenhead, all individually owned and unconnected to each other. The town and its environs were still growing rapidly and the stage was set for further extensions and links between the various lines.

The Street Railway Company still suffered from its early origins as, being without Parliamentary powers, it had no security of tenure. It was constantly under criticism and its ordinary shareholders had never received a dividend. In 1876, the year before Birkenhead received its charter of incorporation, the company was offered for sale and after a period of uncertainty, a new company was formed under the chairmanship of Mr William Abbott, a financier. Three of the other four promoters, Dillinge Parrish, of the New York contractors Fisher and Parrish, Buckley Bent and Thomas Lloyd had been active in Liverpool tramway and omnibus affairs since 1860 and were very experienced. The other directors were R. Stephenson and P. Callender who was to succeed Abbott as chairman. Lloyd had been a coach proprietor in the 1850s and was to become manager of the Liverpool United Tramways and Omnibus Co. and the Chester Tramways Co. His son, George was appointed as manager at Birkenhead. The new owners believed that despite poor financial results in the past, the Birkenhead tramways had potential but needed to be modernised and extended.

The Birkenhead Tramways Act 1877 dissolved the Street Railway Company and authorised a new statutory company, the Birkenhead Tramways Company. The Act authorised 1.5 miles of new line diverging from the existing route in Hamilton Square and passing along Argyle Street, Wilbraham Street, Borough Road and Happy Valley Road (now part of Borough Road) to North Road, Prenton, with a return line round the Haymarket to Hamilton Street. The contract was awarded to D. Parrish but sub-contracted to Joseph Perrin with C. Hopkins as engineer. Preliminary work started on 20 April 1878 and track-laying on 10 May. Double lines were approved on condition that they be removed if the Corporation gave twelve months' notice. The line was inspected on 6 July and officially opened on 11 July by Mr Peter Callender. At 2.15pm two decorated cars left Woodside for North Road where the directors and guests inspected the offices, stables, depot and waiting room. The cars took them back to Hamilton Square and then to the Park Skating Rink for a banquet held amid flags and bunting. The line including eight new cars, stables, depot etc cost £38,000.

Public service did not start until 1 August 1878 suggesting that the cars, built locally by the Starbuck company, had not all been delivered. The eight cars which seated 20 inside and 20 on top carried route boards bearing the extravagant legend 'Higher Tranmere (Borough Road), Woodchurch Road and

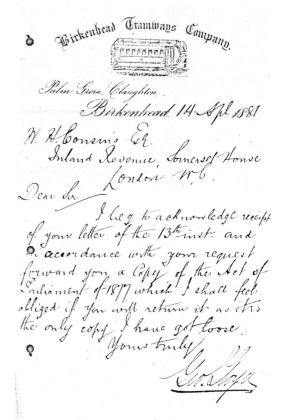

The Birkenhead Tramways Company was formed in 1877 to take over the Street Railway. This letter signed by George W. Lloyd, its managing director shows that the company's office was still at Palm Grove depot.

Kingsland Road, Oxton, Clifton and Tranmere Parks'. A 10 minute service ran throughout the day, reduced to 15 minutes after about 7.45pm on both the Oxton and Borough Road routes and fares were standardised at 3d inside and 2d outside with a 6d fare on late cars to Oxton. The Borough Road cars had cream ends and showed a green light at night whilst the Oxton cars had red ends and displayed a red light.

The Oxton line's outward route along Price Street and Vittoria Street was inconvenient; furthermore, the Price Street line was only a few yards from the Hoylake Railway's Cleveland Street line which provided a service in both directions. In February 1878 the Birkenhead Tramways Co. prevailed upon the Council to allow an outward line to be laid in Conway Street but the use of this was conditional upon every third car continuing to use Price Street and the line being extended across Hamilton Square to Hamilton Street to provide an inward route. The company agreed to this condition or alternatively to provide an omnibus every half hour between Wood-side and the corner of Price Street and Vittoria Street. The second track along Conway Street was in use by October 1878. All cars used this route, a somewhat irregular omnibus service being provided along Price Street until mid-December. Its withdrawal provoked a petition from the residents and in February 1879 the company asked the Council to agree to the withdrawal of the Price Street service altogether, as the patronage was negligible but this request was summarily rejected. Nevertheless by May the Price Street route was withdrawn, a full service being run both ways along Conway Street. In August the Council threatened to take up the second track in Conway Street if the Price Street service was not reinstated and the company reluctantly complied. When it was disclosed that the revenue from the service was only 32/- per week the Council agreed to an experimental abandonment if the company would reduce the Woodside-Park Entrance fare from 3d to 2d. An experiment on these lines was tried in 1881 but revenue fell drastically and the Council finally agreed to fares of 3d inside and 2d outside on ordinary weekdays and the lifting of the Price Street track from 1 November 1881 despite the protests of the local ratepayers. By February 1882 the rails had been removed and complaint was made that the company had failed to reinstate the road properly. The Town Clerk was told to instruct the company to do the work properly or the Corporation would do it and charge them.

From 1 January 1881 the corporation increased the annual charges for use of the lines at Woodside except that for the Docks line which remained at £200. The two companies now paid £75 each for the facilities in the centre of the ferry approach.

Omnibuses, of which there were apparently only five, were to pay £5 each but this was subsequently reduced to £3. The Birkenhead company also paid the Council £50 per year for track maintenance on the streets. The following year the Council was criticised for introducing a conductor's licence costing 6s 6d (32½p) as many conductors were paid less than 10s (50p) per week.

In 1879 the Birkenhead Tramways Co proposed to submit a Bill for powers for extended lines including one to Bidston which was opposed by the Hoylake Railway. This led to discussions during which the Hoylake company indicated its willingness to sell its tramway undertaking to the Birkenhead Tramways Co provided that certain guarantees regarding connections between the railway terminus and the ferry could be negotiated. The growth of industry along the Great Float had brought more local traffic which was now as important as the railway traffic. With plans in the air for extension of the railway to Seacombe, the company did not wish to become involved in a mainly urban tramway scheme requiring new rolling stock to permit the operation of a more frequent service. An Act of 1879 authorised both the purchase of the line by the Birkenhead Tramways Company and the construction of further extensions, some of which were aimed at integrating the Docks line with the main town system.

Late in 1876 the original American-type cars of the Birkenhead Street Railway were replaced by new cars of Starbuck's latest type with convenient quarter-turn stairways. This maker's view of No. 1 carries the name of the newly-appointed managing director, George Lloyd. One of these cars (No.7) has been preserved after operating in both Birkenhead and Southport. *(Science Museum, Whitcombe Collection)*

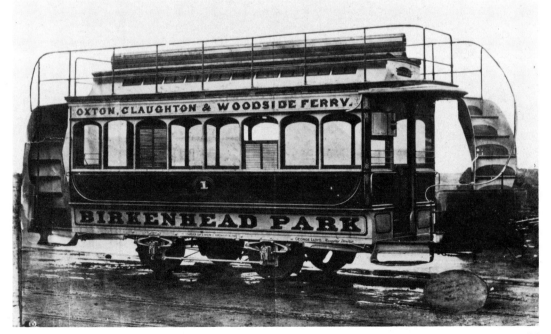

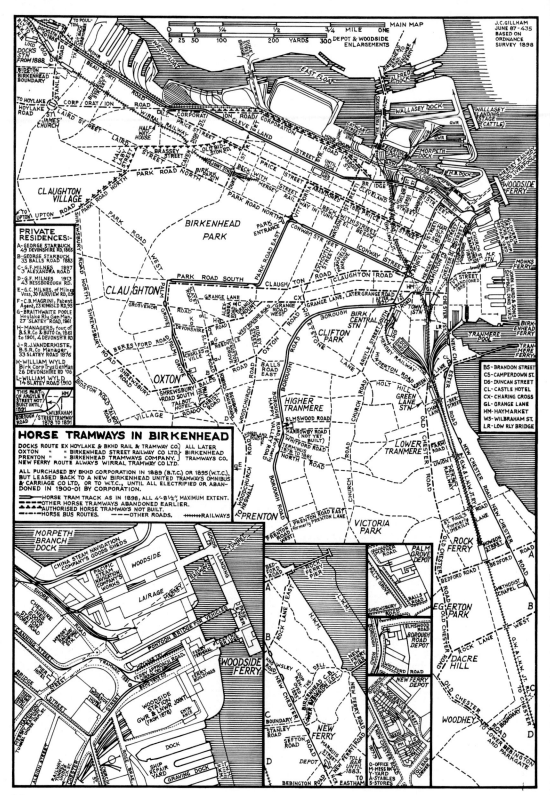

HORSE TRAMWAYS IN BIRKENHEAD

DOCKS ROUTE EX HOYLAKE & BKHD RAIL & TRAMWAY CO.) ALL LATER
OXTON "   BIRKENHEAD STREET RAILWAY CO LTD.) BIRKENHEAD
PRENTON "   " BIRKENHEAD TRAMWAYS COMPANY.) TRAMWAYS CO.
NEW FERRY ROUTE ALWAYS WIRRAL TRAMWAY CO LTD.

ALL PURCHASED BY BKHD CORPORATION IN 1889 (B.T.C.) OR 1895 (W.T.C.)
BUT LEASED BACK TO A NEW BIRKENHEAD UNITED TRAMWAYS OMNIBUS
& CARRIAGE CO LTD, OR TO W.T.C., UNTIL ALL ELECTRIFIED OR ABAN-
DONED IN 1900-01 BY CORPORATION.

——— HORSE TRAM TRACK AS IN 1898, ALL 4'-8½" MAXIMUM EXTENT.
——— OTHER HORSE TRAMWAYS ABANDONED EARLIER.
▲▲▲▲ AUTHORISED HORSE TRAMWAYS NOT BUILT.
——— HORSE BUS ROUTES. ——— OTHER ROADS. ++++++ RAILWAYS

PRIVATE
RESIDENCES:-
A - GEORGE STARBUCK,
49 DEVONSHIRE RD,1865
B - GEORGE STARBUCK,
33 BALLS ROAD 1883
C - G.F. MILNES   1897
3 ALEXANDRA ROAD
D - G.F. MILNES   1913
33 BESSBOROUGH RD.
E - G.C. MILNES, of Milnes
Voss, 30 FAIRVIEW RD, 05
F - C.B. MAGRINI, Patent
Agent,23 KINGSLD RD,95
G - BRAITHWAITE POOLE
Hoylake Rly Gen Man,
27 SLATEY ROAD,1861
H - MANAGERS, four, of
B.S.R.Co & BUTO Co,1861
to 1901, 4 DEVONSHR RD
J - R.J.VANDERKISTE,
B.S.R.Co Manager,
33 SLATEY ROAD 1876
K - WILLIAM WYLD
Birk CorpTrusGenMan
26 DEVONSHIRE RD '06
L - WILLIAM WYLD
14 SLATEY ROAD 1910

THIS PART
OF ARGYLE
STREET NOT
BUILT UNTIL
1891

BS - BRANDON STREET
CS - CAMPERDOWN ST.
DS - DUNCAN STREET
CL - CASTLE HOTEL
CX - CHARING CROSS
GL - GRANGE LANE
HM - HAYMARKET
WS - WILBRAHAM ST.
LR - LOW RLY BRIDGE

J.C.GILLHAM
JUNE 87 - 435
BASED ON
ORDNANCE
SURVEY 1898

26

Each of the three horse tram companies serving Birkenhead Woodside originally had unconnected stub termini, with a two-way single track ending in a pair of short sidings. From left to right, the Hoylake Railway cars left from the tracks alongside the wall; the Wirral company used the centre track, and the original Street Railway was next to it. The car shown here is No. 16 of the Street Railway's successor company. The Albert Dock warehouses can be seen across the river in Liverpool. *(Courtesy Martin Jenkins)*

(1) A short link along the lower part of Argyle Street between Canning Street and Bridge Street.

(2) Borough Road from North Road to Prenton Road East (then known as Prenton Lane).

(3) From Cleveland Street to Shrewsbury Road North via Duke Street, Price Street, Old Bidston Road, Brassey Street, Mallaby Street and Park Road North.

The purchase price for the Hoylake company's tramway was £27,500 including eight cars and a 21 year lease of the sheds and stables at Docks Station, on the same terms as those given to the contractor, Mr. Townson. The Birkenhead Tramways Company was obliged to provide an improved service, to meet all trains, and to run a ten minute service between 8am and 8pm at fares not exceeding 3d inside and 2d outside. Higher fares could be charged by any cars other than those of the regular service, such cars to be distinguished by a 'flag or placard or other adequate means'. The workmen's cars were to continue and there was a duty to continue to run 'Two express through cars at the least, from or in connection with morning trains without stopping for intermediate traffic'. The company was precluded from ever seeking powers to operate tramways beyond Bidston in the direction of Hoylake. The Birkenhead Tramways Co. took over on Sunday 12 October 1879 and, rather short-sightedly, was delighted with its 'bargain' as it thought it could work a branch to Claughton Village from Cleveland Street more cheaply than from the Park and in due course divert some of the Docks cars to the new branch. The commissioners had asked for a Claughton line as early as 1861. In the event, the Docks line was to lead to the ruin of the company as described below.

The Prenton extension was inspected on 21 May 1881 and public service started on 1 June with no additional fare being charged. In November 1881 the Corporation approved the laying of the short Argyle Street extension which connected the town routes at Bridge Street with the Docks route at Canning Street. A further link was laid from Hamilton Street across the ferry approach. This crossed the New Ferry line but there was no connection.

At some date a line was laid apparently without formal powers, along Lord Street between Bridge Street and Canning Street. There were thus short parallel lines in three adjacent streets. The Lord Street line may have been laid as a sequel to a serious accident on 22 July 1882 when car 18 overturned at the bottom of Taylor Street, killing a passenger and injuring several others. Taylor Street was a steep decline followed by a sharp right angle turn and there would be a temptation to increase speed down Taylor Street to gain impetus for the slight incline in Canning Street. Alternatively the provision of the Lord Street line would have enabled the express cars connecting with the railway to overtake the ordinary cars carrying the local traffic.

Following incorporation in 1877, Birkenhead

27

sought numerous powers to undertake public works including authority to own tramways and to lease them to others; the concept of direct operation by a municipality was, at that time, unknown. In 1881 a clause was inserted in a general Act to ensure that certain provisions of the Tramways Act 1870 applied to the Birkenhead tramways which pre-dated the Act and authority was also obtained to make bye-laws preventing overcrowding on any tramway within the Borough.

In November 1882 the company approached the Corporation about a new line which it wished to lay in a proposed new street linking Borough Road with the top of Oxton Road (Balls Road East). The company offered to pay £500 towards the cost of the road and a further £250 if they would make it wide enough for a double line, the gradient being very steep. The cash was offered on condition that the company would be allowed to continue the line along Balls Road and Shrewsbury Road to Claughton but this was refused and the offer was withdrawn. This proposed route and the unused powers in the 1879 Act would have formed a route very similar to the Circle operated during the electric era. During the course of the discussion in Council, Alderman Evans, whose bus route would have been seriously affected, steered the Council into a discussion on acquisition of the tramway tracks but the matter was again deferred.

The Omnibus Companies

At this time there were two other omnibus proprietors in Birkenhead in addition to Thomas Evans and Sons but their activities are obscure. Only Evans had stands allocated at Woodside ferry approach, for which he paid £3 3s per bus per annum. This had risen from £1 5s in 1868. The others were W. W. Townson, who had worked the Hoylake Railway cars, and Edward Davies and Sons of Camden Street. In 1882-83 Evans had 13 hackney licences and Davies had 22 though doubtless most of these were carriages. Inexplicably Townson was not listed. The Birkenhead Watch Committee was liberal in the issue of licences and sometimes licensed omnibuses to run over the tram routes for special occasions, to the annoyance of the Tramways Company. Omnibuses and waggonettes were run to special events such as the Wirral Hunt Steeplechase at Parkgate.

The 1879 amalgamation had been the first stage in the unification of local transport on the streets of Birkenhead. On 29 October 1883 a new company, the Birkenhead and District Omnibus and Carriage Co. Ltd. with an authorised capital of £25,000 in £1 shares was formed to take over the omnibus business of W. W. Townson who was appointed managing director. The other directors were Thomas Henry Brattan (chairman) architect, William Maddocks, contractor, William Askew, innkeeper, William

Walls, saddler, Henry Griffiths, car proprietor, Charles F. Smith, solicitor and George Readdy (secretary), accountant. Townson, a veterinary surgeon by profession, received £3,000 plus valuation of assets comprising land in Balls Road, three omnibuses seating 34, 28 and 16 respectively, two charabancs seating 30 each, one large waggonette to carry 32; 11 carriages and cabs and 20 horses with harness etc. £500 was paid in cash and £2,500 in shares.

Both Townson and Evans had been running services between Woodside and Heswall since the summer of 1882 and it is on record that drivers of both firms were dismissed for racing in Hamilton Street. 'As the cattle was good, there was no accident and the passengers enjoyed the fun but it is fortunate that a dangerous practice has been nipped in the bud' commented the *Birkenhead News*.

The new company started a new service in competition with Evans between Oxton, Claughton and Woodside in December 1883 and in March 1884 William Bulmer, former landlord of the Old Swan Inn and Liverpool omnibus proprietor and Joseph Perrin, a local contractor, were among six directors elected. Reconstruction of the Board heralded the acquisition of the business of Thomas Evans and Sons from 31 March. The Evans family received £14,500, £500 being paid on signature on 25 March; £2,000 cash and £5,000 in paid up shares on 31 March 1884; £2,500 cash within three months (plus 5% interest) and £4,500 cash within 12 months (plus 5% interest). The Evans business had been conducted solely from rented premises and tenancies of 69 Watson Street (£35p.a.), 152 Chester Street (£50p.a.), 42 Balls Road (£65p.a.) and the house, yard and stables at 4 Devonshire Road (£110p.a.) were transferred together with the Woodside coach office at £120p.a. standings for omnibuses at Woodside Nos. 1, 2 and 4 and standings for cabs on the public streets and at Woodside ferry. No vehicles were transferred under the agreement suggesting that they were old and worn out. Ald. Evans, then aged 64, joined the Board and doubtless his chairmanship of the Watch Committee which he retained until 1892, made him a valuable member. He died on 14 December 1894, nine days after his 75th birthday.

Bulmer was appointed manager and under the new regime the Balls Road omnibus route was extended along Shrewsbury Road to Beresford Road. In July 1884 a new route operated half-hourly by 'large and commodious' vehicles commenced between Woodside and the Dock Cottages near St. James' Church via Price Street at a fare of 2d. This competed with the Docks tramway. Carriage hire and funerals were also undertaken. In its first year the company paid a 5% dividend. A letter to the press in October 1884 indicates the greedy practices of the omnibus owners. The writer remarks that the Evanses would withdraw the buses without notice to

G. F. Milnes garden-seat horse car 18 of the Birkenhead United Tramway, Omnibus and Carriage Co Ltd. at the Borough Road terminus of the Prenton route. The bodies of two of these cars were later converted into electric works vehicles. Note the moveable seat on the front platform. *(Tramway Museum Society)*

send them to Chester Races or other events and on 16 October the new company had similarly taken the services off on the occasion of the visit of Mr Gladstone to cut the first sod of the Liverpool and North Wales railway at Bidston.

In 1881 the Hoylake Railway changed its name to the Seacombe, Hoylake and Deeside Railway Co. and proposed an extension from Docks Station to Seacombe. Squire Vyner succeeded in having so many conditions imposed that the line would have been prohibitively expensive to build as then authorised but provision was made for the tramway to be diverted to the relocated Docks Station which would have been built. The Birkenhead Tramways Co. was also to be paid compensation of £500 per annum for four years after extension of the railway to Seacombe. In 1886 these powers were replaced by new schemes to divert the railway to link up with an extension of the Mersey Railway at a new station in Duke Street to be known as Birkenhead Park. A slightly different formula for compensation was enacted.

Construction of the Mersey Railway tunnel affected the tramways in other ways. At 3.30pm on 1 August 1884 part of Hamilton Street collapsed leaving a hole 16ft by 12ft by 10ft deep below the tracks. The sewer below had given way and the subsoil was being washed away into the tunnel workings. There were several cave-ins during the ensuing year resulting in interruption of the tram services and a curve was laid from Argyle Street into Conway Street to facilitate diversion of cars.

The opening of the Mersey Railway to Green Lane on 1 February 1886 had a tremendous impact on ferries, tramways and omnibuses. Ferry passengers at Woodside fell from 10.4 million in 1885-86 to 6.2 million in 1886-87 and to 5.2 million in 1888-89. The trams carried some passengers to the railway stations and the omnibus company put on a special service in February 1886 between Shrewsbury Road and Central Station running every 20 minutes. By January 1888 this was a one-horse bus running at a fare of 1d.

The opening of the Wirral and Mersey Railway extensions to Birkenhead Park on 2 January 1888 deprived the Docks tramway and Woodside ferry of traffic as railway passengers continued on the train to Park Station and transferred to the Mersey's trains for a direct journey to Liverpool. Dock labourers did not use the trams regularly at 2d or 3d a trip and the line was cut back a short distance to the then borough boundary in Beaufort Road. The Corporation agreed to the laying of a branch line from Cleveland Street to Park Station via Duke Street but the company could not finance it. Eventually from 3 March 1894 the Docks route was reduced to half-hourly west of Duke Street where alternate cars terminated.

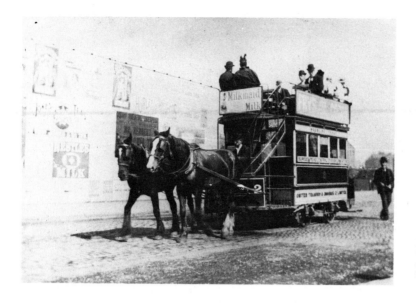

A small garden-seat horse car of the Birkenhead United company passing Central Station. These were originally one-horse cars, but were later used with two horses. The lower destination boards were moveable but the designation 'Woodside Ferry' was painted on the cantrail.
(Courtesy G. Parry)

On 18 January 1888 an auction was held at Docks Station, eight pair horse cars and 30 horses being offered. There was a large attendance and fair prices were realised for the horses but there were no offers for the cars which were presumably those taken over from the Hoylake Railway in 1879. The sale was consequent upon the substitution of one horse cars on the Docks route. A one horse car had made an appearance on the Borough Road route in October 1887 with a view to reducing expenditure on provender. The *Advertiser* commented 'The use of one horse cars and a reduction in fares from 3d to 2d on this route would make all the difference. At present the company's style of management is hopelessly stupid.' The newspaper campaigned regularly for a reduction in tram fares.

The Birkenhead United

In 1887-88 the company made a loss of £700 and the railway extensions were described as a 'staggering blow'. As track and cars needed renewal the company presented a winding-up Petition on 7 September 1888. A liquidator was appointed and the company continued to operate for the time being. Faced with the complete demise of three of the four tram routes in the borough, the Corporation resolved to promote a Parliamentary Bill to buy, work and lease the tramways on the grounds that the company would be unable to meet its obligation to remove the rails and make good the streets. In May 1889 the undertaking, in liquidation, was transferred to Mr. J. H. Brattan on behalf of a syndicate interested in forming a new tramway company. In June the syndicate refused the offer of the Corporation for the rails because in true municipal fashion they attempted to attach conditions placing obligations on the promoters to co-ordinate the running

of the cars with ferry sailings and to obtain Council approval of the fares to be charged. So when the prospectus for the Birkenhead United Tramway, Omnibus and Carriage Co was issued it stated that the rails would be the property of the company. The company was registered on 8 August 1889 with a capital of £45,000 in £1 shares to acquire the business of the Birkenhead Tramway Co and the Birkenhead and District Omnibus and Carriage Co Ltd. The assets which included 27 tramcars, 14 omnibuses, 9 waggonettes, 15 carriages, five hearses, 40 cabs and other vehicles were valued at £43,747 excluding goodwill and the company was to pay £37,500.

On 9 October 1889 solicitors for the liquidator advised the Corporation that they would sell the tracks for £5,000 subject to the approval of the Court and that the Corporation should also buy the land and stables. The Council agreed to the £5,000 but would not buy the land and stables. 34 tons of rails stored at Palm Grove were eventually purchased and the Corporation was obliged to make urgent repairs to the track four months before the formal transfer on 15 August 1890. The directors of the new company included several familiar names in local transport circles. Thomas Sheppard, the chairman, was a director of the Southport Tramways; Thomas Wright, a corn merchant, was prominent in Liverpool and Chester companies; Joseph Perrin and William Bulmer were directors of the previous omnibus company. New names were Andrew Howard, tent and tarpaulin manufacturer of Red Cross Street, Liverpool, a familiar name on shop blinds for many years; Adolphus Aylmer Cleeve, commission agent and Robert Daniel Francis, solicitor. The registered office was moved from 41 North John Street, Liverpool to Ferry Buildings, Woodside in May 1890 but two years later they joined other local companies at the offices of William Knox, now secretary, at 6 Lord Street, Liverpool. Later shareholders were G. F. Milnes, carriage manufacturer and Miles and Charles W. Mason, Liverpool omnibus proprietors.

Birkenhead Corporation granted the new company a temporary lease of the tramways at £50 per month followed by a permanent lease from 1 January 1891 to 31 December 1900. The rent was fixed at £600 in the first year increasing to £825 in the last year. If revenue exceeded £10,000 in any year the company was to pay 10% of the excess to the Corporation. In October 1891 the company sought permission to use electric power but the Corporation's reply was inconclusive.

The opening of the Mersey Railway to Green Lane on 1 February 1886 had not affected the Wirral Tramway Co too badly as it cost passengers the same fare to ride from New Ferry to Green Lane as it did to ride to Woodside. The company had prospered in the early 1880s but from 1 January 1886, in anticipation of a reduction in traffic, wages were reduced from 27s (£1.35) to 25s 6d (£1.27½) per week for drivers and 15s (75p) to 14s (70p) for conductors. In addition a payment of 2s 6d (12½p) for working the late cars was abolished. Comparison was made with Liverpool drivers' wages of 35s (£1.75) though they worked longer hours than the 13-15 per day worked on the Wirral line. At the end of 1887 the company agreed with the Corporation for Woodside ferry tickets to be sold on the trams, the company paying two thirds of a penny per ticket. It is not known how this arrangement favoured the passenger.

The Mersey Railway's extension to Rock Ferry to meet the LNW/GW Joint railway was a much more serious matter and in anticipation of this the tramway was divided into short stages, 1d fares being charged between each adjacent pair viz: New Ferry, Rock Lane, Bedford Road, Chamberlain Street, Green Lane and Woodside. This did not satisfy the vociferous local residents who demanded a 1d fare from New Ferry to Bedford Road (for Rock Ferry station) and a 2d fare to Green Lane to encourage the use of Tranmere Ferry. From 21 December 1891 the timetable was revised so that the cars connected with the trains at Green Lane, the general frequency being quarter-hourly increased to 10 minutes on Saturday afternoons. Fares were reduced, the New Ferry-Bedford Road 1d fare being granted but the 2d stage extended only to Chamberlain Street.

In 1889, before the full effects of competition had been felt the company issued 15 debentures to replace existing securities and on 1 January 1894 £7,500 was due. The mortgage was insured with the Mortgage Insurance Co. which failed and as the Tramway Company was unable to pay the debenture holders it approached the Corporation on 2 February. By this time the track and equipment were in such bad condition that the line was barricaded for

part of the route as the road surface was considered unsafe for ordinary traffic. Repairs were estimated to cost £2,800. On 6 October the Council resolved 22:17 to purchase the tracks on the New Ferry route for £2,250. Lower Bebington Local Board, in whose area 436 yards of track and the depot lay, objected and eventually Birkenhead Corporation purchased only the portion within the borough for £2,054. Inexplicably a 21 year lease was granted to the Wirral company from 11 March 1895 to 10 March 1916 and why it should have been so generous when less than four years earlier the town routes were leased for less than ten years is not clear. One councillor also compared the £850 per mile paid for the New Ferry line with £360 per mile paid for the Oxton, Prenton and Docks lines. The company's rent was fixed at £383p.a. escalating to £410 after five years. The lines along Ivy Street and Church Street were abandoned, a loop being put in in Chester Street near Duncan Street. By 1896 it was clear that the Corporation had made a bad bargain as the track repair and renewal costs were about £4000.

William Lever commenced developing the area around Bromborough Pool as a soap works in 1888 and built the adjoining model village for his employees early in the twentieth century. The rural character of the road beyond New Ferry rapidly changed as more industries were established. From March 1898 to May 1900, the Wirral Tramway Co.

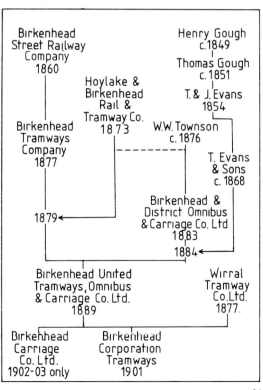

operated a horse bus service half hourly from noon to 8pm between New Ferry tram terminus and Bromborough Cross.

An omnibus service between Upton and Birkenhead was first licensed to the Upton Bus Co on 11 March 1891. It is thought that this probably ran to Park Station but the exact route has not come to light.

The company endeavoured to improve facilities at Woodside. The Corporation agreed to lay a loop line in January 1894, the company's rent to be increased by £5 per year, but a scheme for more extensive alterations and the erection of passenger shelters was rejected by the council in December 1896.

After the track relaying of 1864 cars had used Argyle Street outward and Hamilton Street inward. Argyle Street originally ended at Grange Road, access to Borough Road being by way of Wilbraham Street but a new road was built in 1891. A curve was laid from the inward track in Borough Road into the new part of Argyle Street and the Wilbraham Street track lifted, calls for the diversion of the Conway Street cars via Central Station being ignored. The new line came into use on 21 December 1891 and this is probably when the direction of travel in Argyle Street and Hamilton Street was reversed though it may have happened earlier possibly as a consequence of the diversions which were necessary during the construction of the Mersey Railway tunnel in 1884-86. It seems likely that in the last years of horse traction cars travelled inwards via Argyle Street and Canning Street (involving a few yards of wrong line running) and outward via Bridge Street and Hamilton Street.

By May 1898 Birkenhead town council had decided to purchase and electrify the tramways and obtained the necessary Act of Parliament in June 1899. In consequence of the municipal take-over, described in the next chapter the Wirral company ceased trading in May 1900 and the United company in the following year.

Birkenhead Horse Tramway Rolling Stock

It is unfortunate that few records of the horse drawn omnibuses and tramcars have survived. The basic design of the horse drawn omnibus changed little between the 'forties and the 'eighties — a box like structure with entrance placed centrally at the rear with room for seven or eight passengers on longitudinal seats each side. Ventilation was by top lights in the sides or by means of a clerestory in the roof which also gave extra headroom. When more capacity was required, a vertical ladder was added at the back and seats were provided back to back on the clerestory; additional passengers sat alongside the driver. The addition of top deck passengers seems to have originated in London at the time of the Great Exhibition in Hyde Park in 1851. As the years passed, the stairs became easier and decency screens

were added to the upper decks. In the early 1860s the omnibuses operated by Thomas Evans are on record as having been designed to carry 13 passengers although 15 were apparently permitted to be carried.

1860-type cars

When tramcars first appeared in Birkenhead in 1860, they were imported from America and were thus of a design which had been evolving since the New York and Harlaem line opened in 1832. The main difference between omnibus and tramcar design was that the tramcars were double-ended thus avoiding the need for expensive loops at the end of the line. The much lower rolling resistance of the iron wheel on the iron rail enabled trams to be built to a larger size than the contemporary omnibus. The double deck tramcars weighed about 2 tons 8 cwt unladen and single deckers about two tons. The original four cars are known to have been 24ft long and 7ft wide with interior headroom of 7ft. Longitudinal seats in red plush accommodated 24 passengers. The bulkheads had sliding doors, a completely new feature, and some sources say that the window sashes were raised to open them although contemporary illustrations contradict this. Above each opening window was an ornate fixed top light in decorated ground glass. The wheels were of chilled cast iron and originally the springing comprised air-filled rubber balls in cylinders between axle boxes and the car body. These were probably unsatisfactory as later cars were fitted with a compressed block of vulcanised rubber. In front of each pair of wheels there was a broom to sweep debris from the track. The livery was light green embellished with various armorial devices.

The cars assembled by Robert Main at Canning Street are known to have been numbered 1-2 (double-deck) and 3-4 (single deck). Cars numbered 5-8 were single-deckers imported from the USA in 1861 and these included one one-horse car. The named cars 'Young England' and 'Young America' were of this batch. These eight cars were almost certainly converted to 4ft 8½in gauge in 1864. "Young England" was sold by auction at the Starbuck works in October 1886 where 'it had lain for many years.' The auctioneer apparently described it as the first tramcar used in England, whereupon Robert Main wrote to the local press to correct him.

The Hoylake Company's cars

Eight double-deck cars, numbered 1-8, were purchased by the Hoylake and Birkenhead Rail and Tramway Co Ltd from the Starbuck Car & Wagon Co Ltd in 1873; No. 2 is illustrated on page 18. They retained the primitive 1860-type spiral iron ladder at each end. These cars were acquired by the Birkenhead Tramways Co Ltd in 1879, along with the line upon which they operated. It is believed that they were then renumbered 17-24, and ran until 1887

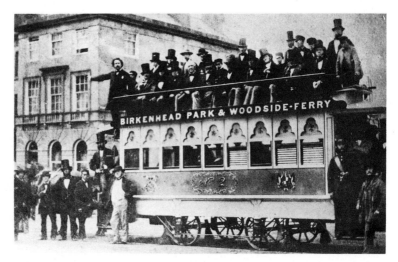

The original photograph of Birkenhead Street Railway No. 2 of 1860 from which the engraving forming our frontispiece was traced. Note the brushes fitted to sweep the track. *(Tramway Museum Society)*

when new smaller cars were purchased. All eight cars were offered for sale by auction in January 1888 but there were no offers and their subsequent fate is unknown.

1876-type cars

Replacement cars, probably eight in number and certainly including cars numbered 1 and 7, were purchased from the Starbuck Car & Wagon Co Ltd soon after the September 1876 change of ownership, to replace the G F Milnes vehicles of 1860-1. Although structurally similar to the 1873 Hoylake cars, they were the first in Birkenhead to have the newly-introduced convenient quarter-turn iron stair and also had a more comfortably shaped top deck knifeboard seat. Car No. 1, illustrated on page 25, has a new type of axlebox suspension, possibly experimental, but car No. 7 had the previous type. They had a 16ft saloon with eight elliptical-top windows on each side and seated 22 passengers on longitudinal seats in the saloon, and a further 24 on

THE ORIGINAL BIRKENHEAD TRAM-CAR

TO THE EDITOR OF THE BIRKENHEAD ADVERTISER.

Sir,—In your publication of the 16th inst. you allude to the sale at the Starbuck Car and Waggon Works of a tram-car claimed as being the first used in England. This is not exactly in accordance with the real history of tram-cars in this country. I had the pleasure of building the first four tram-cars used in England, from designs by Mr. George Francis Train, and the tram-car alluded to in your report of the sale was "Young England," brought from New York some years after the opening of the tramway in Birkenhead.—Yours, &c.,
ROBERT MAIN,
Carriage Works, Claughton-road,
October 27th, 1886.

the knife-board seat on the roof. The livery was varnished mahogany, scarlet red with gold lining, and cream, the cantrail carrying the green-shaded route lettering 'OXTON CLAUGHTON & WOODSIDE FERRY.' The legend 'BIRKENHEAD PARK' appeared in larger letters on the rocker panels, and again in a large semi-circle over the fleet number on the dashes. The fleet number was also carried on each waist panel within an oval garter belt on which appeared 'THE BIRKENHEAD STREET RAILWAY CO. LTD.' At night a green light was displayed.

The interior was of varnished Spanish mahogany, contrasting with an off-white ceiling lined in dark blue. Above each of the eight side windows was an engraved oval mirror, whilst plain rectangular mirrors were fitted in both sides of each bulkhead. Padded seat backs of crimson Utrecht velvet were provided.

These cars were apparently withdrawn and sold when replaced by smaller cars between 1887 and 1890. Car No 7 (probably with others) was sold to the Birkdale and Southport Tramways Co Ltd and operated in Southport until about 1901, then becoming an office and shelter in a coal merchant's yard. In 1972 it was acquired for preservation and is now being restored at Steamport Museum in Southport.

1878-type cars

In 1876 the Borough Road route was opened, requiring additional cars. These were again purchased from the Starbuck works and were similar to the 1876 cars, but slightly smaller. They again had eight elliptical-topped windows, but the saloon was only 15ft 3in long. They seated 20 inside on longitudinal seats and a further 20 on the outside knifeboard seat. The dashes were painted scarlet red to distinguish them from the Oxton cars (now with cream dashes) and a red lamp was displayed at night. Eight cars were required for the service, and it is

33

One-horse Starbuck car No. 8 of the Wirral Tramways Co Ltd. in New Chester Road, possibly on the final day of Wirral Company operations in May 1900. *(M. J. Mitchell Collection)*

A four-horse omnibus of the Birkenhead United Tramways, Omnibus and Carriage Company on the service between Oxton and Woodside which continued for a short period after the electrification of the tramways. *(Courtesy T. G. Turner)*

likely that this was the number purchased and that they took fleet numbers 9-16, but this is unconfirmed. The 1878 cars appear to have operated the Borough Road line until replaced by smaller one-horse cars in 1887, when they were transferred to the Oxton route to replace the 1876 cars. They were replaced in turn by smaller cars in the 1890s.

1887-type cars

In an attempt to reduce the working expenses on the Borough Road line, the Birkenhead Tramways Company in October 1887 purchased a small six-window double-deck car to be drawn by one horse instead of two. It was built by George F Milnes, having the usual longitudinal seats inside but introducing to Birkenhead the reversible garden seats on the roof. The only known photograph of this type of car is one of No 18 at Borough Road terminus. Four additional cars of the same type were purchased by January 1888 and these made their appearance on the Docks route to replace the former Hoylake company's cars. When the Birkenhead Tramways Company's fleet was taken over by the United Company in July 1889 it comprised 27 cars, ten of which were out of use as the Board of Trade return shows only 17 cars in service.

1890-type cars

In order to extend the operation of single-horse cars, ten short double-deck cars of a new type were purchased in 1890 from G F Milnes & Co Ltd. They had five windows per side and seated 18 passengers in the saloon and a further 22 on reversible transverse garden seats on the roof, and were of a more modern design than any of the previous types; fleet numbers included 2, 5 and 12. In practice the 1887 and 1890 cars represented hard work for a single horse and in

later years it became necessary to employ a pair on each vehicle. The arrival of the 1890 cars resulted in a number of older car bodies being offered for sale in August of that year.

The 1887 and 1890 cars continued in service until the abandonment of the horse tramways in 1901. On Friday 13 September 1901 twenty cars were offered for sale by auction at Borough Road depot, and the fate of a few cars is known. One 1887 car was bought by Birkenhead Corporation Tramways and used to build Works Car No 60; another previously sold was bought by the Corporation in November 1902 and became Works Car No 62. One of the 1890 cars survived until the 1950s as a shed on an allotment at Arrowe Park.

The Wirral Company's cars

The Wirral Tramway Company opened its line to New Ferry in 1877 using seven single deck cars built by the Starbuck Car and Wagon Co Ltd. They were presumably numbered 1-7, and seated 18 passengers in the saloon plus two on each platform.

The 1877 cars were found to be rather small for the traffic, and were replaced in 1879 by seven similar but larger vehicles seating 22 in the saloon plus two on the platform. They were built in the Starbuck Works and bore the same numbers as the first batch of cars, which are thought by the authors to have been sold to the Wallasey tramways, as recounted on page 96. The 1879 Wirral cars had seven curved-top windows on each side.

Two more single deck cars, 8 and 9, were purchased from Starbuck in 1880 differing only slightly from the 1879 batch, with more rounded canopies.

Increasing traffic led to the introduction of some double deck cars, all seating 42 passengers. The first, presumably Nos 10 and 11, seem to have arrived in 1894, followed by No 12 in 1895 and No 13 in 1896.

1890-type double-deck Milnes car No. 5 of the Birkenhead United Company outside Palm Grove depot and stables. *(Courtesy M. Jenkins)*

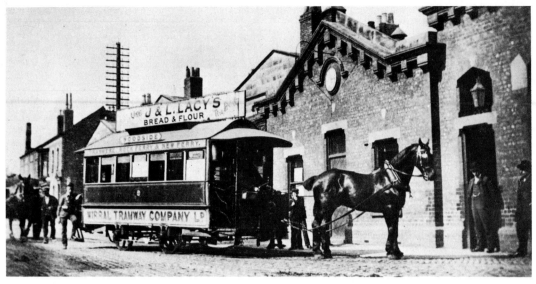

Turtle-back roof car 9 of the Wirral Tramway Company outside New
Ferry depot in the last years of operation.
(Courtesy H. G. Dibdin)

These double deck cars were probably built by
George F Milnes and presumably had transverse
garden seats upstairs. Their arrival suggests the
operation of a part-way service between New Ferry
and Green Lane to feed Laird's shipyard and Green
Lane Mersey Railway station.

All thirteen cars were still in stock on 16 May 1900
when the Wirral company offered its fleet for sale by
auction at New Ferry depot. The cars were sold to
various buyers including the Birkenhead United
Tramways, Omnibus and Carriage Co Ltd, which
purchased about five of the single deck cars, as it was
to take over the working of the New Ferry line
pending electrification, and had no suitable cars of its
own. Nos 4, 8 and 9 were among those purchased.
They were not repainted or renumbered, and
retained the Wirral Tramway Co Ltd fleet name on
the rocker panels. They resumed service on the New
Ferry line with their new owner, and continued to
operate until horse tramway operation to New Ferry
finally ceased. The cars again came up for auction at
New Ferry depot on 24 January 1901 and were sold
for between £4 and £8 8s, presumably for use as huts
and sheds. One of the single deck cars survived until
at least 1930 as a bungalow in Lower Heswall, and
one of the double deck cars went initially to a private
buyer in Lower Bebington.

The Wirral Tramways Company also owned four
omnibuses for its service between New Ferry and
Bromborough. Two were purchased new during
1899, seating 28 passengers with garden seats on the
roof, and were sold at the 1900 auction to a Rhyl
buyer for £80 each. The other two had a knifeboard
seat on the roof and were probably obtained second-
hand; they were sold for £30 each.

Starbuck and Milnes

Birkenhead's unique place in tramway history is
further strengthened by its close involvement in
tramcar manufacture. George Starbuck who man-
aged three short-lived tramway enterprises in London in the early 'sixties, foresaw the potential for
tramcar building in Britain and about 1862 moved to
Birkenhead where he established the first 'tramcar
manufactory' outside the U.S.A. He was probably
also an active director of the Street Railway Company. Starbuck was born in Massachusetts in 1834,
the same state as G. F. Train with whose family
shipping business he had almost certainly been
associated in the 1850s. He started building cars at
the Mahogany Shed, Vittoria Wharf formerly used
by Prentiss and Co. In 1871 he acquired premises at
227 Cleveland Street and took up residence first at 1
Kenyon Place, Devonshire Road but moved to 33
Balls Road upon marrying in 1864. He lived there for
27 years and fathered seven children.

His early production was similar in design to the
1860 Birkenhead cars and examples were supplied to
Copenhagen, Brussels, Pernambuco, Liverpool and
probably Swansea and Mumbles and Portsmouth.
Following the passing of the Tramways Act 1870
orders increased and money for expansion was raised
by the formation of a limited company, George
Starbuck and Co. Ltd. in 1871. This in turn was
replaced in November 1872 by an alliance with a
consortium of London financiers and engineers
headed by William Martineau who formed the
Starbuck Car and Wagon Co. Ltd. George Starbuck
received £20,000 in shares for his business and a
guaranteed income of £700 per year. In 1873-74 the
works was considerably enlarged occupying 227-241
Cleveland Street with a potential output of 150-200
cars per year. Cars were supplied to all the Birkenhead companies and the business remained pros-

36

perous until the 1880s when competition forced prices down to a level at which Starbuck could not compete. Starbuck also provided a repair and overhaul service which was used by the Birkenhead Tramways Co and perhaps others. After the Taylor Street runaway in 1882 Starbuck's foreman gave evidence of having overhauled the car three days earlier. In 1886 the company was wound up on a shareholders' petition but the former Secretary, George F. Milnes, purchased the property, plant and goodwill and started to make 'garden seat' cars. Despite this setback Starbuck continued to reside at 33 Balls Road, describing himself as a 'gentleman'. He moved to a smaller house at 5 Park Road South in 1892 but cannot be traced after 1895.

Birkenhead was also the venue for experiments with steam-powered trams many of which were carried out in the 1870s. The Starbuck company built a bogie single deck Grantham car for Vienna in 1876 and it ran its first trials on the Hoylake company's line which passed the factory, on 12-13 June. Major-General Hutchinson of the Board of Trade was invited to be present and later reported that the car tackled the gradient up from Woodside ferry impressively and achieved a speed of 25-30 mph on the long straight Cleveland Street section. The car later broke down but the possibilities of steam operated tramcars had been effectively demonstrated. The Grantham design was a complete self-contained car as opposed to the engine and trailer concept which found most favour on the systems which adopted steam traction in Britain during the 'eighties. Two more Grantham cars were built in Birkenhead by Messrs. Allan and Dickinson, also of Cleveland Street.

A further trial took place early in the morning of 17 September 1881 using a steam car designed for use in Dundee, a delegation from various Scottish towns attending. This time the Wirral company's line was used and the event evoked such interest in tramway circles that a second trial was held on 20 September at the request of directors of Nottingham, Wallasey, Wirral, Blackburn, Wigan and Leeds tramway companies. The car left New Ferry at 6.15am arriving at Green Lane at 6.25 where Mr. Busby of Liverpool and Mr. Gideon Herbert of Nottingham were picked up. After a standing start on the 1 in 13 Chester Street hill the car proceeded to Woodside; it departed at 6.40am negotiating the 1 in 17 hill, the curve into Church Street and the 29ft radius curve into Ivy Street without difficulty. On Chester Street it was brought to a halt, reversed and started up forward to demonstrate its safety on hills similar to those existing in Dundee. Mr. Herbert then drove the car to New Ferry. The car was said to be quiet in operation and horses regarded it with indifference. Its ultimate fate is unknown.

The Birkenhead Tramways Co. contemplated the use of steam on Cleveland Street but could never afford to do so. It is suspected that there were other steam trials in Birkenhead which have escaped the record and a story of a steam engine running out of control down Palm Grove and overturning on the curve into Park Road South cannot be confirmed. The Board of Trade returns for year ending 30 June 1879 show the fleet as 108 horses, 11 cars and one engine and those for 1884 show capital expenditure of £200 on 'locos/engines'.

3 Birkenhead Electric Tramways 1901-18

By 1895 the reliability of electric tramways had been established beyond all doubt though the merits of different methods of current collection were still being debated. Despite the serious objections made at the time to overhead systems on the grounds of obscuring the daylight, by the last years of the century it was clear that this method had more adherents than any other. Another issue was municipalisation of tramways, the concept of direct operation of systems by local authorities as opposed to that of leasing municipally owned tracks to companies which provided the cars and day-to-day management. The principle was better known in Birkenhead than in most places as Woodside ferry had been municipally operated since 1842. Nevertheless municipalisation was just as controversial a subject as nationalisation was to be half a century later.

Although the Tramways Act 1870 empowered local authorities to acquire company owned tramways after 21 years and then every seven years, the companies frequently continued as lessees as at Birkenhead and the link between municipalisation and electrification was the unwillingness of the companies to finance the conversion in the face of legislation which enabled the local councils to acquire the track and equipment at scrap value. It was the uncertainty of the situation which led many companies to allow their tracks to become virtually derelict. At the end of 1896 Birkenhead Corporation deposited a Bill in Parliament which sought powers "to place and run carriages on and work and use any tramways....including the use of electricity or other mechanical power". This passed into law as the Birkenhead Corporation Act 1897.

Meanwhile on 10 April 1897 a letter was sent to Alderman Gill by a Mr James Ross acting for a Canadian syndicate which was involved in certain tramway schemes in Birmingham. They proposed to form a company to take over, electrify and extend the Birkenhead horse car systems at their own expense and to maintain all track and overhead equipment. The Corporation was offered £1,000 per year but would be expected to grant a 21 year lease. New lines were proposed as follows:—

1. Argyle Street South, Hinderton Road, Queen Street, Old Chester Road, Downham Road, Elm Road, North Road to Borough Road.
2. Balls Road East, Balls Road, Shrewsbury Road.
3. Claughton Road, (Camden Street, inwards) to Park Road East.

4. Egerton Road, Tollemache Road.
5. Park Road North, Upton Road.

The proposed installation was said to be technically similar to that used at Rouen. A special sub-committee was appointed to report on electric tramways to be established by (1) the corporation (2) any other body and (3) the Ross syndicate, and they lost no time in arranging to inspect the overhead wire systems at Rouen and Bristol, the centre conduit system at Blackpool and the experimental "Simplex" system in which the conduit slot was incorporated in one of the rails, at the British Insulated Wire Company's works at Prescot. The members were unimpressed by underground conduit systems and decided unanimously in favour of overhead wires.

There was considerable local opposition to the Ross proposal which in no way compensated for the £15,000 which the Corporation had invested in the purchase and repair of the existing lines. Municipal tramways were being established elsewhere and it became known that the Ross syndicate was already involved in a dispute with Birmingham Corporation. At a disorderly meeting on 26 May the full Committee voted 7:6 in favour of making an agreement with Mr. Ross after consideration of a report which had completely ignored items (1) and (2) of the terms of reference. The whole affair was highly suspicious as people who should have known better such as Dr H. Laird Pearson and Joseph Perrin voted in favour. However, the vote was decisively reversed by the full Council 33-13 and by May 1898 the Council had definitely decided to go ahead themselves. The most pressing problem was that of termination of the company leases and whilst the United lease expired at the end of 1900 the Wirral agreement ran until 1916. Negotiations with that company ensued and the date of acquisition was fixed as 31 December 1899, the purchase to include the short length of line in the Lower Bebington District and the depot and stables at New Ferry.

The Birkenhead Corporation Act 1899 which received the Royal Assent on 20 June empowered the Corporation to acquire the tramways undertaking of the Birkenhead United Tramways Omnibus and Carriage Co. Ltd. on expiry or determination of lease and that of the Wirral Tramway Co. Ltd. before 31 December 1899. There was a proviso in the Act that, should the Corporation wish to re-lay the latter company's line at the Bridge Street — Chester Street Junction where it crossed the United company's line,

The low railway bridge in Chester Street on the New Ferry route had a major influence on Birkenhead's tram fleet, forcing the Corporation to use single deck cars on this busy industrial line. They were later rebuilt as lowbridge double-deckers with knifeboard upper-deck seating. This photograph was taken in 1903/4 when the track was temporarily moved to the side of the road to permit drainage works. The girder bridge shown here had recently replaced a lower stone arch bridge. *(Courtesy R. S. Jones)*

facilities must be provided for that company to carry on its service without interruption. This proved to be impossible, mainly because of the need to eliminate the peculiar "double single track' arrangement between Bridge Street and Woodside terminus. The Act granted very extensive powers for the construction of new lines as follows:—

Tramway No.	Route
1	Ferry Approach, Hamilton Street, Grange Road, Borough Road to Central Station.
1A	From Hamilton Street into Canning Street.
2	Double line substitution for existing single line in Bridge Street between Chester Street and Hamilton Street.
3	Argyle Street (Sidney Street to Borough Road)
3A	From Argyle Street into Cleveland Street.
3B	From Argyle Street into Conway Street.
4	Argyle Street South
4A	From Argyle Street South along a new street (Pearson Road) to Church Road.
5	Whetstone Lane, Church Road and Bebington Road to Dacre Hill.
6	Prenton Road West.
7	From Craven Street along Conway Street, Park Road North, Upton Road, Shrewsbury Road North, Shrewsbury Road, Balls Road and Balls Road East to Borough Road.
7A	From Park Road North into Ashville Road.
8	From Hamilton Street into Conway Street.
8A	From Conway Street into Argyle Street.
9	From Conway Street along Claughton Road to Park Road South.
9A	Camden Street.
10	From Palm Grove along Egerton Road and Tollemache Road into Shrewsbury Road North.
11	From Hamilton Street along Hamilton Square North and Cleveland Street to junction with existing tramway at Pool Street.
11A	From Hamilton Square North into Argyle Street.
12	From Cleveland Street along Duke Street, Ashville Road and Manor Hill into Egerton Road.

No specific powers were granted for the lines to be laid in Laird Street and Mallaby Street, which were originally apparently planned as depot access lines only. Passenger services were run over these lines, technically quite illegally, throughout most of the life of the undertaking. Another section constructed without specific powers was the short single line between Claughton Road and Borough Road via Exmouth Street, Atherton Street, Charing Cross and Whetstone Lane. This was explained to the Board of Trade inspecting officer as a temporary line built under powers in the 1899 Act to lay lines in adjacent streets when major road works were under way. The link between Chester Street and Hamilton Street via Market Place South was separately authorised in 1908.

Orders were placed for a total of 44 cars. Because of the low railway bridge in Chester Street, it was decided to use bogie single deck cars of which 13 were ordered, seven for the New Ferry route and six for Higher Tranmere with its 1 in 13½ gradient over which it was feared the Board of Trade would not authorise the use of double deck cars. This decision reflected the lack of professional expertise prior to the appointment of a manager as maximum traction bogie cars could not be fitted with the slipper brakes necessary on such a steep hill. The remainder of the system was to be served by 31 open top four-wheel cars, but later, when it became apparent that the vastly increased passenger demand had been underestimated, 15 large open top bogie cars which became known as the "Prenton bogies" were ordered.

The Permanent Way

The existing horse tramway track was unsuitable for the heavier electric cars and the lines which were

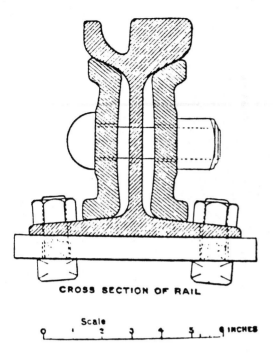

CROSS SECTION OF RAIL

Scale
0 1 2 3 4 5 6 INCHES

Cross-sections of rail and track of the Birkenhead tramways as laid in 1901. The upper sections are of track paved respectively with wood blocks and granite setts. The lower one is of the 100 lb/yd girder rail with fishplates and bolts. (from The Light Railway and Tramway Journal, April 1901)

places on the routes, the total number being 450 men. The following organization was adopted in the large gang: The excavators numbered about one hundred and twenty men, with, say, ten carters. The concretors were divided into two parties, each of about eighteen men, under a banker; the concrete having to be mixed twice dry and twice wet, eight men were required for mixing, four on each side of the stage, with one man pouring and another carrying water, and in addition to these were two men laying, two ramming, and about four wheeling, giving a total of thirty-six, or say, forty concretors; Where the track was to be paved with wood an additional twelve or fifteen men, including two plasterers, were required for floating and bringing the concrete to a smooth surface. The platelaying gang numbered about twenty men, under two platelayers, one superintending the crowing or bending, and the other laying and bolting together of the rails. The paviors, including tar-boilers and labourers, were thirty-five in number. The excavators maintained a distance of three rail-lengths, or 60 yards, ahead of the concretors, who were in turn a sufficient distance in front of the platelayers to allow the concrete to set for 3 days before the rails were placed upon it.

"The rails were bonded with two "Chicago crown" solid copper rail-bonds, each 0.166sq in in sectional area and 29in in length, and having a surface-contact with the rail of 1.37sq in, the track being cross-bonded with bonds of similar cross-section every 40 yards, and inter-cross-bonded, on double-track, every 80 yards. The bond-holes were carefully rimered to give a bright surface for contact with the copper bond. The tracks were paved partly with granite setts and partly with wood blocks, both of which were laid level between the rails, in order not to interfere with the life-guards on the cars. The granite setts, 6in in depth by 3¼in in width, were obtained from Penmaenmawr, Carnarvon, and Ireland. The wood-paving consists mainly of "American red gum" or satin-walnut and Baltic red deal blocks, 9in by 3in, by 5in in depth. The blocks were dipped in boiling tar and laid directly on to the concrete foundation, which was carefully finished smooth to the required levels. The paving was grouted or run, with boiling pitch and tar, with cement grout, or with 1in thickness of boiling pitch and tar finished off with cement-grout. The tops of the rails were coated with lime to prevent the grouting adhering to the metal. A space, ½in in width, was left at each side of the rail and was filled with stiff cement-grout to reduce the disturbing effect on the wood blocks caused by the vibration. Where the sides of the roadway were not also paved, the wood blocks were laid for a width of 18 inches outside the track and the edges were left straight, granite setts being laid longitudinally between them and the macadam. The haunches, or spaces under the heads of the rails, were filled with lime-mortar, manufactured at the Corporation Refuse-Destructors, mixed with Portland cement in the proportion

to be retained were all reconstructed during 1900-01 using steel girder rail of 100lb per yard in 60ft lengths, 7in deep with a 7in flange, 2in tread and 1in by 1⅛in groove. Steel tie-bars 2in deep and ½in thick weighing 17½lb each were fixed 10ft apart and the rails joined by 2ft long steel fishplates weighing 54lb per pair. The whole was laid on what was described as a 6in bed of Portland cement but was in fact concrete. This made the running of the cars non-resilient and vibrations were fully transmitted into the trucks. In particular, the bogies of the 8-wheel cars deteriorated rapidly and this, in turn accentuated track wear. The original specification called for paving with granite setts, but pressure groups succeeded in persuading the Council to provide additional funds for wood blocks on one section after another until eventually over seven miles of route had this quieter form of construction against six miles of setts.

A graphic description of track laying on the Birkenhead tramways is found in a paper by Waude Thompson, Stud. Inst. C.E. read to a meeting of the Birmingham Association of Students of the Institution of Civil Engineers on 12 February 1903, an extract from which follows:—

"The construction of the permanent-way was undertaken by the Borough Engineer's Department without the intervention of a contractor. The workmen employed were formed into one large gang of about 250 to 300 men, and several smaller gangs at various points, finishing off at the more difficult

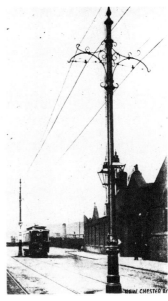

The first route to be electrified was that to New Ferry, mostly with side poles and bracket arms but with centre poles on part of the line. The contractor was Robert W. Blackwell & Co Ltd., whose horse-drawn tower wagon 33 is shown at work while the horse cars were still running; the right hand photograph was taken outside Laird's Shipbuilding yard during trial running in January 1901. *Courtesy M. J. Mitchell; Light Railway & Tramway Journal)*

of 3 parts of mortar to 1 part of cement; and where this has been disturbed for any purpose, it has been found to have set hard and compact, and to adhere satisfactorily to the metal of the rails."

The earliest type of pointwork was only 7ft 6in in length with both grooves straight but later 12ft points with curved grooves were used thus improving the motion of the cars through junctions. Spring points were fitted with the McKnight silent-closing tramway point controller consisting of an oil filled cylinder and piston which by slowing down the return motion of the tongue, rendered the action silent. All points were drained to the sewers.

The trolley wire used was 0.4in in diameter consisting of hard drawn copper of 98% conductivity, with a minimum tensile strength of 25 tons per square inch. It was suspended at an average height of 21ft.

The New Ferry Route

Always isolated from the rest of the system, both in horse and electric days, the New Ferry route can best be described separately. During 1899 the Corporation negotiated with the Wirral Tramway Company and failed to reach agreement as to the compensation to be paid in respect of the unexpired portion of the lease. In November the Corporation asked the Board of Trade to appoint an arbitrator and three months later an award of £22,666 was made. At the end of December 1899 the Corporation was not ready to take over and the company was allowed to continue to operate and to use the New Ferry depot and stables rent free.

On 21 March 1900 the company was authorised to continue running a tramway service at their own risk while the line was being reconstructed. It was intended to relay in quarter-mile sections but the company objected, saying that if more than 200 yard stretches were undertaken it would discontinue the service. Agreement could not be reached and the company wrote to say that they had no alternative but to discontinue the service on 8 May. On 24 April the Committee hastily invited tenders for the provision of an omnibus service and interviewed a Liverpool coach proprietor, Mr. Maguire.

The last Wirral company horse tram ran on the evening of 8 May 1900, being met by a crowd with fog-signals at the New Ferry terminus, and work began six days later on taking up the horse car tracks in New Chester Road. The Wirral company ceased trading, and its stock of 60 horses, 13 tramcars, four buses and one lorry was auctioned at the New Ferry depot on 16 May. The temporary bus service cannot have been satisfactory, for on the same day, 16 May, the Committee approved the operation of a tram service by the United Company. It was, of course, quite feasible to drag horse cars off the track and traverse short sections of paved road, and this is probably what happened when the cars reached a point where track laying was proceeding. As the new heavier track was laid the cars were able to use it. The United company bought some of the single deck cars at the auction, and put them back in service still displaying the Wirral Tramways title, running every 15 minutes. This service continued until 22 January

1901, and the five cars and 27 horses then in use were auctioned on 24 January 1901.

The United manager, Frederick Tidswell, was retained as manager of the Corporation tramways but he was unable to adapt from horse to electric traction and was asked to resign in February 1901. In the meantime Mr A. R. Fearnley, previously manager of the Bradford and Shelf Tramways (a steam line) and the first of three generations of transport managers in his family, had been appointed Tramways Manager in December 1900 at a salary of £300 per annum. Much of his first year in office was spent in persuading the Committee to alter previous decisions.

The New Ferry route had been planned mainly as single track with loops as was the greater part of the Birkenhead system and this proved to be an expensive mistake. In November 1900 the track was nearing completion but the obligation to avoid interruption to the United Company's other services at Bridge Street-Chester Street junction until the end of 1900 made it impossible to complete the line through to Woodside. The first two electric cars were delivered in the last week of December and the first trial trip was made on 28 December over the short distance between New Ferry depot and Parkfield. The Committee made a trial run from New Ferry to the Town Hall at midnight on 2 January. "The din was intolerable" quoted the *Birkenhead News* and the wood block lobby gained ground as a result of this experience. The United Company was given notice to vacate the New Ferry depot on 24 January 1901 and the line was used for driver training until 31 January when Lt. Col. P. G. von Donop, R. E., Inspecting Officer of the Board of Trade, formally inspected the line. As the country was in mourning following the death of Queen Victoria on 24 January, public service commenced without ceremony at 5.30am on 4 February between New Ferry and Brandon Street, behind the Town Hall. It seems

likely that some sort of *ad hoc* omnibus service was again operated during the ten days after the withdrawal of the horse trams.

The dominant feature of the New Ferry route was the low bridge in Chester Street carrying the LNW/GW railway branch to Abbey Street coal sidings and Laird's shipyard. The road was built on reclaimed land on the course of the former Tranmere Pool and further excavation was difficult. The railway companies were unwilling to raise the bridge because of the gradient and the restricted clearance dictated the continued use of low capacity single deck cars. For the opening only six cars were available, the seventh being delivered within a few days. Delays were caused by a snowstorm and there were frequent dewirements. Complaints were made that the cars were running only every 15 minutes compared with the Wirral company's former 10 minute horse car service and the 31-seater cars were quite inadequate as the 1d fares available between Woodside and Bedford Road or Green Lane and New Ferry and the 2d through fare instead of 3d brought regular tram travel within the reach of many working people for the first time. Fixed stopping places were introduced in some haste during the second week of operation in the form of red bands on white-painted portions of the appropriate poles.

In March 1901 attempts were made to hasten arrival of the outstanding six single deck cars and Milnes promised delivery in time for Easter. Originally intended for the Tranmere route, they were urgently needed to increase the service on the New Ferry line. The line down to Woodside ferry approach was completed on 6 June 1901 and brought into service with Board of Trade approval in advance of the official inspection on 27 June. Passenger demand had been seriously underestimated and the single track exacerbated the situation. Only nine days after the line opened, two additional loops were authorised between Green Lane and Bedford Road

Birkenhead's electric trams were built by G. F. Milnes at Hadley, Shropshire but finished off at the company's older works in Cleveland Street, Birkenhead. The New Ferry cars were then hauled across town by teams of horses to New Ferry depot. This shows No.1 in New Chester Road in the last week of 1900. *(Courtesy M. J. Mitchell)*

The Board of Trade Inspection of Birkenhead's New Ferry route was carried out on 31 January 1901 by Col. F. G. Von Donop, RE, and Mr. A. P. Trotter, using car No. 7. Others present included Alderman T. Cook, Mayor of Birkenhead and Councillor Dr. H. Laird Pearson, chairman of the Tramways Committee. Public service began without ceremony on 4 February 1901. *(Courtesy M. Jenkins)*

but by September 1901 the whole length between Chester Street railway bridge and the borough boundary, which included nine loops, had been doubled as a matter of urgency. In heavily industrialised Lower Tranmere with Cammell Laird's shipyard, a tannery and timberyards, huge throngs of men would gather at shift times waiting for trams in both directions. In a report on overcrowding submitted in September 1901 it was stated that inward cars were full on reaching Bedford Road, often to the extent of carrying twice their nominal complement of passengers. Restrictions were removed on the numbers each car could carry and the police were instructed to give the trams priority at all road crossings and to ensure there were no delays due to obstruction at New Ferry terminus.

The Tramways Committee rejected the idea of trailers, but decided to transfer three open top four-wheel double deck cars to the New Ferry route. Although they passed safely under Chester Street bridge (headroom about 14ft 6in) the Board of Trade refused to sanction the carriage of passengers on the upper deck so they were confined to shuttling between Green Lane and New Ferry. Since August 1901 a five minute headway had been provided requiring nine cars leaving only four, until the arrival of the double deckers, for peak hour augmentation

and maintenance. Despite these arrangements, chronic overcrowding still occurred especially at shift times, all day Saturday and on Monday mornings. People took to walking between Green Lane and the town centre as they were frequently unable to board a through car. The Corporation next considered using the high-capacity open top bogie cars Nos 45-59 and No.58 was sent to New Ferry depot to carry crowds attending an Agricultural Show on 10-11 September. It seems to have stayed there being joined by others of its class by December.

In August 1903 the manager was authorised to convert three double deck bogie cars into single deck form by removing the stairs and upper deck seats and fitting a shortened trolley mast. Extra seating on the platforms would give a capacity of 35. No 46 was definitely converted but there is no evidence of any others being done. It remained on the New Ferry service with the four-wheelers until new rolling stock was delivered in 1913.

Lengthy delays in the service caused by wheel slipping with the maximum traction bogies were eliminated by replacing the wheels on the single deckers. The maximum speed of 8 mph was increased by the Board of Trade to 12 mph in August 1903; elsewhere it became 14 mph. A further plan to excavate the road under Chester Street bridge to give

From February to June 1901, the New Ferry cars terminated at Brandon Street while the Borough Engineer's department constructed the six-track terminus at Woodside Ferry approach. The layout included a double slip connection (shown above) giving access to the north sidings. Some of the Irish labourers later became tram drivers and conductors. *(Grosvenor Library Museum, Chester)*

headroom of 17ft 6in was rejected as impractical. When top covered cars were eventually allowed underneath, careful arrangement of the overhead and specially sprung trolley poles were necessary to give adequate clearance.

The initial inadequacy of the New Ferry rolling stock cost the Corporation dearly. Traffic was diverted to the Mersey Railway, particularly after its electrification in 1903, and was thus lost to the ferries also. But the biggest plum was the Lever Bros. traffic to and from Port Sunlight which travelled against the peak traffic flow and was therefore very profitable. This traffic usually travelled by rail to and from Bebington and New Ferry Station but there was dissatisfaction with the railway service and it is apparent that from time to time the workers travelled by tram. In December 1902 Lever Bros. officially approached the Corporation to provide regular travel facilities for 500-600 women employees whose fares were paid by the company. It was said that on the occasions when these people had been conveyed by tram, presumably as a result of railway mishaps, the whole of the New Ferry stock had been required and 70-80 passengers were loaded in each single-deck car. Obviously this disrupted the ordinary service and the Corporation reluctantly had to decline the offer of this lucrative traffic.

The Bromborough Buses

After the electric trams started running to New Ferry in 1901 the United company continued to run its omnibuses between New Ferry and Bromborough and introduced some trips to Eastham. The company tried hard to develop its "Wirral branch" to compen-

sate in part for the impending loss of its tramway routes. Following the Corporation's refusal to meet the request of the Liverpool and North Wales Steamship Co. to run Sunday morning cars, the steamship company arranged for a special omnibus to run from New Ferry to Woodside at 9.55am each Sunday in the summer of 1901, the steamer company guaranteeing the revenue. This developed into a through service between Bromborough and Woodside on Sunday mornings, but the receipts quickly fell and a report dated November 1901 quoted the average receipts as only 5s 3d (26p) a journey in October. In March 1902 12 waggonettes were licensed to convey passengers from Woodside to Hooton races. The company changed its name to the Birkenhead Carriage Co. Ltd. in April 1902, reflecting its restricted activities, but business ceased altogether in October 1903 when receivers were appointed on behalf of the debenture holders, the well-known tramway and omnibus entrepreneurs, Messrs W. Busby and J.A.S. Hassal of Liverpool.

The New Ferry-Bromborough service was taken over by the Oxton Carriage Co. Ltd. a well established firm of coachbuilders, carriage proprietors and funeral undertakers who had built several of the United horse buses. In August 1903 they had been authorised to start a horse bus service between Rock Ferry Pier and Dacre Hill which seems to have been unsuccessful and by 1907 the Bromborough buses were being run from premises at 87 Church Road, Higher Tranmere known as the "New Ferry Bus Stables". An hourly service was run between 1.00 and 9.00pm and this may have continued until 1913 when the first Crosville buses ran between Chester and New Ferry.

44

The Town Routes

The expiry of the United company's lease at the end of 1900 enabled a start to be made on the construction of the main town routes and work commenced in many parts of the town. During 1901 there were many complaints about the state of the roads and the premature disturbance of the surface prior to actual track-laying. In the meantime the United company was permitted to continue running as best it could at a nominal rent of £3 per month subject to one month's notice.

Much of the system was planned as single track even on streets such as Borough Road and Cleveland Street where double horse tracks already existed. The manager pointed out that the section between Laird Street depot and Park Entrance would have to accommodate all the cars running to and from the depot in addition to the ordinary service, yet only one loop was proposed. Eventually after various proposals and counter-proposals, most of the main routes were built as double track, the principal exceptions being Church Road, Higher Tranmere and Shrewsbury Road, where the streets were too narrow. Six passing loops were provided along each of these stretches.

The focal point of all the routes was Woodside ferry approach, with a terminal layout comprising six parallel sidings. Access from the approach tracks was by two crossovers, one facing and one trailing;

The traffic potential of the New Ferry route was seriously underestimated and much of the track had to be doubled within a year of the opening. This wintry scene shows car No. 1 on the new double track at Rock Ferry during the winter of 1901/2. *(Commercial postcard, courtesy A. D. Packer)*

these were replaced by a scissors layout in 1915. Nominal accommodation was for 22 cars although initially the maximum number of service cars meeting any boat was 12. Movements in and out of the sidings were controlled by an inspector and two point-boys whose job it was to memorise the complicated timetables in order to ensure cars arrived and departed at the correct times. Shelter was provided by a wooden hut resembling a sentry box but this was removed in later years. To the east, the terminus was dominated by the 1864 ferry building with its clock and "Ferry to Liverpool" sign which was to stand virtually unchanged for 120 years. On the south side was the imposing red-brick bulk of Woodside railway station and on the north the floating roadway leading to the goods and vehicle ferry. Mingling with the trams were horse drawn cabs and from the 1920s an increasing number of charabancs, buses and private cars.

The two southernmost sidings were used by the New Ferry cars but otherwise positions were not allocated to specific routes. In later years the Prenton bogie cars tended to use the middle tracks and, in order to counteract railway competition, the Circle routes were given priority positions from 1928. Perhaps the most memorable feature at Woodside was the enormous centre pole spanning all six sidings which survived until 1937. Originally there were two such poles but the one nearest the ferry was replaced by individual poles and span wires to give greater flexibility. Elsewhere in the town massive ornate centre poles were used in Chester Street, New Chester Road, Conway Street, Park Road North

CHESTER RD. ROCK FERRY.

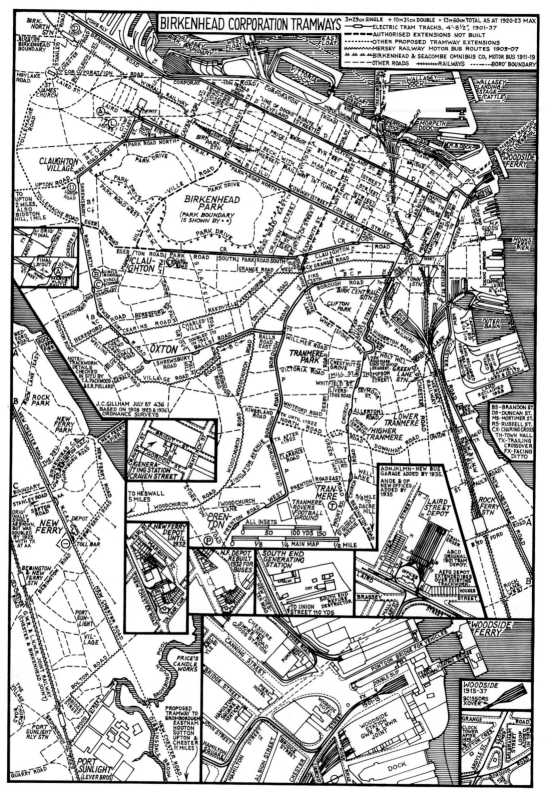

BIRKENHEAD CORPORATION TRAMWAYS

3M29CH SINGLE + 10M31CH DOUBLE = 13M60CH TOTAL AS AT 1920-23 MAX
- ELECTRIC TRAM TRACKS, 4'-8½", 1901-37
- AUTHORISED EXTENSIONS NOT BUILT
- OTHER PROPOSED TRAMWAY EXTENSIONS
- MERSEY RAILWAY MOTOR BUS ROUTES 1905-07
- BIRKENHEAD & SEACOMBE OMNIBUS CO, MOTOR BUS 1911-19
- OTHER ROADS
- RAILWAYS
- BORO' BOUNDARY

and Laird Street and, unusually, in Argyle Street, Hamilton Street and a short length of Borough Road where there was only one track. Elsewhere bracket arms were employed, there being very little span wire in the early days.

A number of the lines authorised in the 1899 Act were not built. Thus the Tranmere route ended at the top of Bebington Road instead of continuing to Dacre Hill, and the Park Road South route terminated in Egerton Road near the foot of Palm Grove instead of linking up with Shrewsbury Road. Of the line through Birkenhead Park only the double junction from Cleveland Street into Duke Street was laid. Likewise a number of sections of horse tramway were not electrified, the network of lines in the Canning Street-Bridge Street area being replaced by a direct line along Cleveland Street from Hamilton Square and double lines in Bridge Street and part of Hamilton Street. The section between Woodside and Hamilton Square Station via Hamilton Street was not built and all cars always approached and left Woodside via Chester Street and Bridge Street. Hamilton Street was used outwards and Argyle Street inwards. On 21 July, a horse car running on the road around the track excavations in Borough Road fell into the resulting hole, ending up on its side.

By late July 1901 the new four-wheel cars were beginning to appear on the streets for trials and staff training and the first derailment, at the Hamilton Street-Conway Street Junction, was reported on 29 July. Some of the bystanders who helped to push it back on the line received electric shocks. On 3 August, the *Birkenhead News* reported that "the trams on the new routes are being run daily. As it is, the Committee is to be complimented upon having done its work in so short a time." A few months earlier it had condemned them for delays! On 13 August 1901, Lt. Col. von Donop using car No. 22 inspected the Higher Tranmere, Laird Street, and Claughton Road routes and passed them as fit for public service.

The opening of the New Ferry route six months earlier had occurred without ceremony because of the Queen's death but the inauguration of the town routes was graced by the presence of the Mayor, Alderman Thomas Cook, members of the Council and invited guests. Tradesmen and shopkeepers were asked to fly as many flags and streamers as they could. Assembling outside the Town Hall in pouring rain at 11am on 14 August the official party set off in car 25 preceded by three other decorated cars.

The first objective was the Higher Tranmere route, on which the engineers had been faced with a major problem in tackling the steep climb as all existing roads included gradients of 1 in 7. Powers existed to solve the problem in any one of three ways, straight up Argyle Street South to Whetstone Lane which even today would involve tackling a gradient so steep

as to be impractical; by Whetstone Lane from the Fire Station, a route followed by the buses since the late twenties or by the construction of a new thoroughfare linking Argyle Street South just above Hinderton Road with Church Road at the top of Holt Hill. Selecting the latter course, the new S-shaped street, 350 yards long with a gradient of 1 in 13.5 was blasted from the solid rock. Curved retaining walls and embankments supported the road and the necessary distance to reduce the gradient was obtained by a system of curves, the sharpest with a radius of 40ft. Reaching the top of Argyle Street South the procession halted, a tape was cut and the new street named Pearson Road in honour of Councillor H. Laird Pearson who had assumed the Chairmanship of the Tramways Committee earlier in the year.

Drivers working the Tranmere route received an additional ½d per hour in recognition of the extra skill required. Slipper brakes were obligatory on all Tranmere cars and a Board of Trade notice was prominently displayed near Holt Hill Convent stating "Drivers must apply slipper brakes". Two stops were allowed during the descent but there were no outward tram stops between Central Station and Holt Hill Convent. Wet weather occasionally prevented some heavily laden cars reaching the top of the incline and the Corporation was careful to watch for excessive loadings. In fact many people were reluctant to travel on the top decks of Tranmere cars, preferring to crowd into the lower saloons and on to the platforms. Even when the cars received top-covers, this fear prevailed.

After the christening of Pearson Road, the procession continued through the narrow length of Church Road negotiating the six passing loops. In places the outer rails were only inches from the kerb. Returning to Conway Street, they then travelled over the Claughton Road line to Bentinck Street where they alighted to inspect the new Generating Station in Craven Street. From there the party proceeded to Laird Street depot for a civic lunch. Coats and hats had to be left on one of the cars in the depot as the offices were incomplete. Public service on all three routes commenced at 2.30pm.

All 14 cars which were available on the opening day were needed to provide a 5-minute service to both Higher Tranmere and Laird Street (five cars each) and a 10-minute service to Claughton Road (four cars). These very high frequencies were found to be excessive once curiosity riding ceased and traffic settled into a normal pattern.

At first the Claughton Road cars terminated at the top of Park Road East, the United Company providing a shuttle horse car service to the top of Palm Grove until the evening of 8 November when it ceased to facilitate preparations for the Board of Trade inspection on 16 November; thereafter the electric cars were extended along Park Road South

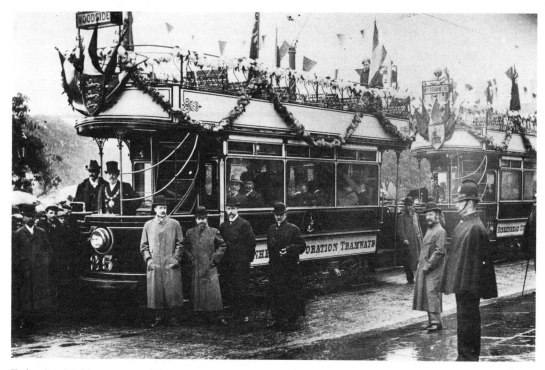

The formal opening of the town routes took place on 14 August 1901, with No. 25 heading a procession of four decorated cars. George F. Milnes, whose firm built the Corporation's first 59 trams, is seated inside the car at the far left, wearing a light trilby hat. *(Tramway Museum Society)*

to the terminus at Egerton Road. The horse car tracks in Park Road East and Palm Grove were not electrified and were abandoned. 8 November 1901 therefore marked the end of 41 years of horse car operation in Birkenhead. The Docks route had ceased on 12 September to facilitate reconstruction and the last horse tram ran along Borough Road on 27 September when Borough Road depot and stables were closed. These were eventually demolished in 1902 but the depot buildings in Palm Grove are still visible today.

Trial trips were made on the Borough Road and Balls Road lines from 16 September and the inspection took place on Friday 27 September 1901 in the usual downpour which seems to have attended all Edwardian tramway occasions in Birkenhead. The Prenton route was extended along Prenton Road West to the then borough boundary at Storeton Road while the Shrewsbury Road line ascended the 1 in 16 hill in Balls Road East (where double track was laid despite the absence of the usual 9ft 6in clearance from the kerb), continued along Balls Road and terminated at Beresford Road. Col. von Donop prescribed the use of track brakes on all cars *descending* Balls Road East, an important distinction when circular working commenced. The first public cars ran at 5.0pm on the same day, 27 September, and the Corporation paid the United company £2 for their clock at the Shrewsbury Road terminus. However the line between Central Station and the

Fire Station, where there were extensive sewer works in prospect, was single and used only in the inward direction, outward cars travelling via Claughton Road, Exmouth Street and Charing Cross. There was much controversy about this one way working and following alterations to the track work, the directions were reversed from 2 February 1902.

In late 1901 work was still proceeding on the Park Road North/Shrewsbury Road North and Line of Docks routes. The latter, double track throughout except for a single track stub outside the Graving Docks Hotel which overlooked the terminus, was opened in the early evening of Christmas Eve. The windswept terminus drove some men into the nearby hostelry and several were reprimanded in 1902 for drinking whilst on duty. The former, single track with passing loops along Shrewsbury Road North and double track along Park Road North, was inspected on 17 February 1902 but not immediately opened. The *Birkenhead News,* seeking an explanation for the delay, learned that no crossover had been provided to enable Circle cars to reach the depot (save by wrong line working in Laird Street) and that it had been decided instead to lay a new double track along Mallaby Street, which was almost ready and would be used by all cars.

Service commenced on 2 March 1902, and the Laird Street and Shrewsbury Road routes were linked to form the "Oxton and Claughton Circle" referred to by the staff as "the Belt." The plans used

To reach Higher Tranmere, Birkenhead Corporation built a new road — Pearson Road — to carry the trams. It included a double S-bend and a gradient of 1 in 13·5. The Board of Trade demanded the use of slipper brakes and refused to sanction the use of top-covered cars on the line. (*Commercial postcards, courtesy T. G. Turner*)

for the inspection did not show the line in Mallaby Street, but it was under construction by 28 February. It is possible that the section of Park Road North between Laird Street and Mallaby Street was used by the Circle cars for a few days, but all cars thereafter ran via Laird Street and Mallaby Street and the centre piece of Park Road North was never again used by service cars. It was useful for assembling cars awaiting football crowds from Birkenhead Park but was otherwise an expensive white elephant. Another unnecessary expense was incurred by providing a junction at Tollemache Road in case the Egerton Road line was extended to meet the Circle; it was later removed.

'Arrangements have been made with the Mersey Railway Co. for the greater convenience of passengers using Central Station. As the inward-bound Prenton and Circle cars draw up at this station, a switch on the overhead wire is operated which turns on an indicator light on the station platform, so that drivers of the electric trains know that a tramcar is there, and so keep their train back half a minute.'

(The Birkenhead News, 13 September 1913)

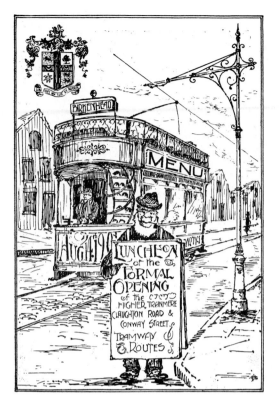

Menu illustration for the luncheon held at Laird Street on 14 August 1901 for the opening of the town routes.

from Woodchurch Road to Slatey Road. On 10 August 1902 the Tramways Committee considered rerouting clockwise Circle cars only along Park Road North in lieu of Mallaby Street, but there is no evidence that this was done.

On 8 February 1902, snow commenced to fall and continued intermittently for four days. The heaviest snowfalls for some years were experienced on 11 February and Borough Road was partially blocked. At 10am four cars together tried to break through on the outward line at Victoria Road and at Whitford Road the leading car derailed. Then the snowplough, together with a New Ferry car fitted with a plough, arrived and with another car coupled behind proceeded to cut a way through to Prenton. The cars charged the snow and derailed frequently. By 1pm the ordinary cars could reach Clarence Road and a car blocked in since 9am could get away. Soon after 2pm, service resumed on both lines. In the midst of all this, the Board of Trade inspecting officer arrived to conduct his examination of the Shrewsbury Road extension, but could not carry it out.

After the opening of the Shrewsbury Road line, the United Company had continued to run its omnibus service using the roads which lay between Balls Road and Park Road South. Services were curtailed to run to and from Central Station, two buses providing a 15-minute service but the company was fighting a losing battle. A small one-horse bus was placed in service in February 1902 but this earned less than the large one which was reinstated within a month. The company changed its name to the Birkenhead Carriage Co. in April 1902 but ceased trading in 1903 when it became insolvent.

At the end of 1902, one-way working in the Charing Cross area was still in force for Shrewsbury Road and Prenton cars because of the planned

Complaints were made about the slow speed of the clockwise Circle, delays being caused by the long single line from Woodchurch Road to Palm Hill. Furthermore there was and still is a blind corner at the top of Balls Road East, so the conductor had to alight and walk forward to see if a car from the opposite direction had entered the single line. If not he would return to give the starting signal but in the interim an opposing car had often arrived and the two would meet. In May 1902 the track was doubled

The Board of Trade inspection of the Line of Docks route on Christmas Eve, 1901, car 44 standing at the terminus near the Graving Docks Hotel. *(Courtesy E. Gray)*

No. 21 travelling between the top of Balls Road East and Slatey Road on the Oxton-Claughton circle. Originally single track, this line was doubled soon after electrification to alleviate delays. *(Courtesy T. G. Turner)*

construction of a sewer in Borough Road. Most passengers wanted the cars to run via Central Station in both directions, and the Manager suggested the construction of a loop in Borough Road to permit two-way working. In January 1903 a complicated arrangement was suggested whereby the Shrewsbury Road and Prenton cars would use Borough Road or Claughton Road in different directions at different times of the day, to endeavour to satisfy the tradesmen at Charing Cross while at the same time providing connections with the Mersey Railway, soon to be electrified.

The scheme adopted from 2 February 1903 was for the Prenton cars to run inward via Borough Road from the start of the service to 4.10pm (except in fog) and then to run via Whetstone Lane and Charing Cross until 6.50pm, since it was impossible to use the Borough Road single line for anything but outward traffic at this time of day because extra cars were run to North Road and Beresford Road. Circle via Conway Street cars ran inward via Borough Road until 10.30am and then via Charing Cross until 6.30pm, after which time all cars operated via Borough Road. The Charing Cross-Claughton Road route on the Circle took 50 minutes instead of 40 minutes via Central Station, and this route was used by all inward cars on Sundays. The sewer was not completed until May 1906, after which the track in Borough Road was doubled and the Charing Cross line fell into disuse.

The main car shed was built in Laird Street. The offices were built with a frontage on to Laird Street and a rear entrance into the depot yard; they were officially opened on 28 July 1903. The Mayor and Council left Woodside in two decorated cars and visited South End Generating Station, New Ferry Depot, Craven Street Generating Station and Laird Street Depot where a dinner was held. The party included Dr. Laird Pearson, A. R. Fearnley and Dr. Napier and R. R. Greene of Wallasey.

As was common practice at the time, very low maximum speed limits were imposed by the Board of Trade inspecting officer. The ruling speed was 8 mile/h with 10 mile/h on long stretches of double track such as Conway Street, Park Road North, Borough Road, Cleveland Street and parts of New Chester Road. Difficult sections such as Balls Road East downhill and Argyle Street South were restricted to 6 mile/h and all curves to 4 mile/h. In June 1903 application was made for increased speed limits and following an inspection on 28 July, most of the 10 mile/h sections were increased to 12 or 14 mile/h and some of the 8 mile/h sections to 10 mile/h. Experiments with speed indicators on the cars were abandoned as the belt drives could not stand up to the work.

By December 1903 there were 3.52 miles of single track and 10.03 miles of double track in operation and the capital cost of the undertaking was as follows:— Craven Street Generating Station, £11,552 plus £27,388 for equipment; South End Generating Station, £5,092 plus £9,588 for equipment; Track £151,854; Electric line work £32,580; Cars £42,760; Laird Street Depot £20,018 plus £2,307 for equipment; New Ferry Depot alterations and equipment £3,173; Legal and General Charges £1.973; Offices £3,221, Cash Office, Woodside and miscellaneous £438; Total £311,944.

The cost of making Pearson Road (£14,678) brought the total expenditure to £326,622.

Railway Buses

Railway companies had been motor bus pioneers in many parts of the country during the early years of the twentieth century and Wirral had its share of railway enterprise.

The Mersey Railway, with some justification, believed that Birkenhead Corporation tramways catered more adequately for ferry traffic than for railway traffic. Complaint was made that cars often filled up at Woodside and along Hamilton Street so that passengers leaving trains at Central Station were unable to board. The absence of double track along Borough Road between Central Station and the Fire Station until August 1906 with cars running in one direction along Claughton Road severely restricted

CM509, one of the Mersey Railway's second batch of Saurer's, in Port Sunlight village on the short-lived service to Rock Ferry station in 1907. *(Courtesy John Cummings)*

access to the station. In 1905 the company decided to inaugurate feeder bus services and ordered four Saurer double deck buses.

Following an announcement of the company's intentions on 29 September 1905 the Town Clerk wrote to protest at the proposal but the company replied to the effect that the omnibuses would be a great convenience to the large number of people who used the railway. In November ply-for-hire licences were sought and the Watch Committee recommended that they be granted. However, the full Council refused to approve the vehicles on the somewhat contrived grounds that less than eighteen inches of seat was allowed for each passenger. The railway company pointed out that only sixteen inches was provided on the lateral seats of the Corporation tramcars. In the course of a long letter to the Town Clerk the General Manager, Mr. R. Bowman Smith wrote:—

"It is apparent that the action of the Corporation is not based upon considerations of public convenience or safety and the only inference which can be drawn is that it is based upon a desire to obstruct the Company's service for other reasons which can form no proper ground for withholding a licence."

The Council held fast and in the absence of local licences the company was obliged to seek methods of operation which did not legally constitute plying for hire. Books of ½d coupons were hastily printed for sale at railway station booking offices at 50 for 2s.

The buses were first used on Saturday 9 December 1905 on the occasion of an international rugby football match against New Zealand at Birkenhead Park. A shuttle service was run between Park Station and the ground and it was claimed that 1,500 passengers were carried. Regular service commenced on Monday 11 December between Central Station and Slatey Road via Grange Road, Westbourne Road and Reedville, a route lying midway between the Circle and Claughton Road tram routes. The through fare was 1½d with ½d and 1d intermediate stages. Three buses maintained a six-minute service and traffic quickly built up. On Boxing Day the buses were operated into the country running between Central Station and Gayton, Glegg Arms via Grange Road, Oxton Road, Woodchurch Road and through the villages of Woodchurch and Barnston. Within a week or two this was extended to Heswall.

Meanwhile six more buses had been ordered and when they arrived, the Slatey Road route was extended on 29 January to Kingsmead Road South in direct competition with the Circle route. From 26 February the bus route was reorganised to traverse a long loop through the whole Oxton district.

A special meeting of Birkenhead Town Council was held on 18 December to determine whether legal action should be taken against the company who had no statutory powers to run motor buses. The Mersey and several other railway companies had applied to Parliament for powers to operate buses and other road transport vehicles in the 1906 session. The need for such specific powers had not been recognised until the London County Council had been deemed to be *ultra vires* in running buses in connection with their tramways.

At the special meeting Dr. H. Laird Pearson estimated that the buses would deprive the ferries and tramways of an eighth of their traffic — a loss of about £9,425 per annum, equal to a rate of 4½d in the £. The Council agreed by 35 votes to 8 to institute legal proceedings. At a two day hearing in March 1906 it was alleged that one third of the passengers carried did not intend to use the railway. The corporation obtained an injunction and services ceased on 8 March. The Mersey Railway's Bill had a fairly easy passage through the House of Lords later the same month but the bus clauses were later rejected by the Commons following strong pressure from a powerful municipal lobby.

The injunction was still in force, and an appeal was lodged. This was not heard until December 1906 when the railway company gave an undertaking to run its buses specifically for railway passengers only. The injunction was rescinded but Birkenhead Corporation was given leave to appeal to the House of Lords and bus services were not immediately resumed. However, on 16 May 1907 the Mersey Railway buses appeared on a new route between Rock Ferry Station and Lever Bros' Works, Port Sunlight, running alongside the trams between Bedford Road and New Ferry every 12 minutes from 7am to 7pm with a through fare of 1d and a ½d fare between The Dell and the Station. Books of 50 ½d coupons were sold as before. On 8 July 1907 the

A noteworthy feature of Birkenhead's tramways was the impressive six-track pole at Woodside terminus, seen here about 1912. Originally it had some ornate scrollwork below the cross-arm. The wires were anchored to poles which projected through the roof of the long shelter, but there had originally been a second six-track pole. *(Tramway Museum Society)*

House of Lords gave judgement for Birkenhead Corporation and the Railway buses were finally withdrawn. These events proved to the Corporation that they could not be too complacent about their monopoly and the double line along Borough Road was completed in August 1906. Thereafter, although the Mersey Railway competed with the Corporation ferries, the tramways and later the buses provided adequate facilities for their passengers.

Consolidation

The Claughton Road route was the least remunerative, yielding revenue of only 3.20d per car mile in September compared with 16.99d on the best route (Docks) and 11.74d on New Ferry. Operating costs were 6.6d per car mile. The half mile of Park Road South between Palm Grove and Park Road East was said to be the fastest on any British tram route. Sunday services were withdrawn on the Claughton Road and Docks routes in September 1904 after which the Circle via Borough Road cars used Claughton Road and Charing Cross on Sundays until August 1906 when, with the completion of a double line in Borough Road, both Prenton and Circle routes used Borough Road in both directions at all times and the short line through Charing Cross was never again used for regular services. From 9

March 1908 the Claughton Road service was run every 10 minutes between Palm Grove and Argyle Street only between 10am and 4pm and after 7pm; at other times a through service was run every 15 minutes to Woodside. A junction was put in at the Camden Street/Claughton Road corner so that the lower part of the latter could be used in both directions when the truncated service was being run.

In 1909 a new line was built along Market Place South and the Claughton Road cars were extended to Chester Street corner off peak and possibly to Woodside in peak hours over the same route from 4 September, with the object of ending the isolation of the New Ferry route following public demand for such a facility. However, patronage was so poor that the diversion was withdrawn on 8 December 1909. A year later, through workmen's transfer tickets were introduced between Laird Street and Green Lane, some cars running to Woodside via Market Place South to facilitate the transfer of passengers at Chester Street. After two months, on 15 February 1911, this facility was also withdrawn and the Market Place South line saw little use until it was abandoned in the late 1920s when part of the street was closed in connection with the construction of the Mersey Tunnel approaches. The whole line was officially abandoned in May 1933.

BIRKENHEAD TERMINI

Car 26 at Higher Tranmere terminus (Bebington Road) soon after the route opened in August 1901. The outer end of this route was single track with six passing loops, due to the narrow roads. This part of the road was widened about 1904 and the poles transferred to the opposite pavement. *(Commercial postcard, courtesy P. Hardy)*

No. 12 standing at the end of the track at New Ferry, about 1909. For a brief period prior to their conversion to double deckers, the New Ferry cars had their clerestory roofs obscured by all-round advertising panels. *(Commercial postcard, courtesy T. G. Turner)*

The postcard from which this picture is reproduced bears the legend 'Laird Street Tram Terminus, Birkenhead', but the car is about to continue round the Circle via Mallaby Street. Laird Street terminus was the track straight ahead, just beyond the Tramway Offices. It was used mainly by peak hour short-workings and by cars returning to the depot. *(Commercial postcard, courtesy T. G. Turner)*

Although normally associated with the Prenton route, the Milnes bogie cars also worked on the Oxton/Claughton circle until 1928. These 1907-10 views show (top) No. 53 at the junction of Borough Road and Balls Road East, No. 57 at All Saints Church, Shrewsbury Road and (below) No. 50 returning to Woodside along Park Road North. In 1910 car 50 was shortened by 5 ft and re-entered service as a single truck car, illustrated on page 68. *(Commercial postcards, courtesy A. K. Kirby and E. Gray)*

Following the abandonment of the Chester Street diversion, the Claughton Road cars again turned short at Argyle Street during off peak periods and transfer tickets were issued to and from Woodside in connection with the Conway Street cars. This arrangement was most unpopular with the travelling public and was superseded from 21 April 1912 by the reinstatement of the through service but with a 15 minute frequency instead of the 10 minute service designed to accord with the ferry sailings.

New Ferry Developments

The inadequacies of the New Ferry rolling stock continued to give problems. During the winter months there was often overloading when the South End Ferries, (New Ferry and Rock Ferry) which had been taken over and been modernised by Birkenhead Corporation in 1897-99, were disrupted by fog. The Ferries Committee issued monthly contracts available on the South End ferries and also at Woodside and somewhat unreasonably expected the already overstretched tramways to absorb the extra load wherever necessary and to carry the passengers at special rates. In November 1906 the Ferries Committee proposed to erect signals on the traction poles to indicate when the South ferries were not running thus saving passengers a long, fruitless walk to the piers. The Tramways Committee agreed to this and the signals, consisting of two white lights, were installed on standards at New Ferry Toll Bar,

New Ferry terminus, 12 September 1913. No. 10 stands at the terminus, with No. 3 approaching. Shopkeepers and other road users frequently complained at two cars standing side by side and blocking the highway.
(Commercial postcard, courtesy T. G. Turner)

Stanley Road, Rock Lanes, Bedford Road and St. Pauls Road. An annual acknowledgement rent was paid by the Ferries to the Tramways. The Ferries Committee having been formed in 1842 considered itself a "senior service" and sometimes acted in a condescending manner towards the Tramways. In 1905 there was criticism of the Tramways failing to give immediate connections with every boat at Woodside and some reluctance to accept the explanation that different tram routes needed different frequencies and it was impossible to dovetail a 6 or 7½ minute tram service with a 10 minute boat schedule, unlike Wallasey where common frequencies made more sense.

A solution to accommodation problems on the New Ferry cars was not found until 1908 when the Corporation designed a "low-bridge" double-deck car which is described elsewhere. New schedules were devised with a saving of 1,600 car miles per week but difficulties were still experienced at times.

In 1909, however, when double deckers had been introduced the Tramways Manager wrote to Lever Bros. and subsequently met the firm's representatives on 1 April. In a letter dated 22 April Levers stated:—

"....we are now prepared to consider the desirability of coming to an arrangement with you for the conveyance of the whole of our employees to whom we grant free travelling facilities provided you are able to offer us suitable service and conditions. Broadly speaking the number of persons to and from our works in addition to those already being carried by you is about 1,000 daily. In addition to those there would be many hundreds of our other

employees travelling back and forward daily who pay their own fares and we would add that we have on average about 60,000 visitors yearly going through our works ..... The lands of the Bromborough Port Estate Ltd. are being developed and it is expected that there will be a considerable influx of population to that district in addition to those of Bromborough and Bromborough Pool Village. If you are able to cope with the additional traffic ..... we would ask you to consider the extension of the tramway system ..... by making a loop line via New Chester Road, Bolton Road, Greendale Road and Bebington Road or ..... alternatively ..... by extending the present system along New Chester Road to Bromborough Pool Road. Without such an extension we do not think we could consider any new arrangements regarding the traffic."

On receiving an assurance that Birkenhead would seek agreement with Lower Bebington Council regarding a tramway extension, Levers agreed to their subsidised workers travelling by tram.

However Lower Bebington insisted that any new lines should be owned by them, and also that the existing section of line within their district should also be transferred to them. Perhaps mindful of the problems which Liverpool experienced with Bootle Council, Birkenhead felt unable to agree to this, particularly as the depot was situated in Lower Bebington territory and future intransigence might leave them with a truncated route and no depot.

Lever Bros. employees continued to travel by tram and walk from New Ferry to Port Sunlight until 1914, when the railway regained the traffic after a new private railway station was built adjoining Port Sunlight works and Levers put two workers' trains morning and evening over their own metals to Bromborough Port. The loss of revenue to the Corporation averaged £208 per month. By 1920 when the number of Lever employees had increased considerably, six special trains were being run from Woodside and two from Rock Ferry.

In November 1917 Levers again sought transport beyond New Ferry, this time for the Margarine Works at Bromborough Port from where workers were sometimes carried to New Ferry in lorries and in two buses bought by William Lever for a service between Prenton tram terminus and Thornton Hough. Because of wartime difficulties there was nothing that Birkenhead could do but in 1920 the Corporation deposited an Extension Bill, one of the objects of which was to extend the borough southwards. This was unsuccessful and the boundaries of Lower Bebington and Bromborough Urban District were altered to form a larger Bebington Urban District. This authority was able to keep Birkenhead at bay for several years and became a municipal borough in 1936.

More New Ferry Cars

In 1911 the Corporation decided to buy six more cars for the New Ferry route. There was considerable local controversy, first in the form of objections from the South End ratepayers, who alleged that as the new cars would be heavier than ever their ears would be assailed by even more noise than at present. They wanted trials with trackless cars, which had just been introduced at Leeds and Bradford, and went so far as to write to the Board of Trade asking that loan sanction be refused. Another source of trouble was the publication in the *Birkenhead Advertiser* of a letter from Thomas Voss of Milnes, Voss & Co. alleging that his tender had not been fairly considered and that information had been withheld from the Committee. There was considerable acrimony

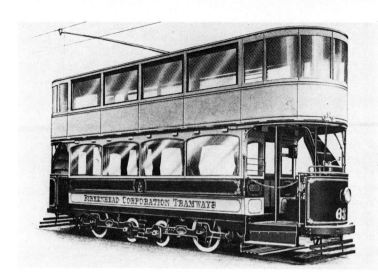

Six additional cars were bought for the New Ferry route in 1913. Nos. 63-68 were built by Hurst Nelson & Co. of Motherwell, with Siemens equipment. *(Hurst Nelson Catalogue)*

and veiled suggestions of irregular practices. The New Ferry cars issue continued to make headlines until 10 July 1912 when a special meeting of the Council confirmed the Committee's original decision to purchase the six cars from Siemens Bros. They carried the numbers 63-68 and were accommodated at New Ferry depot.

No. 63 is recorded as having passed successfully under Chester Street bridge on 5 May 1913 and the cars entered service the same month. There were now 19 cars for the route and this number proved adequate during World War I and the 1920s when new traffic was generated by the opening up of many country bus routes based on New Ferry by the Crosville Motor Co. Ltd. of Chester.

Miscellanea

The Tramways department was originally run from temporary offices in the Sessions House, Chester Street near the present Town Hall. Apart from the General Manager, Chief Clerk and two engineers (one of whom was Mr. R. Stuart Pilcher who in later years became well know as General Manager at Manchester and then Chairman of the West Midlands Traffic Commissioners) the original staff comprised:—

12 Drivers at 5d (approx. 2p) per hour (age limit 35 except for ex-company drivers)
14 Conductors at 4½d (approx. 1.75p) per hour (Age limit 20-35)
 1 Motor Examiner at 35s (£1.75) per week
 1 Foreman Mechanic at 35s per week
 1 Car Cleaner and Night Man at 22s (£1.10) per week
 1 Boy for Car and Point cleaning at 12s (60p) per week
 1 Ticket Clerk at 25s (£1.25) per week
 1 General Clerk at 25s per week
Bell Punches were hired at £1 per annum each punch.

The first manager, Mr. A. R. Fearnley remained with the Corporation until December 1903 when he left to take up a similar appointment with the much larger Sheffield undertaking. He was succeeded by Mr. W. Wyld from Doncaster, who was appointed Tramways Manager and Electrical Engineer at a salary of £450 per year. Mr. Wyld was first and foremost an electrical engineer and when he resigned in April 1913 it was to take up an appointment as Engineer and Manager of the Hampstead Electric Light Undertaking. At this juncture the Corporation decided that the two functions should be separated and appointed the Chief Clerk of the Tramways Department, Mr. Cyril Clarke, as Acting Tramways Manager at £275 per year. It is apparent that the full Council had some reservations about this appointment as they qualified it with the 'Acting' prefix but they need not have worried as traffic increased noticeably under the impetus of Clarke's management and his appointment was confirmed in January 1914. He continued to manage the undertaking with considerable vigour until his retirement in 1942.

The four wheel cars were originally fitted with four sided glass destination indicators but the Prenton bogie cars came equipped with roller blinds and eight four wheelers were similarly fitted in 1903. From late 1901 two black route boards with gold lettering were affixed to the upper deck rails but these were dispensed with after a few years. Advertisements were permitted from the earliest times, each car bringing in £20 per year.

One of Clarke's innovations was the introduction in August 1913 of a system of route letters displayed on 15in square enamelled metal plates mounted on the balcony rails. These carried white letters on a coloured background. Initially there were no plates for Docks or New Ferry cars but later "D" was

From August 1913, Birkenhead trams (except New Ferry cars) carried route letters. No. 26 displaying T for Tranmere turns into Argyle Street South at Central Station. In 1919 a loop for short-working and football cars was built around the Clock Tower in the background.
(Commercial postcard)

allocated for Docks. New Ferry cars never carried letters.

Circle via Borough Road	B in a circle, Blue plate
Circle via Conway Street	C in a circle, Blue plate
Claughton Road	CR, Red plate
Prenton	P, Black plate
Tranmere	T, Green plate

The appearance of route letters in Birkenhead coincided with the introduction of route numbers across the river in Liverpool. Similar route letters had been introduced in Wallasey some months earlier.

Throughout the decade there had been constant complaints about the noise made by the trams in general, a direct result of the concrete foundations. On 13 March 1912 the committee decided that the track in Argyle Street between Conway Street and Market Street should be relaid with longitudinal creosoted sleepers between the concrete and the rails but two weeks later it was decided to relay Bridge Street in this way instead of Argyle Street.

The 1914-18 War

In common with all other systems, Birkenhead's tramways were called upon to carry a heavy burden during the 1914-18 war. Earlier in 1914 the Committee had voted £2,000 for track renewals and suggested the expenditure of £600 on a siding in Wilbraham Street for the use of cars terminating at Central Station. Unfortunately this was not done and by 1919 when the work was put in hand the cost had risen to £885. However, during 1915 renewals costing £4,613, including £1,752 for the scissors crossover at Woodside, were completed and this helped the tramways through the later war years when shortages of materials and labour more or less ruled out

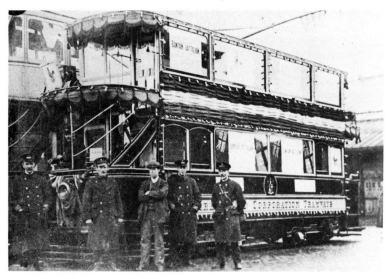

Car 1 or 2 decorated as a recruiting tram for the Bantam Batallion of the Cheshire Regiment standing at Woodside in 1914 or 1915. Unlike 3-13, 1 and 2 did not have twin entrances to the upper deck. In later years these two cars were little used.
(Courtesy T. G. Turner)

59

maintenance other than what was absolutely essential. During 1915-16 mileage decreased but revenue increased (except on the wretched Claughton Road service) reflecting the stepping up of industrial activity and the increased use of the port facilities. As more and more men enlisted, women were engaged as conductors, cleaners and for light repairs and car controller maintenance. The first six women conductors started work on 13 September 1915. They were employed at first on the Claughton Road, Tranmere and Prenton routes. Apparently they were subjected to insults from impudent children in the poorer areas; sticks, manure and street scrapings were thrown at them and disgusting language used. In earlier years the tramways had had trouble with boys jumping on the cars when the conductor was upstairs and jumping off when he came down again. Tranmere cars were mostly affected on their slow climb. Several boys were taken to court and fined one shilling (5p) each in October 1907.

In 1916 it was agreed to pay drivers working with conductresses 2s (10p) per week extra because of the extra work involved in turning the trolley and changing the points. By 1917 practically the whole of the conducting staff was female — there were 84 — and six women ticket inspectors were appointed as the few remaining male inspectors were often called upon to act as drivers.

By 1917 there were serious shortages of materials and labour and it was important to conserve coal. Local Committees on Coal Supplies decided on priorities and after war factories, the ferries and tramways were quite high up on the list of priorities. The Birkenhead Committee suggested the use of the tramways for coal distribution and the department had to point out that not only did they lack the necessary powers but the practical difficulties were insuperable. In October 1917 many stops were cut out to conserve brake shoes and energy and in December the Board of Trade appointed a Tramway Control Board to consider needs for materials and labour essential to the prosecution of the war. A Lancashire and Cheshire Tramways Federation was formed by the operators to secure representation on the Control Board. A requirement to reduce power consumption by 30% was met in Birkenhead, as elsewhere, by cancellation of supplementary journeys and by speed reductions. Coal supply problems continued after the war as labour unrest spread and power generation was often a hand-to-mouth affair.

Throughout the war the tramways participated in efforts to raise funds for war charities. Volunteer workers organised collections on the cars and a decorated car was used as a recruiting office for the Bantam Regiment and for the sale of war bonds and savings certificates. This car was No 1 or 2 and was parked during the day at Woodside. Popular songs such as "Tipperary" were played when it was in motion.

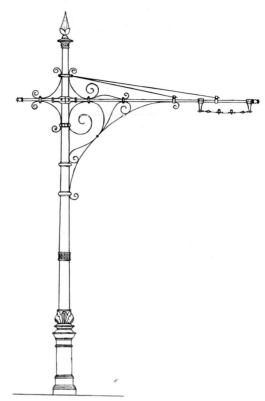

Birkenhead Corporation tramways side pole and bracket arm. This drawing and that of the centre pole on page 1 were drawn by H. G. Dibdin.

The tramways served the town well and, with the armistice signed, the Council and Cyril Clarke looked forward to picking up the threads of development and expansion where they had perforce dropped them in August 1914.

The Birkenhead coat of arms, as used until 1951.

4 Birkenhead 1919-37

The immediate months of peace were beset with many problems. Cars, track and overhead were all suffering from wartime overwork and neglect. Labour was militant and determined to exploit concessions made during the war. Improved conditions, including a 48-hour working week were agreed nationally in 1919 and in the inflationary post-war conditions, a fare increase was inevitable. The Local Government Board had asked for particulars of possible post-war projects as early as September 1916 in order to create employment. Apart from the extensive track and overhead renewals referred to below, Birkenhead Corporation authorised the purchase of new trucks and equipment for the cars and considered extensions to Laird Street and New Ferry depots. The former, designed "to provide additional storage for electric tramcars and other vehicles" started as a £20,000 scheme and expanded to a more grandiose project estimated to cost £48,350. Much was devoted to accommodating the new motor buses and it dragged on piecemeal throughout the decade. Inflation was a serious problem, an example being the price of Brill 21E trucks which was £99 18s. 0d. as tendered in March 1919 but £152 when accepted in January 1920.

At the end of the war when the cost of materials was very high, the track throughout the system was in a poor condition and renewals were absolutely essential. The renewal of underground feeder cables from Craven Street Generating Station to Conway Street, Claughton Road and Borough Road was an urgent requirement authorised in October 1918 at a cost of £2,750 less an estimated £600 for sale of salvaged materials. With the increase in motor traffic the centre poles were now considered a hazard and it was agreed to move them progressively to the sides of the road and introduce span wire suspension of the overhead. Whilst most of the centre poles were reused, many new ones were required. In some cases the work of track renewal and pole replacement was co-ordinated, in others it proceeded separately, an inhibiting factor being the inability of the Street Lighting department to finance the changes which the removal of the poles demanded. In October 1921 it was agreed to suspend work temporarily at the request of the Watch Committee.

In the same month an expensive track renewal programme was drawn up comprising Conway Street £25,731; parts of Hamilton Street, Balls Road East, Singleton Avenue Crossover, Palm Hill Loop,

Church Road (2 loops), Laird Street and Car Shed Junctions £16,669; New Chester Road-St. Paul's Road-Chester Street, £35,600; St. Paul's Road-Rock Lane, £21,800 (total £99,800).

A decision to proceed was rescinded when it was found that the loan repayment period of eight years was too short, but the programme was reinstated on 14 December when the consequences of not replacing the track were brought home to the Council. Assistance was sought from the Unemployment Grants Committee under a government scheme to provide incentives for job creation and much work done in the 'twenties and 'thirties was partly financed under such programmes. In some cases the grants were directly related to the cost of the labour employed whilst in others a proportion of the interest on capital borrowed was paid.

Track relaying using reinforced concrete foundations continued throughout the decade, sometimes with irritating disruption to the lives of residents as witness a petition from Balls Road residents in late 1928 when winter weather had slowed down work. In New Chester Road the New Ferry track between the boundary and Sefton Road was doubled in 1924 in connection with a Bebington UDC road reconstruction scheme; the centre poles throughout the New Ferry route went in 1925 and the track was relaid in the following year. Mallaby Street, Laird Street and Park Road North tracks were renewed in 1926-27. Some work was done on the depot fan during which the line across the yard behind the offices was disconnected.

There were many crossovers throughout the system which never saw regular use but nearly all were replaced during relaying. The North Road crossover was repositioned at Singleton Avenue, to which point the regular short workings were extended. In 1921 most facing points at junctions were made automatic, being activated by the passage of a car over a skate in the overhead. The exceptions were Hamilton St/Cleveland St. and Conway St/Claughton Road where conductors were required to reset points for the straight after passage of the car.

Permanent way work was completed in late 1929 or early 1930 when the Church Road, Higher Tranmere tracks were repaired and the junction of Conway Street and Argyle Street was remodelled to extend the double tracks across the latter street to provide a layover place for supplementary cars.

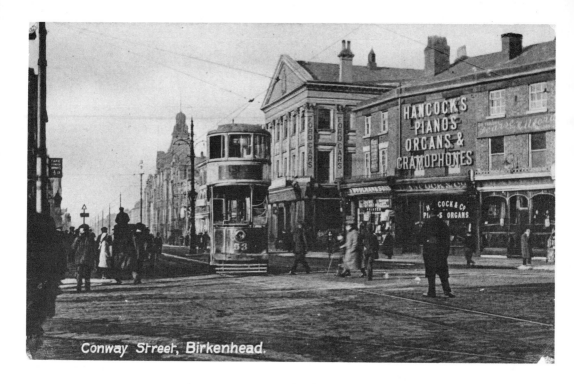

Conway Street, Birkenhead.

In the early 1920s most of Birkenhead's centre poles were replaced by span wire suspension with roadside poles. The upper view published in 1918 shows the centre poles in Conway Street, with car 53 reversing out of the Argyle Street junction to return to the depot. The sign on the left hand pole reads "Fare to end on Conway Street ½d". The lower view published in 1924 shows car 35 en route to Claughton Road with indicator "CR", and span wire suspension. Route CR closed in 1925, the first tramway abandonment on Merseyside. (*Commercial postcards, Philco Series and Valentine, Dundee*)

CONWAY STREET, BIRKENHEAD.   90959.JK

A 1920s aerial view of Birkenhead Woodside, showing (left to right) the joint railway passenger station, the six tram sidings, the floating roadway, the cattle lairages and Birkenhead's first docks. The two river vessels are a passenger ferry and a "luggage boat" (Vehicle ferry).
(Picton Library, Liverpool)

Motor Buses

The Birkenhead Corporation Act, 1914 received the Royal Assent on 31 July 1914, only five days before the outbreak of war. It permitted the operation of Corporation motor buses anywhere within the borough and on six routes outside with the consent of the road authorities. On the very eve of hostilities the Corporation brought a London General B type bus to Birkenhead and members of the Council went on an outing to Moreton. Doubtless but for the war, services would have started quite soon but the five year delay which ensued enabled operation to be started with much more reliable buses than were available in 1914 due to technical advances during the war. The first motor buses entered service on 12 July 1919 on a route between Rock Ferry Pier and Park Station which intersected all the tram routes except the Line of Docks. The following month the route was extended to Moreton and in 1920 another route was opened to Upton. A route to Port Sunlight and joint services across Duke Street Bridge to Wallasey commenced in 1921.

The inaugural bus routes had three basic objectives — to link up the tram routes across town and serve important thoroughfares remote from tramways, to feed traffic to Rock Ferry Pier and to establish a community of interest between Birkenhead and neighbouring districts thus encouraging the residents to shop and seek amusement and recreation in Birkenhead. The original routes were well thought out and considerable entrepreneurial vigour was displayed by the management even to the extent of running a few trips to Hoylake during a railway strike. The wise choice of routes was reflected in the almost complete absence of the withdrawals and alterations which figure so largely in the early history of some motor bus undertakings.

From late July 1921 a bus was run on Sunday mornings from Laird Street depot to Woodside via Shrewsbury Road and Oxton Road to connect with the 10.10am boat to Liverpool. It continued until 30 October but was not reintroduced in subsequent years. The fares were almost double those charged on the trams.

In both 1922 and 1924 schemes were proposed to extend the tramways to St. James' Church from Laird Street, Beaufort Road (via Ilchester Road) and Egerton Road via Tollemache Road. Proposals to continue these extensions across Poulton Bridge to link up with the Wallasey tramways were pursued with more enthusiasm in Wallasey than in Birkenhead. The extension of the Tranmere route to Dacre Hill as had been authorised in 1900 was considered but rejected as there was already a bus route over half the length of the extension. By 1925 Birkenhead was running 40 buses and the Corporation decided to make the extension to St. James' Church with buses and withdraw the loss-making Claughton Road trams. Buses took over on Sunday 30 August 1925 both single deck Lions and double deck Leviathans being used, the latter being the Corporation's first covered top double deck buses. This was the first electric tram route on Merseyside to be replaced by buses and its success ultimately decided the fate of the remainder of the tramways system. However, at the time it was regarded as the right treatment for an isolated loss-making route and no general policy of abandonment was contemplated.

Birkenhead participated fully in the discussions on the Mersey Tunnel scheme for under-river trams (see Chapter 6) and whilst it was hostile to the proposals it would probably have participated if more realistic parameters had been put forward. Essentially despite the success of the buses and the enthusiasm for their development, management's attitude towards the tramways remained dynamic. Cars were re-equipped and standards of comfort improved though there were no proposals for new cars. Under threat from severe competition from the Mersey Railway, the Tramways and Ferries departments co-operated to introduce a range of through tram or bus and ferry tickets covering all routes from 1 April 1928 which was successful in retaining a considerable proportion of the cross-river traffic.

While Birkenhead was developing its own bus route network it adopted a policy of keeping all other operators out of the borough. Crosville buses had been running infrequently between Chester and New Ferry since 1913 and after the war the company's operations were greatly expanded throughout Wirral, depots being opened at New Ferry and West Kirby and later at Heswall when the services of J. Pye were acquired in 1924. These routes terminated at Prenton tram terminus and Singleton Avenue. Other routes from West Kirby terminated at Upton Road (Claughton Village) but eventually penetrated to Park Station. These bus services brought considerable additional traffic to the tramways but the Heswall peak hour traffic was so heavy that the trams could not handle it and the Corporation was obliged to allow "contractors' buses" to run through to and from Woodside. While Birkenhead fought to get its buses out into the countryside, Crosville fought to get to the centre of Birkenhead.

An application by Crosville to extend their services from New Ferry to Woodside in 1923 was unsuccessful, as was a subsequent attempt to run Sunday morning buses from Rock Ferry Pier instead of New Ferry to Chester. The Crosville country services fulfilled a real need and became extremely popular. The Corporation's policy of running no trams on Sunday mornings left the Crosville services with no links with Liverpool or central Birkenhead and whilst the problem was partially solved by running some of the North Wales services from Park Station via West Kirby, the Corporation realised that failure to remedy the situation would ultimately result in Crosville getting facilities to run through to Woodside.

From 4 April 1926 Sunday morning services were provided on the New Ferry tram route and these were soon extended to the Prenton route to feed the Crosville buses at both Singleton Avenue and Prenton terminus. It seems almost certain that the Prenton trips were worked by cars from New Ferry depot as there would be no point in opening two depots on Sunday mornings. This provides a reasonable explanation for various reports of Hurst Nelson cars running on other routes on Sundays. However the Prenton Sunday morning service was taken over by buses to Singleton Avenue only in 1928.

Post boxes were affixed to cars on the Circle via Borough Road, New Ferry, Prenton and Tranmere routes on journeys to Woodside about 9.45pm on Mondays to Fridays from 28 March 1927. They were collected by Post Office staff in the town centre and continued in use until 28 February 1936 when later

Bogie car 55 at Laird Street depot in 1927, showing the dash-mounted trolley retriever. This car is portrayed in colour on the cover of this book.
(Science Museum, Whitcombe Collection)

The scene at Birkenhead Woodside on 24 July 1931, with two of the cars that received six-window Corporation-built top covers in 1923-24 (32 on Circle route B, 24 on route D, Line of Docks) (*G. N. Southerden*)

suburban collections began. The Corporation received £4 per box per year.

By the mid-'twenties a pattern of operating methods had been established which with adjustments continued into the 'thirties. At Woodside the southern two tracks of the six track layout were reserved for New Ferry cars but the other four were used indiscriminately by all the other routes depending upon the order of their arrival. The point boys were kept busy manipulating the levers to ensure that there were no delays. In 1928, following the introduction by the Mersey Railway of a 6d day return ticket between all stations in Birkenhead and Liverpool, the arrangements were changed in order to combat this competition. The Circle route was considered to be particularly sensitive to competition with Central Station on the Borough Road line and Park adjacent to the Conway Street line. The regular use of Prenton bogies on the clockwise Circle was discontinued late in 1928 and the service speeded up from 45 to 40 minutes round trip, this being easily within the capability of the re-equipped four-wheel cars. Circle cars now had priority over all others at Woodside. Various regular supplementary services were operated both at peak hours and midday, the latter to take care of the large number of workers who went home for lunch, including many employed in Liverpool.

In the early morning the Circle ran in two separate parts until about 7.45am, from Laird Street via Conway Street and from Palm Hill via Borough Road. Several peak hour journeys from Palm Hill ran to Central Station only. The Prenton route was also a relatively late starter with cars from Singleton Avenue only from 6.30am and from Prenton terminus from 7.05am. A number of Prenton duties started earlier but first did trips on the Line of Docks route which had a concentrated early peak outward from Woodside. The Tranmere route had no augmentation after 1926 when buses also served the area.

New Ferry was the first to start, the first car leaving the depot at 4.55am. There were frequent short workings to and from Monk Street (Market Place South) and a midday peak service between Green Lane and New Ferry for shipyard workers. The Saturday evening frequency on the New Ferry route was 3-4 minutes.

On the Circle, supplementary midday services ran between Argyle Street and Laird Street via Conway Street and between Market Place South and Kingsmead Road via Borough Road. On the inward journey these cars turned right from Argyle Street into Conway Street then left into Hamilton Street where they reversed. On Saturday afternoons the supplementary cars ran between Woodside and Gerald Road via Borough Road or Upton Road via Conway Street.

About 1922 the route letter plates were replaced by roller blinds and it was probably at this time that some supplementary letters were introduced for part-way cars. These were 'A' — Argyle Street, 'L' — Laird Street and 'U' — Upton Road. The blinds also

Passengers climb on board both ends of
No. 8 at Woodside in the summer of
1930. The 'Port Sunlight' board has
been removed as there was now a
through bus service. *(J. Harold)*

A Hurst Nelson car at Woodside in
1928. These low-ceiling cars were
unpopular with staff and public and
were used mainly at peak hours.
(G. N. Southerden)

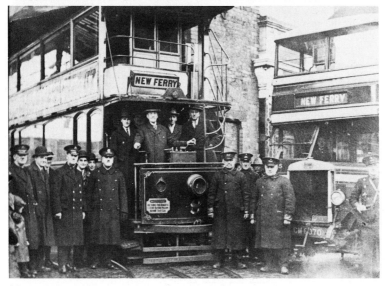

On 28 December 1931, the day after
the closure of the New Ferry route, No.
8 was the last car to leave New Ferry
depot for Laird Street. It was driven by
Inspector John Edom (standing near
headlamp) who had been in charge of
the first New Ferry horse tram in 1877.
(Birkenhead Advertiser)

Football cars waiting in Prenton Road West for the final whistle at Tranmere Rovers ground in March 1934. During football matches the ordinary service was turned short at Woodchurch Road. (*W. E. Williams*)

Car 56 standing at Prenton terminus on Sunday 30 September 1934, the last day of route P. The lower saloon of this car became a shelter in Arrowe Park. (*W. E. Williams*)

The conductor of No 32 swings the pole at the terminus of the Line of Docks route outside the Graving Dock Hotel on the final day of operation of route D, 31 March 1935. (*S. V. Hall*)

included the letter 'X' but this never appears to have
been used. 'A' was used in the inward direction only
so that a car running between Argyle Street and
Laird Street would show 'A' one way and 'L' the
other. Early in 1924 large roller blind destination
indicators were fitted in the middle lower deck
windows except on the New Ferry cars.

The loop at Central Station was used for an
afternoon peak hour service to Prenton and on
Saturdays for football cars to Tranmere Rovers
football ground. After taking one load some of these
cars would return to the Fire Station where an
inspector decided whether the traffic justified reversing them over the crossover. During important
matches cars would be parked for the whole length of
Prenton Road West so that the ordinary service cars
could go only to Woodchurch Lane. With plenty of
cinemas, no television and few motor cars, evening
traffic was considerable especially on Saturdays and
many extra cars were turned out to clear the late
cinema and pub traffic. The exception was the Docks
route which closed down before 8.00pm and never
ran on Sundays.

A very special occasion was 30 June 1927 when
thousands of people went to Bidston Hill to witness a
total eclipse of the sun at 6.00am. Through cars were
run from all termini to Upton Road, New Ferry cars
using both Market Place South and the direct Park
Road North line. Prenton cars ran via Shrewsbury
Road.

The Tramways in Decline

In 1914-15 the tramways had carried 15 million
passengers and this increased gradually throughout
the war until a peak of almost 24 million was reached
in 1918-19. In the post-war slump years it declined to

17 million but picked up again to almost 21 million in
1925-26. Thereafter there was a steady decline and in
1928-29 the buses carried almost a million more
passengers than the trams. Nevertheless there was, at
this time, no official policy of abandonment, cars
being refurbished and track renewals carried out as
necessary.

A bus service between Woodside and Kings Road
via Higher Tranmere had been introduced in August
1926. The buses ran via Whetstone Lane, avoiding
the steep gradient in Pearson Road. Buses and trams
continued to serve Church Road side by side for over
two years until 7 October 1928 when the trams were
cut back from Bebington Road to Whitfield Street to
avoid the need for expensive track renewals. This
eventually proved to be too drastic as such difficulty
was experienced by visitors to Birkenhead Institution (now known as St. Catherine's Hospital) that
the track and overhead were put in order as far as
Allerton Road, outside the hospital gates, to which
point cars were re-extended on 4 February 1930.
However, the whole of the Sunday service was
provided by buses from April 1930.

In June 1930 after months of negotiation Birkenhead Corporation signed an agreement with Crosville whereby the latter's buses previously terminating at Prenton, Singleton Avenue and New Ferry
could run through to and from Woodside and
Corporation buses could run to Bromborough,
Eastham, Irby, Greasby and Heswall. The signing of
this agreement really marks the adoption of a
tramway abandonment policy by Birkenhead Corporation for, from that time buses were run from
Woodside to points beyond all the tramway termini
without a change of vehicle being necessary. From 1
August 1930 when the first stage was implemented,

Car 20 displaying L (for Laird Street) picks its way through the crowds in Conway Street dispersing after the opening of the Mersey Road tunnel in July 1934. *(Courtesy M. Jenkins)*

there was a frequent service of buses over the full length of the New Ferry route and whilst the Crosville buses could not carry local passengers, the Corporation's Eastham buses could and did, albeit at a higher fare. The archaic knifeboard cars were noisy and uncomfortable and it was decided to replace the New Ferry cars by an augmented bus service from 28 December 1931. The last car was No. 8 and after the depot had been cleared it was demolished and a new bus garage built on the site.

From 1 October 1930 buses from Heswall and Parkgate started running through to Woodside via Borough Road and traffic was lost to the Prenton cars. Peak hour augmentation was reduced and the basic service continued unchanged. Much of the Tranmere Rovers football traffic was still, however, carried by tram.

The Tranmere tram service ran for the last time on Saturday 29 September 1934 and the Prenton service on the following day. From 1 October new bus services were introduced using both the Argyle Street South and Whetstone Lane routes to Tranmere though the former route was abandoned after less

Surrounded by buses in the new Birkenhead blue and cream (contrasting with the older maroon and cream) No. 23 stands at Woodside in 1937 shortly before the abandonment. *(R. Crafter)*

Car 32 on the Circle route displaying abandonment window notices announcing the closure of Birkenhead's tramways from 17 July 1937. The driver is Patsy McDonald. *(S. V. Hall)*

than two years. At Prenton, a terminal loop comprising Woodchurch Lane, Storeton Road and Prenton Road West was adopted as it was considered unsafe to turn buses at the tram terminus.

Buses took over on the Docks route on 1 April 1935, the replacing bus service (the North Circle) being linked with the Claughton Road route as had been proposed for trams in 1922. For the last few months, the track in Beaufort Road which had never been renewed was in such a bad state that only the outward track was used. Cars terminated at Ilchester Road and returned, wrong road, to the next crossover. Only the Oxton and Claughton Circle route now remained. There was no bus competition on the Shrewsbury Road and Balls Road section and almost 6 million passengers were carried in each of the ensuing years. The supplementary service continued to run between Argyle Street and Laird Street and to Upton Road on Saturdays. This route continued for more than two years until 17 July 1937 when the tramways were abandoned with the usual nostalgic civic ceremony but with few genuine regrets as the antiquated cars had lost their appeal to the travelling public. The last service car was No. 31, but car No. 22 had been converted to an illuminated car for the Coronation of King George VI earlier in the year and it was adapted as an official last car.

If the tramways had been allowed to extend into neighbouring Bebington and new cars capable of higher speeds had been introduced the system might have survived the war as many of the routes traversed wide roads ideal for tramway operation. As it was, the undertaking was financially very successful having contributed £84,240 to the relief of rates and calling for assistance to the extent of only £6,182 spread over five separate years.

Trolleybuses

The claims of the trolleybus were somewhat cursorily explored and general powers to operate this type of vehicle were obtained in 1930, but not exercised. The electricity department was particularly keen to retain the transport department as one of its principal customers and constantly advocated the use of trolleybuses. A deputation visited Wolverhampton on 12 February 1930 where an extensive system was in operation. In this connection it is of interest to note that one of the first trolleybuses built in Britain had its first run in Cleveland Street, Birkenhead in 1909. This was a "Railless" vehicle bodied by G. C. Milnes, Voss and Co. which was tested by placing the positive trolley boom on the tram wire and trailing a negative skate in the rail. The vehicle subsequently went to the Metropolitan Electric Tramways, London, but never entered service there.

Day and night views of decorated car 22 on the last day of tramway
operation in Birkenhead, 17 July 1937. This car had served as the Illuminated
tram for the Coronation of King George VI in May 1937. On both occasions
it toured the Circle route. *(S. V. Hall and W. E. Cull)*

Birkenhead Corporation Electric Tramcar Fleet as Built

Car Numbers	Type (as built)	Year built	Builder	Seats	Truck(s)	Motors	Controllers
1-13	Single deck bogie (note a)	1901	G F Milnes	28 (note b)	Peckham 14D3 maximum traction bogies (note c)	GE 52-6T 2 × 25hp	BTH B3 (note d)
14-44	Open top (note e)	1901	G F Milnes	22/33	Peckham cantilever 9A	GE 52-6T 2 × 25hp	BTH B3 (note d)
45-59	Open top bogie (note f)	1902	G F Milnes	30/45	McGuire equal wheel bogies (note g)	E & H T11b 4 × 20hp (note h)	E & H (note h)
60	Snowplough	1902	ex-horse car	-	Peckham cantilever 9A	GE 52-6T 2 × 25hp	BTH B3
61	Water car	1902	BCT-made	-	Peckham cantilever 9A	GE 52-6T 2 × 25hp	BTH B3
62	Breakdown car	Converted from ex-horse salt trailer			Peckham cantilever 9A	GE 52-6T? 2 × 25hp	BTH R28?
63-68	Enclosed top lowbridge double deck	1913	Hurst Nelson	28/34	Hurst Nelson swing bolster max/traction bogies	Siemens 250 CT 2 × 40hp	Siemens TA2

Seating figures shown thus: 22/33 are for lower and upper decks respectively.

Notes

(a) Rebuilt 1908-10 as lowbridge top-covered double deck cars

(b) Plus three seats on each platform, for use only at the rear end. Saloon seating increased to 30 in 1903 by removal of interior partitions.

(c) Remounted 1907 on Mountain & Gibson Type 3L swing bolster maximum-traction bogies.

(d) Altered to (or replaced by) type BTH B18 at various dates. 13 cars (probably 24-36) received B49 controllers in 1919 (one in 1914).

(e) 'White' full-length top covers fitted 1903 to 16 and 17; remainder fitted with Brush flat-roof Bellamy top covers 1910-13 except 24-36 fitted with elliptical-roof BCT-made covers in 1922/23.

(f) All fitted with 'White' full-length top covers 1904-05, except car 46 converted to single-deck 1903 and restored to open top 1913. Car 50 shortened to four-wheeler 1910 on Peckham cantilever 9A truck.

(g) Replaced (except cars 46 and 50) by BCT-made Peckham 14B-type cantilever bogies in 1907/08.

(h) Equipments made in Charleroi (Belgium) by Société l'Electrique et l'Hydraulique (later ACEC) and supplied by Witting Bros.

5 The Birkenhead Tram Fleet

At maximum extent the Birkenhead electric tramway fleet numbered 65 passenger cars and three works cars. A natural desire to support local industry probably influenced the Corporation to place their early orders with G. F. Milnes but it is unlikely that any of the cars were actually built there though the 1901 cars were finished at the Cleveland Street works.

George F. Milnes and Co. had been registered as a limited company in 1898 following a successful takeover bid by the German Busch group. One of the directors was James Crosland Taylor, chairman of the Helsby Cable Works. He was later to become the founder of the Crosville bus company which in later years had a considerable impact on passenger transport in Birkenhead. The object of the new company was to mass-produce tramcars to meet the tremendous demand for electric cars and because industrial land was expensive in Birkenhead and labour was considered to be highly paid and too well organised, a new factory was opened at Hadley, Shropshire in 1900, the old Starbuck works in Birkenhead becoming a finishing shop. In 1902 there was a slackening of orders and it was decided to close the Birkenhead works. Some of the men moved to Hadley but others went to work for G. F. Milnes' son, G. C. Milnes who, together with Thomas Voss, the Chief Draughtsman, set up a new partnership, G. C. Milnes, Voss and Co. to manufacture tramway accessories at other premises in Cleveland Street west of Duke Street.

Milnes, Voss established a special relationship with the Birkenhead tramways and an important activity in the early days was the manufacture of top covers for existing open top cars. Open cars presented many operational problems and Birkenhead was in the forefront of experiments with so-called "dry seats" and in 1901-2 four types were tried — Brawn's, the New London, the Never Wet and Voss'. Two cars were also fitted with waterproof aprons supplied by the Universal Apron Co., of London. After some months' trials 30 cars were fitted with Brawn's dry seats which could be assembled on to the existing seat frames. In August 1903 the platform seats on the New Ferry cars were similarly converted.

The long term solution was obviously to cover the top decks and it is surprising that operators were so slow to recognise the advantages particularly as top covered steam tram trailers had been in use in some towns since the 'eighties. Top covers were being actively considered in October 1902 when photographs of Liverpool's canvas sided car were examined. Capt. Kemp's cover at Wallasey was also inspected and a visit made to Huddersfield to view their car 49 fitted with a Milnes Voss "collapsing cover".

Under Board of Trade regulations, all cars had to be fitted with lifeguards designed to prevent a pedestrian falling under the wheels. The original Birkenhead cars were fitted with the Peckham Tray Guard but, following a fatal accident in 1901, experiments were made with other equipment and in December 1901, it was decided to fit 12 cars with the Tidswell lifeguard. This consisted of a vertical gate hanging across the front of the car four inches from the ground. Should it meet an obstruction, the second part of the guard, a lattice tray, immediately fell and scooped up whatever had fallen on to the line. It was most effective and was said to have been instrumental in saving eleven lives in the first two years of the electric tramway. The extent to which Frederick Tidswell influenced the design of the lifeguard which bore his name is unknown. It is certain that A. R. Fearnley, the Birkenhead manager, had an interest which he declared at a Committee meeting in June 1901 and as municipal managers were inclined to eschew public acknowledgement of their technical inventions, it may be that Fearnley was the true inventor. It is clear that the claim that A. Hardy and D. Voss of New Brighton were the inventors of the Tidswell lifeguard is false. The committee gave the manager permission in February 1903 to try Hardy and Voss patent lifeguards on one car. Later Hardy and Voss patented modifications to the Tidswell guard, experiments being made on Wallasey cars in early 1903, and in due course founded the Tidswell company.

All 4-wheel cars in the Birkenhead fleet, including the works cars, were given slipper brakes which could operate on the track in an emergency. Although special cars were confined to the steep Tranmere route, the hill in Balls Road East on the Circle route although shorter was considered to be almost as hazardous. As delivered all cars had chilled iron wheels and in June 1903 the manager persuaded the committee to authorise the purchase of two sets of steel tyred wheels and axles from John Baker and Co., Rotherham. This type was in due course adopted as standard.

Although the Birkenhead cars retained an old fashioned appearance throughout their 36 year life, the Tramways department showed considerable innovation particularly during the 1920s. On 27 September 1922 the committee approved the purchase of 65 pairs of spring loaded trolley retrievers consisting of a drum on the end of the rope fitting into a socket on the dash plate. Numerous items of second-hand equipment were purchased and considerable improvements made in passenger comfort even when it was known that the days of the system were numbered.

The original livery was maroon with pale cream rocker panels and upper works. The maroon was ornately lined out in gold whilst the cream was lined in maroon. In the 'twenties the maroon was continued from waist to cantrail level and the lining out simplified but large heavily shaded numerals carried below each headlamp were a prominent feature to the end. The dark wood interiors were decorated with ornate wood carvings including the borough arms at each end of the saloon and the ceilings were adorned by a complex design in blue. The maroon of the trams was lighter than the deep chocolate brown (actually termed Scotch purple) used on the Corporation buses in the late 'twenties and early 'thirties. Window curtains were fitted until 1922/23.

Nos 1-13 G. F. Milnes & Co.
Bogie, single deck. 1901

These single deck cars were 31ft. 6in. long, had open platforms and clerestory roofs and were mounted on Peckham 14D3 maximum traction bogies. They were equipped with 2 × 25hp GE52 motors and BTH B3 controllers. There were six slightly arched windows each side, two large fixed central ones and two small drop-lights at each end. As built there were three compartments with offset doors in the four bulkheads. The central compartment seated eight a side lengthways with 2 × 3 seats in the end compartments and a seat for three on each platform, increasing the seating capacity to 31; passengers were not allowed to sit on the platform at the driving end. Originally the two end compartments were for smokers and the centre for non-smokers. The disadvantages of this system are obvious and after only a week or two's operation, smoking was restricted to the compartment at the Woodside end only. In March 1902 smoking was prohibited altogether except on the platform seats. Another difficulty was caused by the partitions being fitted with mirrors as when the cars were crowded with standing passengers and the conductor was at the front of the car, he was unable to see if the platform was clear before giving the starting signal. The mirrors were replaced by clear glass and eventually, in 1903, the partitions were removed and the seating capacity increased to 33, 15 each side and three on the rear platform.

A four sided rotating glass destination indicator was mounted on the canopy at each end; this could be turned to show "WOODSIDE", "MONK ST.", "NEW FERRY" or "HIGHER TRANMERE". The latter was never used as the cars were used exclusively for the New Ferry route. In addition, a

board inscribed "FOR PORT SUNLIGHT" was carried centrally on each side above the window.

By December 1906 the non-resilient track foundations had pounded the trucks almost to destruction and there were frequent derailments. Tenders were invited and it was decided to order 14 pairs of Mountain and Gibson swing-bolster maximum traction bogies as early delivery was promised. Alderman Gamlin thought that Milnes, Voss should have been given the order as it was a local firm but the result would have been the same as Mountain and Gibson were suppliers of trucks to Milnes, Voss.

In 1908 a mock-up of a double deck conversion of one of the single deck cars low enough to pass under the Chester Street bridge, was built in Laird Street workshops and, after an inspection by the committee on 3 April, approval was given for the conversion of one car. Car 1 was rebuilt at Laird Street at a cost of £257 12s. 10d. (£257.64) and had its trial run on 1 June. The design was approved by the Board of Trade inspector on 21 August but, in the meantime it seems that the Corporation had converted a second car. The committee decided that all 13 cars should be converted and following a discussion on tenders, Thomas Voss attended the committee meeting on 30 September and suggested modifications to the design. After listening to his presentation, the committee authorised Milnes, Voss to convert one car to their design. The original conversion consisted of constructing a knifeboard seat over the clerestory and enclosing the upper deck with a flat roof which did not extend over the platforms. Access to the upper saloon was by a right-angled staircase with rather narrow treads as the platforms were not extended and the end layout was very cramped. One door in the upper deck bulkhead led to one side of the knifeboard seat and there was cramped access at the ends to the other side; upper deck headroom was only 5ft 6in. The Voss modification provided a transverse gangway at the head of the staircases and two bulkhead doors. Despite their low height construction, the cars were still nearly 15ft high from rail to trolley base.

Tenders were invited for the conversion of the remaining 10 cars in November 1909 and Milnes, Voss got the order at £200 per car. All were done by 1910. In practice there were considerable variations in detail within the batch. Some retained the offset doors in the lower deck bulkheads whilst others were converted to centre doors thus eliminating the three-seat with its back to the bulkhead. Most retained the slightly pointed' lower deck windows but others received new cantrails with straight topped windows though the characteristic Milnes curved upper corners were retained.

Reports that car 11 was withdrawn after a head on collision with car 64 in fog on 23 October 1913 or that it was rebuilt resembling a Hurst Nelson car and numbered 62, appear to be incorrect as there are

Birkenhead's "New Ferry" cars 1-13 began life in 1901 as single-deckers, built by G. F. Milnes of Hadley, Shropshire on 14D3 Type trucks made by the Peckham Truck Company of Kingston, N.Y, USA. They were retrucked in 1907 with Mountain & Gibson Type 3 maximum-traction bogies, and rebuilt in 1908-10 as double-deck cars with knifeboard top-deck seating. Nos. 1 and 2 were rebuilt by the Corporation, with flat-topped saloon windows, Nos. 3-13 by Milnes Voss, retaining the round-topped windows. The lower photograph was taken in Laird St. depot yard for Robb's, Birkenhead's premier store. *(Tramway Museum Society and M. Jenkins)*

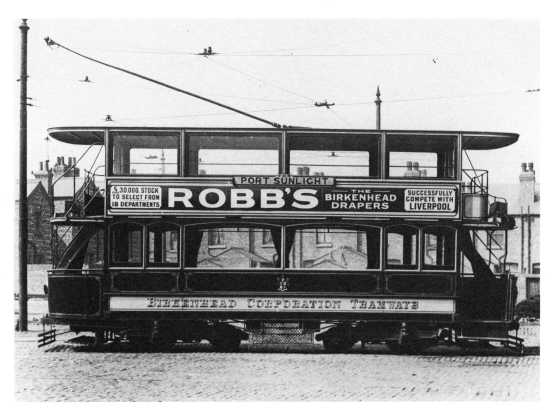

Car No. 1, the first low-bridge conversion, standing at Woodside in 1908. In this car (and No. 2) there was only one door at each end of the upper deck. *(Tramway Museum Society)*

A close-up of No. 8, taken by Dr. H. A. Whitcombe in 1927 from the top deck of No. 2 to show the outside landing and the full-length longitudinal top deck seat, a layout unique to Birkenhead. *(Science Museum, Whitcombe Collection)*

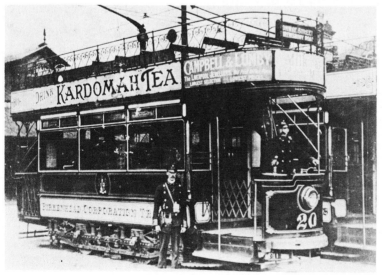

The most numerous Birkenhead trams were the four-wheel cars of the series 14-44, built by G. F. Milnes in 1901. No. 20, seen here at Woodside, has been recovered for preservation after serving as a hut at Farndon. Note the cutaway dash to clear the track brake operating wheel. *(R. L. Wilson)*

other reports of it lurking at the back of the depot in the 'twenties and of its occasional appearance looking very drab and run down.

In 1914 one car received new GE58-4T motors and B49 controllers. The war held up the conversion of the others but they were all done after 1919. However, by the time they were withdrawn when the New Ferry route closed at the end of 1931, all these cars had B18 controllers. Early in 1932 the bodies were broken up and the frames, complete with bogies are believed to have been exported to Bombay.

Nos. 14-44   G. F. Milnes & Co.
4-wheel double deck   1901

These 31 four wheel cars, delivered in the second half of 1901, were 27ft 7in long and were mounted on Peckham 9A cantilever extension trucks of 6ft wheelbase. Power was provided by two BTH GE52 25hp motors; B3 controllers were fitted. As delivered they seated 22 inside on longitudinal seats and 33 outside on reversible transverse seats and ordinary stairs turning through 180 degrees were fitted. Very ornate wrought iron rails were fitted around the upper deck and originally there was a wrought iron grille between the dashplate and the saloon but these were removed and the dashplates extended in later years. The saloon had double doors at each end giving a wide entrance to speed loading and unloading. Destination equipment consisted of boards along the upper deck rails on each side and rotating glass indicators at each end to which paper labels were affixed. These were replaced by roller blind indicators, rather longer than those used in later years, towards the end of 1903. Spencer's patent slipper brakes had been fitted to 18 cars by March 1902. Eventually to achieve flexibility in the use of the fleet all the four-wheel cars were fitted, the dash being cut away on the nearside to accommodate the brake wheel. Some of the crews called these cars 'buckjumpers'.

In the autumn of 1903 the Committee decided to experiment with top covers and approved the simultaneous treatment of two cars — one by the Corporation's own staff and the other by Milnes, Voss. The design chosen was very advanced for its time and covered the whole car from end to end with a shallow clerestory for light and ventilation. It was known officially as the "White" top cover after its originator, H. L. White of the Great Grimsby Street Tramways Co. The Corporation fitted car No 17 at a cost of £138 whilst Milnes, Voss worked on No 16 for £132. This firm called their version the "Birkenhead cover" as it incorporated some features of the "Magrini" patent which included a mechanism for opening all the windows on each side simultaneously with the aid of a detachable handle. This design was used extensively on Merseyside and was probably invented by Messrs. Bellamy and Mallins of the

Experimental windscreens were fitted to two cars late in 1913. The one used on No. 28 was similar to those used in Aberdeen (note the hand holding the screen in position). The second was designed and made at Laird St depot and fitted to No. 25. *(Courtesy E. Gray)*

Liverpool Tramways, Magrini being the name of a patent agent behind whom they sheltered.

The Committee inspected the two cars on 30 December 1903 and, satisfied with what they saw, authorised two further conversions. However for reasons unknown nothing was done and it was not until 1910 that ten cars were fitted with covers by Brush workmen. No more four wheel cars were fitted with the rather expensive "White" top cover, others being covered only in the centre with the balconies left completely open. The ornate wrought iron railings were retained on the balconies. The roof which was fitted eventually to cars 14-15, 18-23, 38 and 41 was of Milnes, Voss design but manufactured by Brush. In August 1913 the Manager reported on the need to fit covers to another six cars and this work was done by Corporation staff at a cost of £119 10s. 0d. (£119.50) per car early in 1914, cars 43-44 re-entering service late in February. The other cars were 37, 39, 40 and 42 and these six included three cars recently returned from service on the New Ferry route. Cars 24-36 were left open as the Board of

In 1903 Birkenhead Corporation
adopted the "White" full-length top
cover patented by local firm G. C.
Milnes, Voss & Co Ltd. They were
fitted to three four-wheel cars
(including No. 16, shown here) and to
thirteen of the fifteen bogie cars 45-59.
One of them, No. 58, was later given
driver's windscreens. The photograph
was taken on 24 July 1931.
(G. N. Southerden)

Trade still refused to allow top covered cars to run on
the Tranmere route. Cars 24-31 usually worked to
Tranmere whilst 32-36 were used on Claughton
Road and occasionally on the Circle.

During their lifetime these cars underwent many
changes of equipment. As early as October 1901 the
committee authorised the purchase of a pair of BTH
GE58 motors to be fitted to a Tranmere car to give
extra power for snowploughing on the Tranmere
route. The displaced GE52 motors were to be used
with a spare truck and a horse car body to make a
snowplough and these were apparently the origins of
works car No 60, described later. The long gradient
of Pearson Road and Argyle Street South always
caused anxiety and in 1914 a pair of B49 controllers
with GE200K motors was purchased. The B49 had
automatic runback and cross-field braking and it
must be assumed that this equipment was fitted to
one of the 24-31 batch. In 1919 a further 12 sets were
purchased and presumably all 13 cars (24-36) were
then equipped but this is not certain. Commencing in
1911, work began on strengthening the lower saloons
of four wheel cars by means of trusses. Over the next
four years, 23 cars were trussed and given new lower
saloon floors.

The Ministry of Transport, successor to the Board
of Trade in tramway affairs, relaxed their attitude
and agreed to top covered cars running to Tranmere
in 1922. By March 1923, 36, 26, 25, 24 and 34 had
been covered, in that order; the others followed. The
Advertiser said on 5 September 1922 that several
people thought 36 was a new car, and would not go
on it initially as they thought it was too dangerous on
the Tranmere route. The design was quite different

Below: No. 22 at Laird Street depot after being fitted with its 1910-type top
cover with three large side windows. 22 cars were thus fitted between 1910
and 1914. This view also shows the double saloon doors and the dash cut
away to clear the slipper brake wheel. *(Courtesy M. Jenkins)*

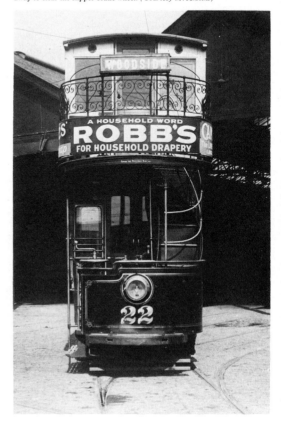

from that of the flat roofs previously fitted. There were six windows each side instead of three, the roof was elliptical and the seating a mixture of longitudinal and transverse. Strangely enough, open balconies were retained at a time in tramcar development when it could have been expected that canopies would have been fitted over the balconies. The ash, oak and elm was supplied by the Parks Department from trees grown in Birkenhead Park and the work was carried out by departmental joiners at Laird Street at a cost of £150 per car. The cover weighed only 6cwt (305kg). 18 cars were fitted with 21E trucks, 10 of them purchased from Brush, during 1920. These were 15, 19, 20, 22-24, 26, 28-30, 34, 36-7 and 40-44. The origin of the other eight trucks is obscure as no purchase was authorised. Several cars had their controllers replaced. 23 and 38-40 received reconditioned BTH B18s whilst 14-22, 27, 29-33, 36-7, 41-4 and another five cars not specified received BTH 510s by 1929. Some BTH magnetic track brake equipment was bought in the 'twenties but, apart from 50, it is not known which cars were fitted. 16 cars received BTH 200K motors whilst three received GE 200Ks.

About 14 cars were refurbished internally at a cost of £200 per car in 1929-30. Two-and-one reversible sprung seats in dark red leatherette as used on the buses were fitted on both decks of a few cars but conductors complained of the difficulty of collecting fares when there were standing passengers and subsequent conversions received upholstered longitudinal seats with three cushions on the lower decks. Other improvements included better lighting, oak faced plywood ceilings, replacement of gongs with reciprocating ones and installation of 'Numa" pneumatic bells in place of cords. Cork floors were laid in saloons and on the platforms but these proved unable to stand up to hard wear and laths were put back after a time. But externally the cars retained their Edwardian mien. The drab, heavily lined out body panels, ornate shaded lettering and numerals and metal advertisement plates which obscured the upper panels remained unchanged to the end. Two experimental drivers' screens had been tried experimentally in October 1913 but abandoned.

In 1931 cars 18, 36 and 42 were fitted with platform vestibules similar to that fitted to No 58 in 1921. In the absence of auxiliary circuits, windscreen wipers could not be fitted to assist drivers in wet weather so the windscreens needed to be partially lowered to give reasonable visibility.

It is believed that cars 24-26, 28, 34 and 35 were withdrawn in 1931. After 1935 when only the Circle

Steep grades on the Tranmere route prevented the use of top-covered cars until 1922. After the ban was lifted, the Tranmere cars (24-36) were fitted with six-window top covers built of timber supplied from Birkenhead's parks. By this time No. 34 (shown here) had been given a Brush type 21E truck, of which Birkenhead had bought eighteen. *(R. M. Morris, Birkenhead)*

The last improvement made to Birkenhead's trams was the fitting of driver's windscreens to cars 18, 36 and 42 in 1931. No 36 is seen here passing Borough Road Library in July 1937. The original Birkenhead Library was demolished to facilitate construction of the Mersey Road tunnel. *(S. V. Hall)*

route remained, cars which developed serious faults were parked so that at the end only some 20 cars were serviceable. Many bodies were sold off as summer-houses especially for sites along the North Wales coast. A "White" top cover was rescued but unfortunately scrapped, and a 1910-type top cover became a kennel for the guard dog in the former Milnes Voss works when used by a scrap dealer. No 20 is currently being restored in open top form.

Nos. 45-59   G. F. Milnes & Co. Ltd.
Bogie double deck   1902

When it was realised that the original orders would be insufficient to serve all the routes, a third order was placed in August 1901 for 15 large bogie cars. Having considered various tenders the Corporation decided to save £58 per car by ordering the bodies, trucks and electrical equipment separately. The body contract was awarded to G. F. Milnes at £300 per car. The trucks were McGuire equal wheel bogies (£135 per car) and the electrical equipment — four 20hp TIIb motors were manufactured by l'Electrique

et l'Hydraulique of Charleroi, Belgium and imported by their U.K. agent Witting, Eborall and Co. at £330 per car. Milnes persuaded the Corporation to revise the original specifications to include overall upper deck canopies in lieu of short canopies which would not have covered the platforms. This increased the capacity to 75–45 outside and 30 inside. The cars were 34ft 6in long. Their appointments were similar to the four wheelers except for the dash which had a peculiar protruding centre portion behind which the controller was mounted thus providing a more spacious platform. All cars had curtains and seat cushions which were removed after about five years. Leathers' patent ventilators were originally fitted but removed in early 1904. The Tramways Committee minutes record the adoption of a new painting style for the class. The first car entered service on the Laird Street route on 22 March 1902 and others were in service before Easter. There were soon complaints of noise and vibration.

In late 1903 car 46 had its staircases and upper deck seats removed and a shorter trolley mast fitted.

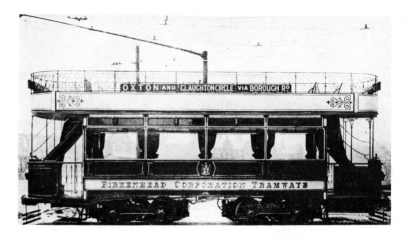

The 1902 additions to Birkenhead's tram fleet comprised 15 G. F. Milnes bogie cars, Nos. 45-59, on McGuire equal-wheel trucks. They were known to the staff either as 'Dreadnoughts' or 'Big Cars.' *(Tramway Museum Society)*

Seats were placed on the platforms giving a seating capacity of 35 and in this single deck form it ran on the New Ferry route until 1913 when it was reconverted to an open-top double decker. The Committee minutes refer to converting cars to single deckers and it is possible that at least one other car of this class was also altered. Passengers complained that the big cars were higher off the ground and difficult to board and the bodies were apparently lowered on the trucks.

By the end of June 1904 52 emerged with a top cover similar to those on 16 and 17. At least four more had been done by July 1905 when slipper brakes were ordered for five cars presumably because the extra weight gave rise to braking problems. The Board of Trade would not permit these cars in their original condition to run on the anti-clockwise Circle route because of the steep descent in Balls Road East but these five were excepted. All this class were eventually top covered except No 46. They were nicknamed 'Dreadnoughts' by the crews. When originally covered, car 52 had its destination indicators mounted below the canopies at an angle but all cars eventually had destination equipment in the end windows of the upper deck. 47 was given continuous dash plates with louvres replacing the wrought iron grilles.

Before long, the Corporation discovered that very heavy bogie cars gave rise to various problems, in particular excessive noise and track wear which could not be justified by the traffic. In August 1906 the committee considered a petition from residents in the neighbourhood of Prenton Road West requesting that bogie cars be withdrawn on Sundays and after 10pm on weekdays purely on the grounds of excessive noise. The manager reported that the trucks were in poor condition as a result of the track foundations and small cars were put on the Prenton route every day for several months. It was decided to have a special meeting at Laird Street depot on 27 August. A truck was inspected and it was decided that a truck of a different design should be built up in the works. This was inspected on 23 January 1907 and, having expressed their satisfaction, the committee authorised the construction of 15 pairs at Laird Street.

The truck was an equal wheel bogie of similar design to the Peckham 14B which had gone out of production in 1906. The Corporation accepted tenders in March 1907 for steel castings from Robert Wilson and Sons of Bishop Auckland and for iron castings from Summerson and Sons of Darlington. Other tenders accepted during April were that of George Salter and Co. of West Bromwich for axle box and other springs, Robert Smith and Sons of Birkenhead for mild steel channel and the Consett Iron Co. Ltd. for mild steel flat bars. It is not certain

if the full 15 pairs were built as a four wheel truck was built at Laird Street in 1907-8 and it may be that an order for this was substituted for one car set of bogies. One car, 49, was remounted in August 1915 on a pair of Mountain and Gibson maximum traction trucks of which there was a spare set for the New Ferry cars. It is possible that 45 and 48 retained their original trucks.

It is apparent that retrucking the large cars did little to reduce the noise and in August 1908 there was talk in the council of scrapping them and replacing them with lighter vehicles. Other councillors wanted to dispose of the undertaking to a private company. In 1910 car 50 was taken into Laird Street workshops and cut in half. A complete section 5ft 4in long was cut out, the remaining pieces being joined together and mounted on a Peckham four wheel truck. The shortened car weighed six tons less (10 tons instead of 16) and seated 24 inside and 38 on top. It re-entered service on 3 October 1910. The Council then approved the conversion of the remainder of the class at an estimated cost of £135 each but for one reason or another the work was postponed until the outbreak of war made it impossible. The high capacity of the cars was doubtless found to be useful in handling the extra wartime traffic and in any case Clarke considered that top covering should have priority over any other reconstruction work. In the event, no further conversions were made.

In 1919-20 the cars were fitted with four GE52 25hp motors which were somewhat faster and restored the power-weight ratio which had applied in open top days. About 1923, car 50 was fitted with BTH controllers and BTH 200K motors. Car 58 was equipped with platform vestibules in the autumn of 1921, becoming the only totally enclosed car in the fleet. No 46 was probably not remotored, and was used from time to time as an illuminated car often with a band playing on the top deck. In later years it saw only occasional service as a football special and it was almost certainly the last car to use the Charing Cross line.

In 1929-30 car 50 and at least seven of the bogie cars (probably 51-57) were refurbished internally to the same standards as cars in the 14-44 class. 50 was the first to be done and was the only car to have uncut moquette seats on the lower deck. It also had BTH magnetic brakes and black "Exorite" covered handrails. The bogie cars had red leather upholstered longitudinal seats on the lower deck and similar transverse reversible seats upstairs. 51-59 are reported as having second-hand Westinghouse 90 controllers by 1929. Several of the batch, including 45-49 and 58 saw little service after 1930-31. The others continued in service until the Prenton route was abandoned on 30 September 1934 but at the very end there were insufficient bogie cars to run the supplementary peak hour workings between Singleton

No. 52, seen here at Prenton terminus, was the first Birkenhead bogie car to be top-covered (June 1904). The design was that of Mr. H. L. White of the Great Grimsby Street Tramways, which was taken up by the Birkenhead firm of G. C. Milnes, Voss & Co. *(Courtesy T. G. Turner)*

In 1907-08 at least twelve of the bogie cars were remounted on Peckham 14B type trucks made in Birkenhead. The Corporation may have hoped to obtain the quietness and smooth riding of the similar trucks in Blackburn, but if so, they were disappointed, for the cars were still noisy. *(G. N. Southerden)*

Known to enthusiasts as the 'Prenton bogies' because of their normal duties, the bogie cars had a protruding central portion of the dash to provide more room on the platform. The circular mounting near the headlamp is for the trolley retriever. *(M. J. O'Connor)*

Avenue and Woodside in the mornings and Central Station and Prenton in the afternoons.

In addition to their regular Prenton duties these cars were to be found on the Circle until 1928 and on duplicates on the Line of Docks route in the early mornings where their large capacity was useful. Car 50 survived until the final abandonment in 1937 and the lower saloons of all the bogie cars were sold to the Parks Department for use as shelters. Some were in use in Arrowe Park until the early 1970s.

Nos. 63-68 Hurst Nelson
Bogie double deck 1913

The last cars to enter service at Birkenhead were six low height cars for the New Ferry route, delivered in 1913. The contract was awarded to Siemens Bros. at £4,374 but Hurst, Nelson of Motherwell were sub-contractors for the 62-seat bodies and swing bolster type maximum traction bogies of their London type. The upper saloons were totally enclosed and the Corporation spent £466 modifying them before entering service. The height from floor to ceiling in the upper saloon was on 5ft 4in; other dimensions were height to trolley base 14ft 7¾in, width 6ft 8in (upper saloon 7ft 2in), body length 20ft 2in plus 5ft 3in platforms, truck wheelbase 4ft 6in, overall wheel-

base 12ft 6in. Their internal arrangement of a monitor ceiling surmounted by an upper deck knifeboard seat was the same as that used in the cars which Hurst Nelson had built for Southampton.

These cars were used only on the New Ferry route though one report states that they also ran on Sunday morning to Prenton for a time. They had a reputation of being very unsteady; they not only pitched but at high speed they tended to tail-wag. They had a fair turn of speed and in later years notches 10 and 11 of their controllers were blanked off. Eventually they were confined to peak hour service and were withdrawn at the end of 1930, a year or so before their older stable mates.

Nos. 60-62 Works Cars, 1902

Most British tramway systems had a works car but Birkenhead had three. Heavy snowfalls persuaded the Corporation that they needed a snowplough tram especially for clearing the tracks up to Tranmere and Prenton. Car 60 was built as a snowplough

Newly-delivered Hurst Nelson lowbridge car 63 standing in the little used section of Park Road North in 1913. These cars had back-to-back knifeboard seating upstairs and were assigned to New Ferry depot. Instead of a route letter, 63-68 displayed a triangle of three coloured lights on the canopy, above the brake handle. (*Motherwell Library, Hurst Nelson Collection*)

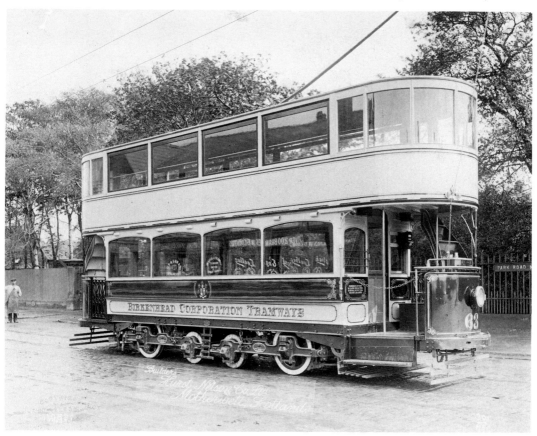

Birkenhead Corporation Electric Tramcar Fleet in 1928/29

Car Numbers	Type (in 1928/29)	Year built	Builder	Seats	Truck(s)	Motors	Controllers
1-13	Covered top lowbridge bogie double deck (open stairs)	1901, rebt. 1908-10	G F Milnes	30/34	Mountain & Gibson Type 3L max/traction bogies	GE 58-6T 2 × 28hp (note d)	BTH B18
14-44	Covered top, Bellamy roof (note a)	1901 rebt. 1910-23	G F Milnes	22/33 (note e)	Peckham cantilever 9A (note b)	GE 200K 2 × 40hp (note c)	BTH 510 (note c)
45,47-49, 51-59	Enclosed top double deck bogie	1902 rebt. 1904-06	G F Milnes	30/46	Peckham cantilever 14B bogies (made by BCT) (f)	GE 52-6T 4 × 25hp	51-59 W'house 90, others E & H
46	Open top bogie	1902	G F Milnes	30/45	Peckham cantilever 14B bogies (BCT)	E & H T116 4 × 20hp	E & H
50	Enclosed-top 4-wheel car	rebt. 1910	G F Milnes	24/38	Peckham cantilever 9A	GE 200K 2 × 40hp	BTH B510
60	Snowplough & rail grinder	1902	ex-horse car	-	Peckham cantilever 9A	GE 52-6T 2 × 25hp	BTH B18?
61	Permanent way car	1902	BCT-made	-	Peckham cantilever 9A	GE 58-4T? 2 × 28hp	BTH B18
62	Breakdown car	Ex-horse car, returned to horse car condition for 1927 anniversary	?	Rigid frame	-	-
63-68	Enclosed top lowbridge double deck	1913	Hurst Nelson	28/34	Hurst Nelson swing bolster max/traction bogies	Siemens 250 CT 2 × 40hp	Siemens TA2

Seating figures shown thus: 22/34 are for lower and upper decks respectively.

Notes
(a) 'White' enclosed full-length top cover on cars 16 and 17 (also on car 50).
(b) 15, 19, 20, 22-24, 26, 28-30, 34, 36, 37, 40-44 remounted 1920 on 21E type trucks, mostly by Brush.
(c) 16 sets purchased 1923, 5 sets 1924, 12 sets 1925.
(d) these motors may have been purchased at second-hand.
(e) Seating 22/35 for cars 24-36.
(f) Car 49 remounted 1915 on Mountain & Gibson Type 3L bogies.

using a six bay horse car body. It was mounted on a Peckham 8A cantilever truck and powered by two GE52 motors. It originally had BTH B3 controllers but had B18s fitted in 1924. It was equipped for towing and initially was used also as a salt sprinkler. It was in service by February 1902. In 1910 it was equipped with carborundum blocks for rail grinding. There was a hand wheel at each corner of the body to screw down the abrasive blocks.

Car 61 was quite different consisting of a large rectangular water tank with open platform ends. It was apparently filled with salt water to be sprayed on to the tracks to clear snow and ice. Facilities existed at Woodside to replenish the supply from the River Mersey. In later years it was used to tow a welding trailer which ran on solid-tyred rubber wheels. Electrically it was identical to 60. The car was well described in *Birkenhead Advertiser* of 22 November 1902:

"It has a thoroughly business look about it with its compact solidity but from a mechanical point of view it has likewise its beauty. The car is a rail washer and sprinkler and part of it is a large tank which has been constructed to specification by the Cleveland Construction Co. The tank is 5ft 6in deep, it has a similar breadth and is 12ft long and its holding capacity is 11,000 gallons. It is divided into two compartments with an equalising pipe to feed the compartments. An ordinary manhole is at each end and the tank is filled from the top. The car contains two double spray sprinklers and four rail washers. There are also four scrapers for the purpose of cleaning the grooves of the rails and which

are exceedingly useful in case of snow . . . . When there has been a downfall of snow the tank is filled with salt water. . . . It is calculated that the tank will water a track five miles long. . . ."

In September 1902 the manager was authorised to purchase an old horse car for use as a salt truck and this was almost certainly the origin of car 62. Salt was probably shovelled out through empty window spaces. Eventually it was motorised using a similar truck and equipment to 60-61 and carried jacks, lifting gear and dolly bogies to place beneath a car with a broken axle. It was normally parked on the extreme left hand track at Laird Street depot whilst 60 occupied the extreme right hand track. Eventually the breakdown gear was transferred to 60 and all the evidence suggests that the remains of 62 were converted into the horse car used in the Jubilee celebrations in 1927. In 1935 the car reappeared as part of the centenary celebrations for the establishment of municipal government. On 12 January 1936 it narrowly escaped destruction in a fire which consumed one bus and damaged 12 others. It was earmarked for preservation but in 1940 it was taken over by the Home Guard. One report says that it was destroyed in the air raid of March 1941 but another states that it survived, cut into two halves, until 1945.

Birkenhead had three works cars, 60-62, of which 60 and 62 were former horse cars. In 1927 No. 62 was returned to horse car condition to celebrate the Jubilee of Incorporation of the borough, displaying the dates 1860-1877 of the Street Railway Co. It was thereafter stored in Laird Street depot but was damaged in a 1941 bombing raid and never repaired. The electric car is No. 27. *(Courtesy T. G. Turner)*

The department possessed a hand operated tower wagon with cart wheels which was towed behind one of the works cars. The clatter of iron clad wheels on granite setts must have been deafening. In 1916, tenders were invited for a motor tower wagon and the Mersey Motor Company's offer of a Daimler for £820 was referred back to the Committee by the full Council. A Halley was ordered for £870 and this was in service by November. In 1927 it was replaced by a Straker Squire "A" bus which was rebuilt as a mobile workshop and tower wagon. This vehicle (CO 3399) had been bought by the Corporation from Plymouth Corporation in March 1922 and it served until 1936. In the last few months of operation a tower wagon of the Street Lighting department was used. All the works vehicles were finished in grey.

BIRKENHEAD.

Birkenhead's horse drawn tower wagon was built by J. Houlgrave & Co. of Liverpool. This photograph was taken in the maker's yard.
(Courtesy M. Jenkins)

6 Other Tramway Schemes

Most electric tramway systems in Britain were entirely urban in character but there were some exceptions. A continuous chain of tramways eventually existed from Liverpool Pier Head to the Pennines above Oldham and Mossley and many sections of this network were rural throughout their whole existence. Two rural tramway schemes were proposed for the Wirral peninsula both to be linked with municipal tramway systems. Neither was built, but had they come to fruition many of the more rural districts would have been opened up much earlier.

In 1900, mindful of the impending loss of their business, a consortium of directors of the Wallasey United Company proposed to form the North Wirral Electric Tramway Company. The intention was to lay a line starting in Upton Road, Birkenhead at a junction with the proposed Birkenhead Corporation line and running through Upton, Greasby, Frankby, Caldy, West Kirby, Hoylake, Meols, Moreton and Leasowe, to Wallasey Village. In Wallasey the promoters proposed to continue the line via St. Hilary Brow and Wallasey Road to join the proposed Wallasey U. D. tramways over which they sought running powers to Seacombe Ferry. The standard gauge line was to have been constructed under the provisions of the Light Railways Act 1896 which were less arduous than the Tramways Act 1870 and would have included unpaved sections on roadside reservations. Ordinary and "express" cars were to be run.

In November 1900 solicitors acting for the proposed company wrote to both councils enclosing plans and seeking some arrangement whereby they could run their cars from Hoylake and West Kirby to both Woodside and Seacombe. Birkenhead appointed a sub-committee but deferred making any decision. Wallasey was outraged and dismissed the application as being "a measure decidedly hostile to the interest of the Council's tramway scheme".

All the local authorities and the Wirral Railway were hostile and no progress could be made with the scheme. The company is believed to have had plans to extend to Heswall and perhaps beyond as the railway stations for the Deeside communities were all on the river bank at some distance from the villages.

The other scheme was that of the Birkenhead and Chester Tramways Co. Ltd., registered on 18 November 1902 with a capital of £5,000 in £1 shares. Its objects were "to carry on the business of railway and tramway proprietors, carriers of goods and passengers, omnibus and van proprietors and to carry on the business of an Electric Light and Power Company". The promoters were influential men, the Chairman being Sir James A. Willox, proprietor of the "Daily Courier" a Liverpool morning paper which survived until 1929. Others were John Holt, merchant; Edwin Adam, an Edinburgh advocate; Cecil Edward Maples, a Liverpool solicitor and Arthur Stanley M. P. of Knowsley, brother of Lord Derby, who could be relied upon to lend his name to add respectability to any ambitious company promotion. Later on James and Jacob Atherton, leading lights in British Insulated Cable Works at Prescot and the South Lancashire Tramways, took 500 shares each; the Eastham Ferry, Pleasure Gardens and Hotel Co. Ltd. took 100 shares and Thomas Montgomery, a brewer with an interest in the Eastham Ferry Hotel, took 75.

The scheme provided for about 15 miles of standard gauge single track tramway with passing loops extending from New Ferry Pier to Chester Town Hall, passing through Bromborough, Eastham, Childer Thornton, Little Sutton, Great Sutton and Backford. A short connecting line was proposed with the Birkenhead Corporation New Ferry line at the Toll Bar and a long branch to Eastham Ferry. A depot and power station were to have been built on the bank of the river near Eastham Lock, the entrance to the Manchester Ship Canal. No plans existed for another depot but in practice another shed nearer Chester would have been essential. At Chester the line would have ended on double track in Northgate Street opposite St Werburgh Street outside the Cathedral and the Town Hall; the first loops would have been laid at the junction of Liverpool Road and Parkgate Road. There was also to have been a short double track siding leading into the forecourt of the Liverpool Road Station of the Great Central Railway. These proposals were incorporated in the Birkenhead and Chester Tramways Bill 1903.

The Bill was controversial in many respects and the company's objectives suggested that the carriage of passengers in such a sparsely populated area would be secondary to power generation and the carriage of goods. The L N W and G W Joint Railways objected to the building of a competitive parallel line even if it were laid on public roads. The proposed siding to the Great Central at Chester would have given that company a collection and delivery network in the heart of Joint territory. Furthermore, the Birkenhead to Chester road was little more than a country lane. Provision was made in the Bill for no fewer than 37 road widening and

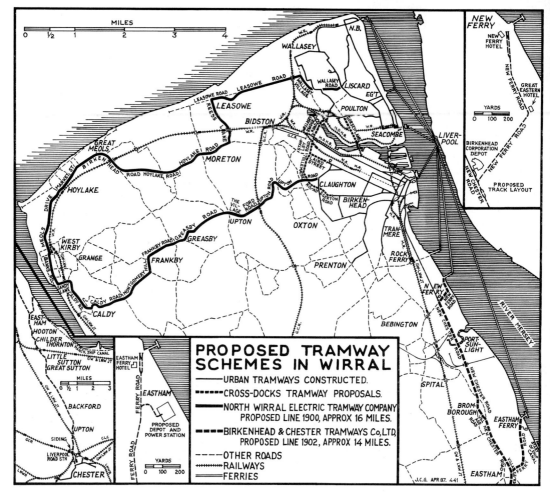

MILES
0   ½   1   2   3   4

PROPOSED TRAMWAY
SCHEMES IN WIRRAL

——— URBAN TRAMWAYS CONSTRUCTED.
••••••• CROSS-DOCKS TRAMWAY PROPOSALS.
▬▬▬ NORTH WIRRAL ELECTRIC TRAMWAY COMPANY
        PROPOSED LINE 1900, APPROX 16 MILES.
▬▬▬ BIRKENHEAD & CHESTER TRAMWAYS Co.LTD,
        PROPOSED LINE 1902, APPROX 14 MILES.
----- OTHER ROADS
++++ RAILWAYS
==== FERRIES

NEW
FERRY

YARDS
0   100   200

PROPOSED
TRACK LAYOUT

YARDS
0   100   200

improvement schemes which would have added greatly to construction costs. A scheme for a line along Liverpool Road, Chester to Upton had been deleted from the Chester Corporation Bill 1901 due to opposition and it is significant that because of the restricted width of the mediaeval streets in Chester the city's tram system, which would have been 150 yards from the proposed line at its nearest point, was converted from standard gauge to 3ft 6in on electrification.

The concerted opposition from railway companies and road authorities was such that the Bill was withdrawn and the company was wound up in February 1905. However, it is interesting to speculate on the course of events if the line had been built. Port Sunlight, Bromborough and Eastham would have developed as suburbs much more quickly and ribbon development along the Chester Road advanced by ten years or more. Birkenhead cars could have carried Lever Brothers' traffic and perhaps a branch would have been built to Bromborough Port. New Ferry, closed in 1922 following

damage to the pier, might have become a major ferry and its life prolonged. Similarly, Eastham, a privately owned ferry operated on a shoestring until 1929, might have prospered particularly if a goods and parcel service had been started.

Cross Docks Schemes

The presence of the Dock Estate with its moveable bridges and myriad railway tracks presented serious obstacles to communication by road over the short distance between Birkenhead and Wallasey. The dock railways in Liverpool had been used by specially adapted omnibuses in the nineteenth century but circumstances were different on the Wirral side of the Mersey. Most people either walked across the Dock Estate or crossed the river by ferry to Liverpool then recrossed to the other town and this was still a popular method up to the middle of the present century. A horse tramway between Birkenhead, Seacombe and New Brighton had been unsuccessfully proposed by the Street Railway in 1861. The omnibuses connecting the Hoylake Railway with

One of the Birkenhead and Seacombe Omnibus Company's ancient omnibuses standing at the Seacombe terminus in Birkenhead Road in 1913. These 20-seat vehicles with their crude ladders to the upper deck were bought secondhand many years earlier from the Birkenhead Carriage Company.

Seacombe crossed the Pool but provided no local facilities and the only other omnibus to run, a vehicle known as the Black Maria, supplied under contract by Thomas Evans for £5 a month to convey prisoners between Wallasey and the court in Birkenhead, was discontinued in May 1881.

During 1902 Birkenhead manager Cyril Clarke and his opposite number at Wallasey, R. R. Greene, had informal discussions but came to the conclusion that there was no practical means of linking up the tramways of the two towns at that time. The Dock Board was unco-operative, as in Liverpool.

On 7 September 1903 after some initial licensing difficulties, Thomas Peters, a "cocoa rooms proprietor" of 181 Price Street, Birkenhead, started a horse bus service under the title "Birkenhead and Seacombe Omnibus Company" using small vehicles purchased second-hand from the Birkenhead Carriage Co. Ltd. He also took over some former omnibus company premises at 2-4 Devonshire Road together with stables in Watson Street and Back Menai Street, near Charing Cross. The route ran from Charing Cross to Seacombe Ferry via Exmouth Street, Watson Street and the Four Bridges. The buses came to be known as the "Seacombe, or Penny Joggers" and eventually ran half-hourly from 10am to 11pm with extras at rush hours and on summer Sundays. In 1911 some Ford model T buses with specially built 12-seat wooden bodies were operated over the route but the horse buses seem to have continued throughout the war until 1919 when the service was taken over by the Birkenhead Motor Works using Dennis buses. Apart from some hotel buses in Liverpool these were the last horse buses to run on Merseyside.

Wallasey had sought powers to make agreements with other tramway authorities in its unsuccessful 1906 Bill but did not pursue the matter in subsequent legislation. Meanwhile in 1911 the Town Clerk of

Wallasey had requested the appointment of representatives from Birkenhead to discuss with Wallasey councillors the question of improvements in the means of access by road and tramway between Birkenhead and Wallasey. A Joint sub-committee examined schemes for a high level bridge or a tunnel and recommended purchase of Poulton Bridge on which tolls were charged until 1936. A double track tramway was proposed from the Pool Inn, Poulton to the Line of Docks terminus in Beaufort Road with a line up Stanley Road to Laird Street depot. The Poulton and Docks routes were only ¾ mile apart and there were, at that time, no railway tracks on Poulton Bridge. The Mersey Docks and Harbour Board opposed the scheme and a report dated 24 July 1912 concluded that "no scheme for improving the means of communication is feasible of which the estimated cost is not prohibitive". The early under-river tunnel proposals (see below) would have enabled trams to pass beneath the docks between central Birkenhead and Seacombe.

Birkenhead obtained motor bus powers in 1914 but the war intervened and it was only after Wallasey had started its own motor bus service in 1920 that serious discussions on cross docks services began. The first joint route between Seacombe Ferry and Charing Cross via Duke Street Bridge began on 19 March 1921 and further routes serving Liscard and Harrison Drive were soon added. However, interest in tramway schemes did not die immediately. About 1923 a plan for linking the Claughton Road and Docks routes via Tollemache Road and either Stanley Road or Ilchester Road with a connecting line along Wallasey Bridge Road to Poulton was proposed. Again, in 1924, when Wallasey was upgrading Gorsey Lane, there was serious talk of seeking powers for a tramway along it as far as the borough boundary at Duke Street bridge. But the powerful Dock Board remained the stumbling block.

It did not want the complication of tramway track on its roads many of which already carried paved railway tracks nor did it want overhead wires which might obstruct the movement of outsize loads. With improvements in vehicles, the buses of the two towns solved the problem and no more was heard of joint tramway schemes.

The Tunnel Tramway Scheme

In 1923 the Merseyside Co-ordination Committee, a loose association of local authorities under the chairmanship of Sir Archibald Salvidge received a report on the practicability of building a bridge or tunnel between Liverpool and the Cheshire bank of the Mersey. The report was compiled jointly by Sir Maurice Fitzmaurice, Mr. Basil Mott and Mr. John A. Brodie. Bridges had been suggested on two occasions in the 1860's by Dock Board engineers and in 1880, when work on the building of the Mersey Railway tunnel had commenced, Parliamentary powers were obtained for the construction of a subway between Liverpool and Birkenhead. Suspension bridges were proposed on two occasions, in 1898 and 1912 but none of these schemes came to anything. The present scheme was prompted by the knowledge that over the 20 years between 1901 and 1921 the population resident within a rough 10 mile radius of Liverpool Town Hall had increased by an average of 11,000 per year to almost 1.25 million. In the same period cross-river passengers by public transport i.e. ferries and railway had almost doubled from 33 million to 62 million. The number of vehicles conveyed by the goods ferries of Birkenhead and Wallasey had likewise increased from 380,000 to 640,000.

The report ruled out a bridge on grounds of cost, £10.5 million, headroom required for shipping at high tide (185ft), length of span (2,200ft) and gradients of the approaches and recommended a tunnel of 44ft internal diameter with four 9ft traffic lanes. The entrances on the Liverpool side were to be at New Quay and Whitechapel and on the Cheshire side near the Woodside Hotel, Birkenhead and at Victoria Place near Seacombe ferry. Both Cheshire branches were to be of full 44ft width but the New Quay entrance was to serve only a two lane tunnel 26ft wide.

The tunnel was to consist of a cast-iron tube lined with concrete and grouted in to the sandstone rock by cement or lime mixtures under pressure thus rendering pumping unnecessary. The carriageway was planned to be built just below the diameter of the tube with 17ft headroom. Below the vehicular carriageway was to be a separate section for a double track tramway. The remaining space either side of the tram tunnel and above the main carriageway would have been utilised for ventilation. In view of the fact that at that time transport to and from the ferries on both sides of the river was almost

exclusively by trams the scheme for tunnel trams was quite logical and in fact the first scheme on these lines had been proposed by C. W. Mallins, the Liverpool tramways manager in 1908. J. A. Brodie, Liverpool's City Engineer and the architect of Liverpool's grass tracks which were spreading across Liverpool's suburbs in the early twenties, was originally a protagonist of a bridge but by 1923, recognising the strength of the shipping lobby, he, too, favoured a tunnel. Separate tramway entrances and exits would have been required and whilst the ruling gradients in the vehicular tunnel were planned to be 1 in 30 with some 1 in 20, steeper gradients for the trams were envisaged. A gradient of 1 in 10 as used at the northern end of the Kingsway tramway subway in London would have been practicable but much more powerful cars than were then running on any of the three systems would have been desirable. It is of interest to note that whilst the principal objective was to provide for cross-river traffic, communication between Birkenhead and Wallasey by tunnel thus avoiding the dock bridges was also envisaged. This would have enabled through tram services to run between the two towns.

Liverpool, with its own extensive tramway system but no stake in the ferries, was understandably enthusiastic about through trams from Prenton to Prescot or New Brighton to Old Swan. Some quite astonishing figures were produced in support of the idea and the opponents of the scheme, which included both Birkenhead and Wallasey, had little difficulty in refuting them. The tunnel structure to accommodate the trams was estimated to cost £1,650,000 with a further £100,000 for permanent

A 1925 artist's impression of the original Mersey Tunnel, showing the main deck level higher than actually built and two elderly trams in the lower section. Note the horse drawn cart and pedestrians, neither of which were ever permitted in the tunnel. *(Liverpool City Engineer)*

way and equipment, £67,000 for loan charges and £33,000 for running charges. Estimated annual revenue at 1d per passenger for the under river section was £112,500 with a car mileage of 750,000. Working expenses were thus estimated as 10.56d per mile and receipts as 36.00d per mile, figures which were quite out of line with current experience in Birkenhead and Wallasey. In 1924 Birkenhead tramways produced 25.72d per mile with total expenses of 22.69d (including loan charges) whilst Wallasey's receipts stood at 25.30d per mile with expenses of 16.70d. In arriving at the tunnel estimates it was assumed that 77% of ferry passengers would transfer to tram (27 million).

Birkenhead Corporation which had more to lose than any of the other parties, readily agreed to the control of the ferries by the proposed Tunnel Authority but would have nothing to do with tunnel trams. In Wallasey there was opposition to the Seacombe tunnel *per se* and the Corporation at first insisted on retaining control of both ferries and tramways though agreeing to pooling the losses on the vehicular ferry. In February 1925, Salvidge, impatient with Wallasey's earlier hostility, stated that he was indifferent to their problems and Wallasey Council then voted 41:4 in favour of handing their vehicular ferry to the Tunnel Committee plus a 6d rate. They also agreed to trams through the Seacombe tunnel despite an estimated loss equal to a 1/2½d rate due to falling ferry traffic. Their agreement came too late and the Mersey Tunnel Joint Committee comprised 10 from Liverpool and seven from Birkenhead.

The Mersey Tunnel Act became law in 1925 and provided for a main tunnel with one branch serving the docks on either side. Protection was provided for the Birkenhead ferries for 40 years from the tunnel opening.

It is of interest to speculate on the possible course of transport history on Merseyside if tunnel trams had become a *fait accompli*, particularly in view of Liverpool's Everton Tunnel scheme, a plan for a tramway tunnel from Anfield to a point quite near the main Tunnel entrance. Liverpool Corporation obtained Parliamentary powers for this scheme in 1927 and bought one single deck car as a prototype

for use in tunnels, but work never started. By the time the first Mersey road tunnel was opened in July 1934, Wallasey's trams had already been scrapped and Birkenhead was committed to a policy of abandonment. On the other hand, Liverpool had just started to renew and modernise its system and the existence of what would have amounted virtually to a rapid transit network might well have kept the tram on the streets of Birkenhead and Wallasey for many more years. In post-war traffic congestion, the value of such a segregated system of public transport would have been immense.

Map of the first Wallasey tramway scheme to be authorised, described in the next chapter.

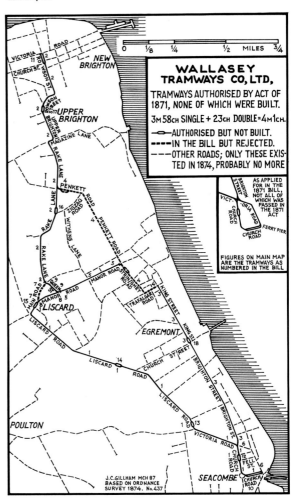

7 Wallasey Horse Tramways

The need for purely local transport in Wallasey had first arisen during the 150 years that Wallasey was host to one of the country's earliest racecourses which ran for five miles from Wallasey Village across the windswept dunes to Leasowe Castle and back. Between approximately 1635 and 1770 carriages and wagonettes conveyed punters from the ferry at Seacombe to the course by way of a track which hugged the north shore of Wallasey Pool crossing its many tributaries by tiny wooden bridges. In 1732 the principal event was transferred to Newmarket where "The Wallasey Stakes" survived for some years. Excursions continued to be provided to Leasowe Castle, being publicly advertised by the owners of the Seacombe ferry and hotel in 1840. In February 1847 they obtained four hackney carriage licences from the Town Commissioners to carry ferry passengers to any part of the district at 3d for the first 1000 yards and 6d for any distance beyond.

On 1 August 1861 the Wallasey Local Board assumed control of the three Wallasey ferry stations, Seacombe, Egremont and New Brighton and on 10 October the Board's Works and Health Committee received notification that James Hall, employed by them to carry goods and luggage to and from Seacombe, had started a bus service between Seacombe and New Brighton, with double-deckers at a fare of 3d inside and 2d outside. Owing to the paucity of roadways, the buses probably went via Victoria Road, Liscard Road, Liscard Village, Rake Lane and Rowson Street. On 31 October 1861 the same committee rejected a proposal to extend the Birkenhead Street Railway from Birkenhead to New Brighton via the Dock Estate and Seacombe Ferry.

By the terms of the Wallasey Improvement Act 1867, the Local Board obtained general powers "to lay down, maintain and renew" tramways "provided always any such rails, plates or trams shall be laid along the middle of the street so that the upper surface of the rail, plate or tram shall be even with the upper surface of the road". This proviso had been inserted to guard against the use of step rails which had caused so much trouble at Birkenhead. Winter receipts on the two northern ferries, Egremont and New Brighton, were poor and the Board's Surveyor was asked to submit estimates for a tramway running from Seacombe to Trafalgar Road so that Egremont could be suspended between October and March each year. Quoting a figure of £4,446 the Board now sought legal advice as to whether they could close both northern ferries either permanently or temporarily and replace them by tramways to and from Seacombe. They were informed that they would require Parliamentary approval and that they themselves were not permitted to operate trams. By 1868 several bus operators were serving Seacombe most of them running to New Brighton. However, Adam Fox of Church Road, Seacombe wrote to the Board complaining that his bus had been prohibited by the Wallasey Pool Bridge Company from plying between the ferry and Docks Station. Fox may well have been one of the operators who stepped into the breach when the Hoylake railway was curtailed in 1870, as already described.

Sufficient numbers were using the Seacombe boats to encourage a syndicate of business men headed by Algernon Warner, Joseph E. Dowson and Charles P. Gibbons to promote the Wallasey Tramways Bill in 1870, the object of which was to form a Wallasey Tramways Company with powers to build just over five miles of route. There were to be two main lines linking Seacombe and New Brighton — one would run from the Marine Hotel along Victoria Road, Liscard Road, Liscard Village, Rake Lane and Magazine Lane where it would meet the other route which would travel from the ferry via Brighton Street, King Street and a private reserved track (Seabank Road at this time was not built throughout). They would descend into New Brighton by "an intended street to be called Grosvenor Road". A third route would link the others by way of Manor Road. A maximum fare of 6d was proposed. A powerful lobby of local landowners stifled the project.

Using the less costly procedure permitted by the newly passed general Tramways Act 1870 a second attempt was made in 1871. After a local enquiry, the Wallasey Tramways Order 1871 authorised the construction of certain lines by the Wallasey Tramways Company Ltd., registered on 8 May 1871 with a nominal capital of £30,000 in £10 shares. The shareholders were Messrs. Glen, Lucas, Smith, Harvey, Morris, Larson and Gratham. The controversial private track was replaced by a line up Trafalgar Road, Stringhey Road and Manor Road where it joined the other main route again as in the 1870 proposal running via Liscard Road and Rake Lane. This time a line the length of Penkett Road connected the two routes. Nine passing loops were included and at Seacombe the cars could approach the Marine Hotel either via Church Road or Victoria Road. Victoria Road, Seacombe was later renamed Borough Road to avoid confusion with Victoria Road, New Brighton and will be referred to as

Borough Road hereafter. The company also sought powers to operate omnibuses and railways advising prospective investors of the potential for "considerable freight and animal traffic". The requisite capital failed to materialise and the company was dissolved on 23 February 1874. The only creditor was William Morris, who received the entire assets of £911.

In 1876 the Local Board embarked upon the complete rebuilding of Seacombe ferry. The existing facilities were all swept away in a major land reclamation project, the boats being transferred to a temporary stage in a former shipbuilding yard off East Street. It was from this stage that the ferry boat p.s. *Gem* set sail one foggy morning in November 1878 and collided with the s.s *Bowfell*. Although never in danger of sinking, panic ensued and several passengers were drowned.

It was against this background of despondency that the new terminal was opened to the public on 5 January 1880. It was an ideal gateway and gave birth to several major thoroughfares including the extension of Seabank Road in the same year. Travel patterns changed. Hundreds still walked to one of the three ferry stations but the improving road system and the eventual housing boom demanded improved transport.

Anticipating these trends, a delegation consisting of Messrs. William and Daniel Busby and Charles H. Beloe had approached the Local Board on behalf of Messrs. Wright, Hackley and Beckett on 10 October 1876 with a view to building a tramway from Seacombe to Upper Brighton. Upper Brighton was a fashionable residential district but also a thoroughfare (later incorporated into Rowson Street) running between Field Road and Mount Pleasant Road. The Board rejected their first proposals, the Busbys returning on 10 July 1877 this time on behalf of the Wirral Tramway Company. A special sub-committee was appointed to advise on the practicality of laying tramways in the districts proposed. In mid October the Busbys presented detailed plans for a single track tramway with passing loops running from Seacombe to the Assembly Rooms, New Brighton via Church Road, Borough Road, Liscard Road, Rake Lane, Earlston Road, Sandrock Road, Mount Pleasant Road, Mount Road and Albion Street, at its junction with Montpellier Terrace. The sub-committee recommended acceptance providing the promoters also included a line from Seacombe to Liscard via Brighton Street and Church Street which would cover for Egremont ferry in the event of it being closed as proposed in 1867.

Having agreed, the Busbys, anxious to tap the wealthy middle-class residents living in Upper Brighton, announced plans to build a two-way steeply-graded loop from the Assembly Rooms along Albion Street, Atherton Street, St. James' Road, Rowson Street, Upper Brighton and Rake Lane to Earlston Road where it would rejoin the original route.

On 24 November 1877 Beloe presented his detailed Parliamentary plans for lines estimated to cost £20,999. They were fiercely opposed, so a Select Committee of the House of Lords sat to hear evidence from both sides. In his submission, Beloe stated:— "The object of the tramway is to bring residents of New Brighton, Liscard and Egremont, which are all in the district of Wallasey, to the Seacombe Ferry, which is the shortest ferry across the Mersey to Liverpool and generally to facilitate intercourse in the district". The residents of Upper Brighton clearly wanted intercourse with no one, as they vigorously opposed the building of the tramway claiming it would destroy the exclusivity of the neighbourhood. Their Lordships were unimpressed but recognising the strength of feeling allowed the promoters a maximum of four years to complete the loop instead of the two years for the remainder of the system.

The Wallasey Tramways Act 1878 received the Royal Assent on 16 August and authorised the Local Board to lay the following tramways to the gauge of 4ft 8½in, the outer rails to be never less than 9ft 6in from the kerb:

a) From Seacombe (Church Road) along Victoria Road (Borough Road) and Liscard Road to Falkland Road (Tramways 1, 1A, 2, 2A, 2B);

b) From Seacombe (Church Road) along Brighton Street and Church Street to Liscard Road (Tramways 3, 3A, 3B) plus a line along Falkland Road (Tramway No. 4);

c) From Falkland Road along Liscard Road to Liscard Village (Tramways 5, 5A, 5B, 5C);

d) From Liscard Village along Rake Lane to Earlston Road, with an alternative single line in Manor Road and Queen Street, Liscard (Tramways 6, 7, 8, 8A, 8B);

e) From Earlston Road along Rake Lane and Upper Brighton to Dalmorton House (Tramways 9, 10, 10A);

f) a loop in Upper Brighton via Albion Street, Mount Road, Mount Pleasant Road, Sandrock Road and Earlston Road to rejoin Tramway No 8 in Rake Lane (Tramways 11 to 14)

Passing places, of which there were to be eighteen, were designated by the letter suffixes (1A, 2A, 2B, etc.); the seven not listed above were on the Upper Brighton loop. The course of all these proposed lines is shown on the map.

The tramway was to be operated by the Wallasey Tramways Company, with its head office at 6 Lord Street, Liverpool, the centre of the Busbys' tramway empire. The directors were Daniel Busby, William Busby, John Carson (a Liverpool omnibus proprietor), Harry Sheraton (timber merchant) and Thomas Russell Lee J P who was elected chairman. The Company Secretary was accountant William Knox, whose name appeared on the sides of the cars. The capital of £30,000 was divided into 3,000 £10 shares. The Act authorised the Company to borrow a maximum of £7,500 restricted to £1,250 for every £5,000 of subscribed capital, providing that they did not borrow £5,000 before 30 May 1879.

The Local Board had the right to purchase the company and all its assets after 15 years providing they gave six months' notice in writing. Should the dividend exceed 7½%, the Board was entitled to demand 50% of the surplus profits (minimum £100) for highway improvements, priority to be given to the tram route. If the company became insolvent or ceased operation for more than three months, the Board was authorised to take over all assets without compensation. The Company was prevented from

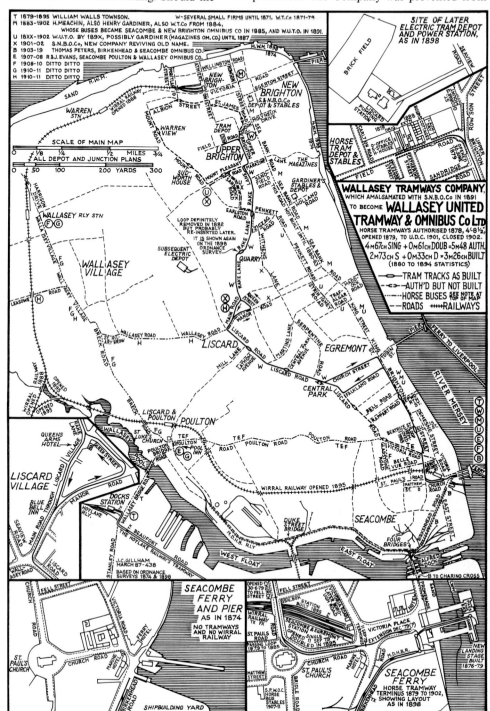

seeking powers for further lines until five years had elapsed, they had to seek permission to abandon all or part of the system, and they had to pay two thirds of any road widening undertaken. Once the tramway had been constructed, the Company had to pay the Board an annual rental of £100.

The Company guaranteed to provide a regular service "at the same time as the ferry boats" between 8am and 7.30pm on weekdays and from 10am to 8.30pm on Sundays. Provision was also made for operating early morning and late evening cars for artisans at fares not to exceed ½d per mile. This statutory obligation was ignored, the Company stating 'Wallasey had no work people'.

The Board whilst generally welcoming the tramway had been determined throughout to protect their own interests. Their solicitors had explained to the Select Committee why they were insisting upon precise fare details being incorporated into the Parliamentary Bill. They argued that if the Company charged less than 3d it would jeopardise the future of the New Brighton ferry. They wanted the combined tram/Seacombe ferry fare to be 4d, a penny more than the New Brighton boat. Parliament fixed only the maximum fares the Company could charge:—

1.	From Seacombe to Upper Brighton or vice-versa a sum not exceeding	3d
2.	From Seacombe to Liscard or vice-versa a sum not exceeding	2d
3.	From Liscard to Upper Brighton or vice-versa a sum not exceeding	1d
4.	Beyond the above distances, for every mile or part of a mile a sum not exceeding	1d
5.	From any distance less than 2 miles, any sum not exceeding	2d
6.	Between 9pm and 5am double the above rates	
7.	Children in arms under 3 years of age — free	

The Act authorised 5.48 miles of track of which 0.61 miles would be double; however, only 3.26 miles was actually built, giving a total route length of 2.70 miles. The powers for the alternative line to Liscard via Borough Road lapsed after two years and those for the Upper Brighton loop after four, although various attempts were made to revive the idea. However, by 1883 the Company declared their outright opposition, dismissing the area as undeveloped.

The route had been planned to link Seacombe ferry to the growing communities of Liscard and Upper Brighton but it also passed through several sections of open country with impressive Georgian villas, ancient cottages, fields, brickworks and quarries. The line started in Church Road, Seacombe (at its junction with Fell Street) then proceeded via Brighton Street (a major shopping thoroughfare), Falkland Road (outbound), Church Street (inbound), Liscard Road past Liscard Hall and Central Park into Liscard Village with its flour mills, slaughter house and Welsh speaking community, then

Queen Street/Manor Road (outbound), Rake Lane (an extremely narrow road skirting a quarry) and Upper Brighton, terminating at its junction with Field Road. Eight passing loops were built, of which two fell into disuse; the main loops were one in Brighton Street, three in Liscard Road, one in Rake Lane and one at the junction of Mount Pleasant Road and Upper Brighton.

Beloe's estimates were based upon his own method of track construction which he had employed at Southport and Birkenhead. However, the Board advised that they wished the Company to use the Benjamin Barker system used in Leeds and Manchester and against Beloe's advice, the Company acquiesced. On 29 October 1878 the Board gave permission for the Company's contractor, Mr. Hawkes to stack setts along the length of the proposed route. Hawkes intended to employ direct labour thus providing work for local men. On 13 November the Company approved the appointment of a Mr. E Cornish to act as the Board's supervising engineer at a fee of £5-5-0d per week to be paid by the Company. He was later accused of spending insufficient time on site but the Board declared themselves satisfied with his bi-monthly reports.

Excavation began on 16 December 1878. Barker was the first engineer to employ cast-iron longitudinal sleepers to afford a continuous bearing for the rails and adjoining paving. He used grooved rail, the lower surface being indented longitudinally and formed with a central flange or web by which it was fastened to the sleeper by a cotter-pin or hardwood edge. The Company adopted the lightweight version of Barker's system, the rails weighing 34lbs and sleepers 90lbs per yard; they were 10in wide and lay 5in below the level of the rail. The Board insisted that they should rest upon a one-inch layer of rough mortar to provide adequate packing. The excavations were to a depth of 8in and a width of 8ft except at passing loops, where the width was 17ft. The road surface was reinstated to the statutory 18in either side of the outer rail with 4in by 6in granite setts. The Company was responsible for the subsequent upkeep of the track and paving within the 18in limit. The rest of the road was often left unmade, encouraging other traffic to use the tram track and subjecting it to extra wear and tear. Work proceeded well, over a mile of paving and track being in position by 11 March 1879.

Two places presented the engineers with difficulties, particularly both ends of Falkland road where the Company was forced to acquire land to allow curves of sufficient radius. When completed they were said to be "easier than those in Birkenhead". Secondly there was the sharply-angled curve from Manor Road into Queen Street, which the Company sought permission to abandon on 22 April 1879. William Busby and John Carson personally attended the Board's Works and Health Committee explaining that due to acute clearance problems they wished to replace the outbound avoiding line by a passing loop in Liscard Village. Following an on site inspection, the Committee whilst refusing the deviation from the approved Parliamentary plan, agreed to delay construction until the remainder of the line was completed.

The passing loop in Liscard Road immediately north of Church Street was deemed unnecessary as the decision had been made not to proceed with the line via Borough Road. Permission to omit this loop was granted on 25 March 1879. In late April, a short extension to the Marine Hotel, Seacombe and a spur from Upper Brighton to the depot site in Field Road were approved by the Board.

Cars, Depot and Stables

The line was to be operated by seven Starbuck built single deck cars, seating 18 plus two seated on the platform. They had seven windows per side, and were very similar to those employed on the Wirral Tramway in Birkenhead. In view of the close connection between the two companies, the authors consider it likely that these cars were those built by Starbuck in 1877 for the Wirral company (see page 35) and subsequently replaced by larger cars. They were given the Wallasey numbers 1 to 7 and were painted in red and ivory lined out in black. Their relatively low price of £1,152 (£167 each) further supports the contention that they were transferred from the Wirral line.

The depot and stables (see below) were built in Field Road, New Brighton and although extended in 1884 and 1888, additional stabling for the bus fleet was acquired at 20 Egerton Street, off Rowson Street. Five staff houses built alongside the Field Road premises in 1891 were named Busby Cottages and were still there in 1987. The first cars were delivered in late May 1879 and 48 horses were acquired at the same time. A good tramming horse

cost approximately £25 with a working life of about five years on a relatively flat system like Wallasey. Feeding and grooming cost 7d per mile compared with 1d for track maintenance and ½d to maintain the cars. The capital outlay on the trams had been £1,540, the horses £1,250 and the track, depot and stables £17,000. A mile of Barker track had cost £3,784 — concrete bed and rails £2,031, granite setts £1,144 and paving £609.

The company engaged a complement of coachmen (drivers), conductors, horsemen (stablemen), coach-builders, farriers, yardmen and tip boys. The crews worked seven days a week for anything up to 15 hours for 25s a week (coachmen) or 9s 6d (tip boys). Horses worked up to a maximum of four hours. No uniforms were issued, the men wearing the warmest possible clothing. Although offering regular employment, turnover was high and drunkenness was a perennial problem. Another member of the Busby family, Henry Busby, was appointed as Manager.

Two Board of Trade inspections were necessary before the line was declared safe for public use. Both were conducted by Maj. Gen. C. S. Hutchinson. On 28 May 1879 he toured the system and inspected the depot and stables accompanied by Mr. Skinner, Chairman of the Board's Works and Health Committee, committee members Messrs. Alltree, Sillitoe and Walmsley, directors of the Company and the engineers, Beloe and Cornish. He listed a number of faults which needed rectifying. Two weeks later on 10 June, he again listed further deficiencies but agreed the line could open if notification was received in writing that all faults had been rectified.

Large crowds assembled to watch the official opening ceremony which took place at 11.45am on 28 June 1879 when two decorated and heavily laden cars left Church Road, Seacombe for Field Road and then to the Concert Hall, Liscard for a lunch at which hopes were expressed that the line would stimulate

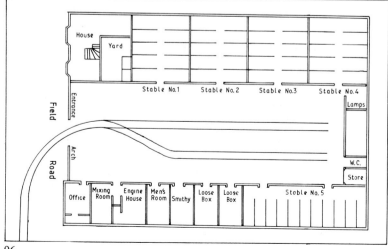

Tracing from an 1879 plan drawn by Robert A. Busby of the Field Road horse tram depot and stables at Upper Brighton. There was stabling for 51 horses. The tracks are shown as surviving in 1959, but the layout originally included a turntable. The buildings were still standing in 1987. The yard measures 124ft by 40ft. *(from an original drawing, courtesy Wirral Borough Libraries)*

high-class housing development. Free rides were offered until public service began at 2pm.

Regular service began on Monday morning 30 June with five cars operating every 15 minutes between 8am and 8pm; shortly afterwards the schedule was extended to 11pm but at reduced intervals. Although not advertised to connect with the boats, there was usually a car waiting at Church Road — sometimes two. The journey to Rowson Street took 25 mins. at an average speed of 6mph. There were no fixed stopping places, passengers flagging the cars anywhere en route. Parcels were transported free except if between 28lbs and 56lbs for which the charges ranged from 3d to 9d according to weight and distance. No unaccompanied goods or livestock could be carried and large accompanied items could be conveyed at a pre-determined price.

The carnival atmosphere surrounding the opening quickly evaporated as loadings failed to match expectations. The tram terminus was half a mile from the temporary ferry stage which was used during a major reconstruction of the ferry between 1876 and 1880.

On 11 September 1879 Maj. Gen. Hutchinson revisited Wallasey and passed for immediate use the short extension to the Marine Hotel, now situated at the top of Victoria Place, the new ferry approach road. Anxious to serve the terminal buildings, the company entered into a long and outspoken negotiation with the Local Board each accusing the other of deliberate provocation. As the company had no powers to operate into Victoria Place which was privately owned by the Board, it was finally agreed they should pay an annual rent of £1 providing they maintained the track and the surrounding surface. The agreement was signed on 23 October 1879 but it is not known when the short 150 yard extension was opened. It comprised a single line and a one car spur normally used for housing a spare tram for use as a waiting room.

The pull up from the ferry was one of only two taxing grades on the line; both required the use of a "chain", "trace", or "tip" horse. One was permanently stationed at Seacombe to assist all afternoon and evening departures as far as St. Paul's Church where it would be unhitched from the front or side of the regular team by the tip boy who would then lead or ride it back down to the ferry. The other grade, from Upper Brighton into Rake Lane, demanded an extra horse only at peak times.

In the course of his inspection on 11 September Maj. Gen. Hutchinson had again examined the track along Rake Lane and advised that the loop along its narrowest parts should be confined to emergency use only. The points at the Quarry loop were set so that all cars used the outbound track, the inbound line eventually being lifted in 1882.

The Eades Cars

Despite poor loadings during the day, larger capacity vehicles were required to handle the increasing number of commuters. On 15 May 1880 *The Birkenhead Advertiser* reported 'The Wallasey Tramways Company has just introduced onto their line several new patent cars fitted with outside seats on the roof. They are handsomely constructed, and will doubtless be appreciated.' These cars, five in number, were of the Eades Patent Reversible type; the first two cost £210 each, and were followed in 1883 by three more at £208 each.

William Busby was a director of the Ashbury Carriage and Iron Co. whose chief designer, John Eades, had patented a new type of lightweight double-deck tram in 1877. First used in Salford, it had been developed in an effort to reduce operating costs. Being single-ended, construction costs were lower but the biggest saving was in horse power, each vehicle requiring a daily stud of eight, as opposed to the more usual 12 horses per day. The cars incorporated a turntable underframe whereby the body

No photographs are known of Wallasey's original horse trams, but the Starbuck single-deckers were very similar to those on the Wirral Tramway and the Eades type resembled those used on William Busby's other tramways. This one ran in Bolton. The body of an Eades car could be turned on the underframe.
(*Tramway Museum Society*)

could be reversed on the truck frame, eliminating the need for pole-shifters at each terminus. Wallasey's Eades cars were 17ft 6in long overall with a 12ft × 6ft 6in saloon with six windows a side. The two axle truck had 30in diameter wheels with cast iron naves, wooden spokes and rims and flanged steel tyres. One wheel on each axle ran loose. A tare weight of only 34cwt was achieved. They seated 18 inside and 20 outside, probably on knifeboard top deck seating, and were allotted the numbers 8-12.

Initially, the Company was able to pay a reasonable dividend — 5% for the year ended 31 December 1880 (gross receipts £2,526, expenditure £1,862), 6% in the first half of 1884 and 4% in the second. However, these payments were only possible because the Company neglected to maintain the tramway in a proper state of repair. The demands of the shareholders forced the Busbys to cut corners, and relations between Company and Local Board were hardly amicable.

By 1882 much of the line was in poor condition as the lightweight Barker system had proved inadequate. The cotter pins had worn or fractured but replacement often resulted in cracking the iron sleepers: Furthermore, the road metal trapped between the rail and sleeper was crushed into abrasive powder causing erosion. The loose rails combined with defective joints were having a disastrous effect on the cars, which were described as deplorable. In places the rails protruded above the road surface; elsewhere they had sunk below. The Board and the company blamed each other. In October 1882 they jointly inspected the track in Liscard where it was discovered that the foundations were of sand and not good concrete as specified. Accepting liability, the company undertook immediate repairs.

Another grievance was overcrowding, and there were several reported instances of conductors being fined for allowing too many passengers on board. The fleet of 12 cars was probably never all in use together. In November 1884 licences were obtained for 12 trams at 5s 6d each but the application named only eight coachmen and conductors. As the depot could only house nine cars, the others must have been stored off the tracks. The Board of Trade returns, which indicated the number of cars in use (not those in stock) showed seven cars from 1879 to 1881, five in 1882-3 and eight in 1884-7. The stud of horses varied from 42 in 1880 to 66 in 1885.

Expanding Bus Routes

In 1883 the Works and Health Committee of the Wallasey Local Board issued individual licences to all the bus and tram operators. Various earlier applications had been made for services between Docks Station and Seacombe, and locally in New Brighton, but records are scant and some may not have started.

The Tramways Company failed to respond to an 1883 request from landowner Edgar Swinton Holland to provide a bus service along Seabank Road, which had been completed through from Trafalgar Road to Molyneux Drive by February 1880. Holland then approached fellow landowner Henry Gardiner and persuaded him to set up the Magazines Omnibus Company, with one bus from stables in Holland Road. The object was to provide a direct route to Seacombe and to stimulate house building.

On 26 April 1884, this Company was re-registered as the Magazines, New Brighton and District Omnibus and Carriage Company, with two buses and a capital of £5,000 in £1 shares. There now followed a period of intense competition. With the assent of their shareholders, the Tramways Company started running buses over the same route as Gardiner in November 1884. By May 1885 Gardiner's yellow buses and the Tramways Company's red buses were both offering a 15-minute service with four buses each.

Mr Holland, having deliberately acquired shares in the Tramway Company, challenged the legality of their action, forcing them to withdraw their buses on or shortly after 29 July 1885. Undeterred, the Busbys launched the Seacombe and New Brighton Omnibus Company in August, with a nominal capital of £5,000. This company's articles empowered it to operate buses along Seabank Road, as well as tramways, railways and omnibuses within the County of Chester or elsewhere in England. The shareholders of the new company were the same as those of the Tramways Company. The service started in early September 1885, worked by four-window knifeboard-seat double-deckers manned by separate crews under an independent manager.

The rivalry between the two main operators and with others who joined in the increasingly lucrative trade in summer continued unabated until a price cutting war which reduced the through fare to one penny forced Gardiner to sell his assets to the Seacombe and New Brighton Company in December 1887. Newspapers of the day were full of accounts of excessive speeding, dangerous races and cruelty to horses, several of which collapsed in harness. Local sympathy was strongly in favour of Gardiner's original yellow buses but there had been increasing public concern over the tactics employed by both companies. Gardiner's buses had never descended into New Brighton, always turning at Molyneux Drive, but the Seacombe and New Brighton buses, anxious to capture additional seasonal traffic, went down Rowson Street (gradient 1 in 15) to the junction of Victoria Road.

The Battle For New Brighton

The miles of golden sand stretching from Egremont to Harrison Drive were a magnet for hundreds of day trippers from Liverpool. In 1863 the Hoylake Railway had had ambitions of serving the

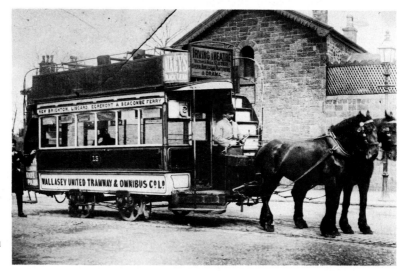

From 1893 until electrification in 1902, Wallasey's 2.70-mile horse tramway was worked mainly by seven garden-seat Milnes cars built in 1893. This view is of car 13 at Upper Brighton terminus at the top of Rowson Street, probably early in 1901. The rest of Rowson Street was too steep for horse tramways, so horse trams never reached New Brighton Pier.
(P. Priestley & Sons, Egremont)

resort and capturing some of the lucrative summer trade, then the monopoly of the Board's ferry boats. Powers to build a line to serve both New Brighton and Harrison Drive had been allowed to lapse but the Railway's successor, the Seacombe, Hoylake and Deeside renewed them in 1882, announcing their intention to start construction work in 1886. The Board and the Tramways Company feared the competition, especially as the trains would connect with the new under-river Mersey Railway which had opened on 1 February 1886 with a service from Liverpool Central to Green Lane, Birkenhead.

Abortive attempts had been made to reach the shore by tram, the Board having refused an application from a Mr. Millward in 1879 and from another applicant in May 1884 who had proposed a route from Wellington Road to the Springs, a local picnic spot. This last attempt was linked to the Tramway Company's expressed wish to extend their route, Wellington Road being close to the new railway station. In July 1885 they formally applied to extend to Molyneux Drive and in October to Wellington Road. In November, Robert Busby deposited plans for the extension including two mid-way loops at Molyneux Drive and Pickering Road at an estimated cost of £2,181.

The Board rejected the application due to the steepness of Rowson Street and the preponderance of omnibuses and William Busby, supported by Carson, Knox and Lee, personally failed on 24 November to persuade them to reverse their decision. However, two weeks later the Board did authorise the short length down to Molyneux Drive, providing the buses running into New Brighton were withdrawn. The company refused. Despite a number of subsequent proposals, the horse trams were never extended, being confined to their somewhat remote

terminus at Field Road. The railway eventually reached New Brighton on 30 March 1888, offering passengers a 25 min journey to the centre of Liverpool with one change at Birkenhead Park.

Company versus Board

By 1884, relations between the Wallasey Tramways Company and Wallasey Local Board had become extremely poor. For the 18 months to December 1884 the company refused to pay the £100 annual rental on the track in Victoria Place, Seacombe, dismissing the sum as 'unfair'. The Board's repeated demands for payment were ignored. In retaliation, the Board threatened to order the Company to remove their rails from Victoria Place, which would have denied the trams access to the ferry buildings. The two sides finally agreed on 5 January 1885 that the Company should pay £50 per year in two equal half-yearly instalments.

Trouble flared again in May 1886 when the Board threatened legal action unless the track in Brighton Street was repaired. This dragged on until July 1887, when following an inspection the Company agreed to rectify the faults. The old loop outside St Paul's Church was removed during 1885.

Seabank Road

Several attempts were made in the 1880s to obtain powers for a tramway along Seabank Road, the route which was eventually to carry Wallasey's heaviest electric tram service. The Busbys, through their various representatives, sought powers for a line from Molyneux Drive to Egremont and their solicitors, Wright and Beckett, deposited a parliamentary bill seeking powers to operate steam, compressed air, mechanical or electrical tramways in Wallasey. The initial intention to use compressed air trams was dropped in favour of steam.

On 8 December 1885 the Local Board gave permission for the use of a steam tram and trailers on the line, but allegations were made of corruption and that a Board member had been 'got at'. The Board thereupon reversed its decision, and a period of prevarication followed whilst the Board considered seeking powers to operate tramways in their own right.

When on 16 September 1886 the Board announced that they intended to seek powers to build a publicly owned line along Seabank Road, the Tramway Company directors reminded them that they had been refused a similar line in 1877 and that such a move would represent unfair competition. On 7 October 1886 Wright and Beckett renewed their own application for a horse line along Seabank Road, this time on behalf of the Seacombe and New Brighton Tramways Company, and continuing through to Seacombe by way of a new line on the river side of Brighton Street. The Board refused the application because of the threat it posed to Egremont Ferry, and took no further action.

The Wallasey Tramways Act, 1887

Aimed at regularising bus operation, this Act gave the Local Board the power to authorise and approve routes and fare scales. In practice it spelt the end of competition along Seabank Road, the Board vesting the future of the route solely in the Seacombe and New Brighton Company. With this new monopoly, the Busbys' abandoned their plans for steam trams. They also decided not to proceed with the extension to Wellington Road, even though the Board had dropped their opposition and powers for the line were embodied in the Act. High operating costs were quoted as the reason, 55% of all receipts (or 6½d per car mile) being spent on the horses. Drivers and other staff cost 9% or 1d per car mile; traffic expenses 17% (2d) and repairs and maintenance 19% (2½d). Total expenditure was 1s per mile run or 75% of gross receipts which amounted to about 1s 4d per mile run; this left a dangerously small profit margin, restricting dividends and limiting investment and capital expenditure.

The Act acknowledged that powers for the Church Road/Borough Road line and the Upper Brighton loop had lapsed. It also paved the way for the merger of the Busbys' Wallasey interests into the Wallasey United Tramway and Omnibus Co. Ltd. which was incorporated on 20 April 1888 with a nominal capital of £40,000 divided into £10 shares. The Secretary was William Knox and the registered office at 6 Lord Street, Liverpool. The eight shareholders were William Busby and Messrs. Carson, Russell Lee, Sheraton, Wright, Gill, Moresy and Knox. The final amalgamation did not take place until 8 May 1891,

two months after the Wallasey Tramways Company had become limited. The Seacombe and New Brighton Company was wound up on 2 February 1892 although the title was to be revived in 1901. From May 1891 buses and trams carried the United title and crest.

Gardiner's business including his horse buses was taken over some time in 1889. Older residents referred to his buses as "Gardiner's originals". The stables in Holland Road were sold for building land.

By 1888 the Tramways Company had hit an all time low. With the track in Rowson Street declared unsafe, the cars were cut back to Mount Pleasant Road, the length to Field Road being used only for depot journeys. Prompted by local residents who objected to the new terminal arrangements, the Board accused the Company of causing an obstruction by parking illegally. Receiving no satisfaction, they threatened legal proceedings in December warning the Company that as they had ceased operating to Field Road for over three months they could seize their assets without compensation. Proceedings were started on 8 January 1889 but, suitably chastened, the Company relaid the track from Mount Pleasant Road to the depot entrance but excluding the terminal spur in Rowson Street. They also relaid several passing loops.

Both ferries and trams had suffered from the opening of the railway to New Brighton. By 30 June 1890 the fleet had been reduced to five licensed cars and 46 horses. During the year they had carried 609,544 passengers, run 145,784 miles and earned £4,994. Expenditure totalled £4,101 giving a small profit of only £843 which forced the directors to cut maintenance to a minimum. Only £168 was spent on the permanent way as opposed to £1,282 on animal upkeep and fodder, £1,264 on wages, new horses £361, car repairs £261 and management £300.

Matters improved with the absorption of the Tramways Company into the United Company in May 1891. The Rowson Street spur was relaid in February 1892 although the Company blamed the poor weather for its failure to renew cracked paving.

In contrast, the buses were going from strength to strength, offering a 15 min service on Seabank Road between 8am and 10.30pm at a through fare of 2d. However, shortly after the formation of the United Company, the Board using their powers embodied in the 1887 Act banned all buses from descending Rowson Street, the route being permanently curtailed at Molyneux Drive. Sometime after 1891 the network was expanded with the introduction of a route from the corner of Mount Road/Mount Pleasant Road to Seacombe via Sandrock Road, Penkett Road, Stringhey Road, King Street, Brighton Street and the lower part of Borough Road. Believed to have operated only at peak times, this route may well have been started by Gardiner. During its life the route varied — Serpentine Road,

Liscard Road and Borough Road. It is possible that this was an entirely separate short-lived service. By 1892 the buses appeared in the tram livery of maroon and cream lined out in black with the Company title and destinations in white lettering.

The decade 1891-1901 marked a period of extraordinary population growth in Wallasey from 33,000 to 53,000. Other events included the replacement of the Local Board by an Urban District Council (1894), the opening of the Wirral Railway branch to Seacombe (1895) and the start of "The Dodger" a purely local rail service between Seacombe and New Brighton; the erection of the Tower (1897-1900)

railway station (1894), the lower part of Church Road was reconstructed and a double track installed reviving the former St. Paul's Church loop abandoned in 1885. At the same time it is thought the loop in Brighton Street opposite Nelson Street was lifted.

In 1896 the Council declared their interest in converting the Rake Lane tram route and the Seabank Road bus route to electric tram operation. They requested W. H. Travers, the District Engineer and Surveyor, to relay the existing route with rail suitable for heavier electric cars.

Anxious to retain control of the town's transport, the directors of the United Company including

Milnes-built double-decker 6 of 1893 standing at the Upper Brighton terminus of Wallasey's horse tramways, fitted with curtains and top deck seat-aprons. One of these cars was retained after electrification as a salt trailer.
(Courtesy G. H. Peers)

which at 621ft (higher than Blackpool) dominated the whole Mersey Estuary. The commissioning of the Council's electricity generating station (1897) and the decision to acquire and electrify the tramways operated by the United Company (1896) were to lead to a hard fought legal battle.

Determined to capture some of the potential new traffic, the Company revitalised the tramway by purchasing seven double-ended double deck two-horse cars from G. F. Milnes in 1893. With a 6ft wheelbase the cars had improved springing and stairs, and integral decency boards. With six windows per side, they offered accommodation for 16 upstairs on reversible garden type seats and 18 downstairs on longitudinal seats provided with seat carpets or cushions. Their original fleet numbers are unknown but by 1901 they carried the Nos. 6, 7, 10-14. Most of the older cars were withdrawn except for two Eades cars retained for standby duties and possibly one single-decker for Sunday working. To improve riding conditions, the Company undertook cosmetic improvements to the track and paving. They may have reduced the through fare to 2d.

During the building of Seacombe and Egremont

Russell Lee, the Chairman, William Busby and J. A. S. Hassal, the Secretary who had succeeded Knox, met the representatives of the U D C. After a year's deliberation they offered on 3 February 1897 to improve travel facilities by :—

1. Laying down a tramway from Egremont to Molyneux Drive where it would link up with the existing route.
2. Seeking powers to move the tramway carriages by electricity.
3. Suggesting that the U D C provide the Company with electricity from their generating station.
4. Inserting certain powers in a Provisional Order to be applied for by the Company.
5. Constructing a tramway along Borough Road and Liscard Road at a later date.

Later they added a line from Seacombe to Wallasey Village via Poulton Road and Breck Road. The company offered to rent any new lines at 6% per annum of a previously agreed sum. They recognised that road widening would have to be undertaken in King Street and in Seabank Road between Trafalgar

Road and Maddock Road. Receiving no positive reply from the U D C, they announced their intention of applying for powers to lay the Seabank Road tramway in 1898.

The Council declared their outright opposition, announcing their intention to acquire the United Company and electrify the tramway for the benefit of the ratepayers. The first meeting of the Council's newly formed Tramways Committee was held on 12 May 1898 under the chairmanship of Mr. W. G. Ellery. They approved Travers' track plans for three routes (Rake Lane, Seabank Road and a new line linking Seacombe with New Brighton via Warren Drive) and recommended the preparation of a detailed Parliamentary submission. Presented on 10 October 1898, it was opposed by the Wirral Railway, the Mersey Docks and Harbour Board and the New Brighton Pier Company.

The Wirral Railway realised tramway electrification was a considerable threat, and accused the U D C of deliberately damaging their interests. They objected to the use of heavy vehicles over their railway bridges, but mainly they feared a loss of revenue. In an arrangement with the Ferry Department they received 7d from every 9d return ticket issued to people travelling from Liverpool to Harrison Drive via Seacombe ferry as well as ⅓d for every railway passenger using the boats. In the summer "The Dodger" did good business transporting hundreds from the beaches to Seacombe, especially when extremely low tides prevented the boats from landing at New Brighton. The Pier Company argued that the trams would encourage exploration of other parts of the town, whilst the Dock Board was determined to squash any consideration of an inter-town link between Wallasey and Birkenhead. The objections were unsuccessful and the various proposals were embodied in the Wallasey Tramways and Improvements Act 1899 which gave the UDC powers to operate electric trams.

There now followed a complex legal wrangle as the U D C sought to implement the powers. They wished to serve notice to purchase the tramway side of the United Company under the provisions of the 1870 Tramways Act, which gave local authorities power to acquire a tramway undertaking after 21 years and thereafter every seven years. The Company maintained that the special purchase provisions of the Wallasey Tramways Act 1878 superseded the general provisions of the 1870 Act and, therefore, not having exercised its option within 15 years, the U D C had forfeited its right of compulsory purchase. Events proceeded as follows:—

1899
6 June — The U D C applied to the Board of Trade under section 43 of the Tramways Act 1870 for approval to serve notice in writing on the United Company requiring them to sell their undertaking.

7 July — Approval received.

20 July — Council resolved to issue Notice to Purchase as above and this was served on the Company on 17 August.

18 August — Company obtained injunction claiming Council was not entitled to purchase.

6 September — Company refused to accept arbitration and denied ever having discussed a purchase price with the Council.

25 October — Company obtained interim injunction restraining the Council from asking the Board of Trade to appoint a Referee to adjudicate on the acquisition of the tramways undertaking and on 8 November this was extended until date of trial.

16 November — Injunction discharged and Council's act deemed to be legal.

1900
4 Jan — Company appealed to the House of Lords.

13 December — Lords found in favour of the Council. Parties subsequently appeared before the Referee, Sir Frederick J. Bramwell at the Surveyors' Institute, Westminster and undertaking valued at £20,500.

1901
30 March — Company transferred undertaking to Council at midnight.

The Company's final timetable (that of 1901) required seven cars on Rake Lane, ten buses on Seabank Road including extras at peak hours, and one bus on Mount Road. The total stud was 142, 64 for trams and 78 for buses. Hours were still long, the tram crews averaging 90 hours per week with no holidays. Missed days were deducted from the weekly wage packet even down to ¼ days. On 23 January 1901 the total staff involved with the trams was 38 excluding the Manager Tom Hale who received £2 10s.0d. per week. Under him was a cashier (33s. per week), three checkers or inspectors (25s.), five coachmen (28s.), eight horse-keepers(22s. to 25s.) four of whom were also drivers working summer months and peak hours only, one washer (18s 6d), one blacksmith (32s), a blacksmith's lad (16s), a tip lad (12s 6d), 15 conductors many of whom worked part-time (10s to 14s), yardman (15s) and a line repair man (26s). The wage bill for one week was £33 3s. 0d. and on the buses £37 15s. 10d., the bus manager Henry O'Neill of Field Cottage, Field Road receiving £2 5s. 0d. Drunkenness, still an habitual problem, was only partially alleviated by the provision of a coffee stall at Seacombe. Run by

Wallasey United Tramways and Omnibus Company horse tram 6 in King Street, Egremont in 1900 in the annual May Day Parade. The picture also shows one of the company's horse buses on the Sea Bank Road route. Both services were replaced by Corporation electric trams in 1902. *(Priestley and Sons, Egremont)*

the Women's Temperance Society and opened in 1897, it dispensed mugs of coffee for 1d and cakes for ½d.

The tip lad referred to above was Robert McElney, who joined the United about 1898. His day began at 9am when he would start three hours of grooming the tip horse and cleaning its bridle. At 1pm, after an hour for lunch, he would ride down to the ferry and from 2pm until the last tram he was available to assist every departure up to St. Paul's Church. As the early morning cars were lightly loaded no assistance was needed. He also helped the pole-shifters whose job was to unhitch and re-harness the teams on the double-ended cars; these men were stationed at both ends of the route and were usually spare conductors. Operationally little had changed since inception; there were no official stops and those wishing to alight simply pulled a bell cord. On entering and leaving loops the conductor (or guard as they were usually called in Wallasey) blew a whistle. At night, oil lamps were used and a red tail light; in winter straw was laid on the floor. If two cars met on a single line one would be dragged off the rails, usually after a heated argument. The horses were fitted with collar-bells as a warning device at night. A good "trammer" cost in the region of £30. The Eades cars were only used as extras during the 10 minute service, McElney stating one car was No. 5. According to John Eades Jnr. Wallasey was the last system to use his father's cars, other tramways having dispensed with them due to their costly pivoting arrangements and the cumbersome problem of turning the bodies in confined spaces. By 1889 the through fare on all routes was 2d with a range of intermediate 1d stages. No workmen's cars were ever operated.

Operation By The Council

At midnight on 30 March 1901 the keys of the tram depot and stables were handed over by a representative of the Wallasey United Tramways and Omnibus Co Ltd to the Council's newly-appointed tramway manager, Major R. R. Greene. The Council took over nine cars and 60 horses, many in poor condition. On the advice of the council's veterinary surgeon, Stafford Jackson, £912 was spent in three weeks buying 16 former tram horses from Warrington and Liverpool. Short-term repairs were carried out to the trams, including a new axle for car 6 and re-wheeling three others. On 26 April the fleet was augmented by three second-hand double deck cars purchased from the Liverpool tramways at £5 6s. each. In July a further ten horses were purchased, mostly through auctioneers but including four from Liverpool and one from the Warrington Omnibus Co. Another six inspected in Liverpool were rejected.

Most of the company's 38 employees were re-engaged and their wages considerably increased, the average working hours per week reduced from 90 to

62. The company had given drivers and conductors one Sunday off in each fortnight, their places being taken by bus crews, but Greene employed additional staff allowing every employee one day off per week. Seven days' paid holiday were granted after twelve months' satisfactory service. The conductors and inspectors were given cap badges, but the purchase of uniforms was postponed until the opening of the electric tramway. The waybill-only method of revenue control was discontinued almost immediately, the first fare-stage tickets being issued in April and the first Bell Punches were hired in July. Additional revenue was raised by charging an extra penny on Bank Holidays. Temporary offices for Greene and his staff were provided above Price's baker's shop in Rowson St for £20 per year. In December a waiting room for the tramway crews was rented at 1 Sandridge Road.

From 18 July 1901 a ten-minute service was provided on the tram route between noon and 2pm on Saturdays only, and that month Greene was asked to cost the provision of a temporary horse-car service along the newly-laid electric track along Seabank Road. To provide a six car service he estimated it would cost £2,355 including £1,650 for 30 horses, £139 for additional harnesses, £16 for a further two second-hand trams and £550 for extra stabling facilities. Owing to the short-term nature of the operation, the proposal was dropped.

By September 1901 construction of the new electric tracks began to affect the operation of the horse tram service. The Falkland Road line was closed from 9 September and outward trams diverted along Church Street. From 28 October the horse cars were re-routed from Church Street to Seacombe along the newly-completed track in Liscard Road, with penny stages from Liscard Village to Lloyd's Corner and St John's Church to The Queens Arms. From 1 Decem-ber the horse cars were diverted to use the Seacombe ferry loop, their old stub tracks being removed, and the next day they were re-routed again, this time from Seacombe to Molyneux Drive via Demesne Street (inbound via Church Road), Brighton St, King St, and Seabank Road, with a through fare of 2d and intermediate penny stages. Through an oversight, the Board of Trade inspection from King Street to Molyneux Drive was not carried out (by Lt Col von Donop) until 5 January 1902. It is not known when the trams reverted to their original route.

For the period of this major diversion, a bus service was operated wherever possible along the course of the former tram service by the Seacombe and New Brighton Omnibus Co as successors to the United. At two Extraordinary General Meetings of the United Company on 30 March and 15 April 1901 it had been resolved to liquidate the company, to repay the preference shareholders and distribute the remainder of the £20,500 award to the ordinary shareholders, and to transfer the assets of the United Company to a new company. The final directors' meeting of the Wallasey United Tramway and Omnibus Co. Ltd. was held on 25 September 1901.

The new Seacombe and New Brighton Omnibus Company was incorporated on 25 May 1901, with a nominal capital of £5,000 in £1 shares of which 4,938 were to be allotted to holders of ordinary shares in the old company. Operating out of Egerton St, the horse buses continued to run from Seacombe to New Brighton via Seabank Road and from Seacombe to Mount Road via Penkett Road with a stud of 78 horses and a fleet of 14 buses and one wagonette. The tram-replacement service in the winter of 1901-2 approached Seacombe via Wheatland Lane.

After the completion of the council's electric tramway system, the Omnibus Company continued

Wallasey's horse tram depot and stables in Field Road were still standing in 1987. The chimneys belong to five cottages built for Company employees in 1891 and named Busby Cottages. Four members of the Busby family were connected with the Company.
(R. T. McMahon)

for a time to operate a truncated service from Mount Road to the Queen's Arms, Liscard, probably via Withens Lane and Manor Road. This ceased about 5 April 1902 and the Company's horses and buses were sold, although some were kept for a short time to run excursions with the wagonette from New Brighton into the Wirral countryside and as far as North Wales. The manager was John Worrall, who subsequently ran the taxis and landaus of the Birkenhead Carriage Co. Eventually the Egerton Street site was disposed of, the whole area being destroyed in the bombing of 1941. The Omnibus Company was finally dissolved on 5 May 1910.

Following the opening of the Rake Lane electric service on 17 March 1902, the horse trams appear to have been diverted to operate along Seabank Road for a final two days until shortly after mid-day on 19 March 1902, when the Seabank Road electric service was inaugurated. The last day of operation of the horse trams has been variously quoted as 17, 18 and 19 March, but in the handwritten minute book for the monthly meeting of the Tramways Committee in April 1902 Greene wrote "the traffic return for the Horse Cars for the four days ending the 19th March (the last day on which the horse cars operated) amounted to £50.11s.6.". The authors accept this date as correct.

During the 50 weeks and four days the horse cars were administered by the Council, they earned a total of £7,942 16s. 1d, over £1,000 more than the last annual return made by the Company. The cars carried on average 110,000 passengers each month, operated 13,500 miles and earned £700, receipts being 12½d per car mile and expenses 8½d per car mile. On 4 April the stock was sold by auction, the horses realising £23.13s. each and the cars £5 each, a total of £1,628; other items fetched an additional £1,380. One chestnut mare, Jessie, was retained and housed in a small stable at Seaview Road; she was used to pull the overhead tower wagon and for hauling heavy materials around the depot.

A Milnes horse car was also taken to Seaview Road, the electric depot. Painted in an overall muddy brown, it served as a mobile works car. Latterly without windows, it was used to carry grit to be shovelled on the road, and survived until scrapped in 1933. Several other bodies survived in the town, including one as a summer house in Wellington Road and another as a shed close to Wallasey Village station.

The formal start of electric tramway construction by Wallasey Council at the top of Tobin Street (near Egremont Ferry) on 24 June 1901. The tracks were first used by a temporary horse car service in the winter of 1901-2. *(Courtesy J. McWatt)*

8 Wallasey Electric Tramways, 1902-1918

As recounted in the previous chapter, Wallasey Urban District Council had decided in 1896 to introduce municipally-operated electric tramways, and had instructed their District Engineer and Surveyor, W. H. Travers, to draw up plans. He recommended a system that would provide three different routes linking Seacombe Ferry to New Brighton (via Seabank Road, via Rake Lane, and via Seaview Road and Warren Drive). These were approved by the Council's newly-formed Tramways Committee at its first meeting on 12 May 1898, and application was subsequently made to Parliament. They were authorised in the Wallasey Tramways and Improvements Act 1899, but owing to stiff resistance from the United company the Council did not take over the horse tramways until midnight on 30 March 1901.

The 1899 Act authorised 8.5 miles of standard gauge tramways, corresponding exactly with the initial system opened in 1902 and shown in map form on page 110. The double track sections (mainly passing loops) totalled just under two miles, the rest being single track (mainly used in both directions) but with one-way working in separate streets approaching the two termini. Most of the passing places were of two-car length (88 yards). The depot was to be built on land off Seaview Road adjacent to the Council's electricity generating station, with separate two-storey administrative offices fronting on to Seaview Road. The estimated cost was £72,871 including track at £2,189 per mile, paving at £2,229 per mile, £9,000 for cars and £5,129 for the depot.

The Tramways Committee, having appointed sub-committees to deal with specific issues, decided to adopt standard gauge (4ft 8½in) and overhead current collection. Visits were made to inspect tramways at Glasgow, Leeds, Liverpool, Halifax and Hull and to the Preston works of the Electric Railway and Tramway Carriage Works Ltd. (ER&TCW). The initial requirement was 20 trams and the Committee considered the following tenders:

Electric Railway & Tramway Carriage Works Ltd, £11,800 without air brakes or £12,700 with air brakes;
British Westinghouse Electric & Manufacturing Co, £11,940 plus £1,000 for air brakes;
Brush Electrical Engineering Company, £13,200 without air brakes;
Robert W. Blackwell & Co Ltd, £13,923 with air brakes.

The Committee accepted the first tender, without air brakes, as the Board of Trade had meanwhile ruled

that despite grades of 1 in 15 and 1 in 16 the cars would need neither air nor slipper brakes.

During the legal battle with the Company, work had begun on the future Seabank Road line. The first rail of the new system was laid in King Street on 24 June 1901 by W. G. Ellery, now Chairman of the Council. The track bed was excavated, and buildings demolished at the corner of Seabank Road and Trafalgar Road to accommodate an S-shaped length of double track. The Council used direct labour, and the men completed a mile of single track per month.

On 20 February 1901, Major (later Lt-Col) Robert Roughley Greene, aged 48, was appointed Tramways Manager, at a salary of £250 per year. He had been accountant with the Dock Board, and was general secretary of the Liverpool Dispensaries. He came from a local family and, having been chairman of the UDC in 1897, was fully conversant with municipal procedure. He also commanded the New Brighton company of the 1st Cheshire and Carnarvonshire Artillery Volunteers, a predecessor of the Territorial Army.

As owners of the tracks used by the horse trams, the Council had already relaid much of the horse car route between 1897 and 1898 with heavier rail suitable for electric cars, but all passing loops, junctions, and sections not scheduled for electrification had been left untouched, with the result that repairs had to be carried out in May 1901. Mean-

Richard Roughley Greene, manager of the Wallasey Tramways 1901-1923.

Wallasey Council Tramways roadside overhead standard and bracket arm, with WCT monogram on pole base. (*H. G. Dibdin*)

WALLASEY.

DRAWN BY
H.G. DIBDIN

Except for the track laid by R. W. Blackwell & Co Ltd in the car sheds and along the depot approach road, all other track-laying was under the supervision of Council engineer W. H. Travers and his two assistants, Howdle and Jackson. Laid on a concrete bed 6in thick, the rails were 7in deep with a 1⅛in groove, weighed 98 lb/yd and were supplied in 60ft lengths by Barrow Haematite Steel Co Ltd, costing £7 7s. 6d. per ton, with 37lb soleplates and 24-inch six-hole fishplates. Askham Bros. and Wilson Ltd. supplied the points and crossings, tie-bars, fishbolts, drain boxes and Dawson's patent drain rail, the points being 8ft 6in long and the crossings being of crucible cast steel. Special work was pre-assembled to specification on a concrete platform in the Council's yard at Mill Lane. Anchors were placed under rails on the steeper gradients, the most severe being the 1 in 15 out of New Brighton terminus and for a 20 yard stretch of Rowson Street. Transition curves were employed; the sharpest had a radius of 40ft in the centre of the curve. Brown's rail bonds were used, and flexible "Crown" cross bonds were installed at all points and crossings and at 100ft intervals on plain track. The paving used was 4in to 6in granite setts, except for Allcott's 5in hardwood blocks on the most select stretch of Seabank Road.

The feeder cables (11 miles) supplied by the British Insulated Wire Co. Ltd. were laid and jointed by the Council's staff, in single earthenware troughs filled with bitumen. The overhead equipment was supplied and installed by R. W. Blackwell & Co Ltd., using 400 poles bought from the British Mannesmann company. The standard poles tapered in three sections from 7in to 5¼in outside diameter, but heavy poles of 8in to 6in diameter were used for pull-offs at curves; the bases were of cast iron with a neat scroll and the Tramways monogram (WCT) artistically entwined. Span wire construction was used at curves, crossings and main road junctions, side poles with bracket arms elsewhere; the bracket arms varied in length from 10ft 6in to 18ft 6in and included ornamental scrollwork and rosettes to take arc lamps if required. The trolley wire of 3/0 gauge hard drawn copper was hung 21ft above road level. The overhead included guard wires of ⁷⁄₁₆in galvanised steel, bonded to the poles and rails at every fifth pole. Telephone wires linking the depot with Seacombe and New Brighton were carried on insulators fixed to the bracket arms. Cast iron rectangular section boxes bearing the Council monogram contained switches and fuses for the feeders and the overhead lines.

The first of the 20 new electric cars were delivered complete at Wallasey Station in mid-January 1902, and were dragged along Grove Road and Hose Side Road by teams of horses, the wheels gouging grooves in the surface. All subsequent deliveries were to Liscard & Poulton station. At the end of February it

while, new tracks were laid to form the anti-clockwise "horse-shoe" or "Balloon" loop outside New Brighton ferry, as well as the connecting length between Molyneux Drive and the horse tram terminus at Field Road which was completed by late September 1901. Work began on 16 August on the line between St. Paul's Church, Seacombe and the Falkland Road/Liscard Road corner, which took two months and involved a new street, Mainwaring Road, directly linking Lloyd's Corner and Liscard Road.

The Falkland Road horse car line was closed from 9 September 1901 and trams used Church Street in both directions; this allowed new track to be laid in the very narrow part of Liscard Road between Falkland Road and Church Street. The successive diversions of the horse cars between this point and Seacombe Ferry in the last weeks of 1901 were described in the previous chapter, and included a horse car service along the electric tracks from Seacombe to Molyneux Drive via Seabank Road which commenced on 1 December 1901, permitting work to begin on the renewal of loops and pointwork along part of the original horse tramway between Church Street and Field Road, with major road widening in Liscard Village and Rake Lane. When this work was complete, the horse trams reverted to their original route and the construction teams joined those already at work on the Seaview Road portion of the Warren Drive route.

No. 12 in Liscard Road during the first week of operation which commenced on 17 March 1902 after a successful Board of Trade inspection on 14 March. The car has no destination displays, but a notice on the bulkhead announces the start of workmen's service on 24 March. *(Wirral Borough Libraries)*

was announced that the Seabank Road and Rake Lane routes would open in mid-March, with Warren Drive to follow later. On Saturday 8 March a tour of inspection was held for Council officials and representatives of the construction firms. Driver training was now in progress, some men having previous experience at Birkenhead or Liverpool, others being Irish labourers formerly employed in the tracklaying gangs.

The Board of Trade inspection took place on Friday 14 March 1902, the inspectors being Major Druitt RE for cars and track and Mr. A. P. Trotter for the electrical installations. The party assembled at the depot at 9.45am, and the inspectors accompanied by Greene, Travers, Council officials and representatives of the contractors boarded car No 10 and departed first for Seacombe via Wheatland Lane. The car then proceeded to New Brighton via Rake Lane and back to Seacombe via Seabank Road. The inspection was completed by taking the car along Liscard Road to the top of Church Street, reversing and returning to Seacombe via Brighton Street. Having witnessed an emergency stop and examined all track and overhead junctions, especially those at either end of Rowson Street hill, the inspectors declared themselves satisfied, except

for the "horseshoe" at New Brighton where the curve on the south side was too sharp. Temporary terminal arrangements were still in force there in late April.

The System Opens

With the inspection successfully concluded, Wallasey Council officials announced that public service would begin on the Rake Lane route at 8am on Monday 17 March. The intervening weekend was spent completing driver training and running cars at frequent intervals along both routes. There was an increasing sense of excitement in the town as people prepared to welcome the new electric cars.

Leaving Seaview Road depot at 7.30am on Monday morning to take up duty as the 8am from New Brighton, the first car lost its trolley head whilst reversing at Liscard. A second car was hastily despatched and left New Brighton at 8.10am. Between 8.30am and and 9am another car derailed, finishing on the footpath near Osborne Avenue, whilst in a third mishap a car jumped the points at the foot of Rowson Street, narrowly missing the frontage of the North and South Wales Bank on the opposite corner. There were no injuries, and a ten minute service was provided until 11.45pm.

The opening ceremony, attended by dignitaries from all over Merseyside, was held two days later on 19 March when the Seabank Road route was inaugurated. At noon the Chairman of the Tramways Committee, Dr. T. W. A. Napier and other council members, officials and guests assembled at Seacombe Ferry and after declaring the system open from the top deck of a decorated car, travelled past lines of schoolchildren to New Brighton via Seabank Road, returning along Rake Lane to Liscard Village and the depot. Dr. Napier drove the car, and apparently the circuit breaker blew whilst ascending Rowson Street. The car started to run back, and he quickly brought it to a standstill by applying the emergency short-circuit brake.

After inspecting the depot and power plant the party then made their way to the Council offices in Church Street for lunch. After the loyal toast, Mr. Ellery, Chairman of the Council, proposed "The Wallasey Tramways." In his speech he said that the system must not be considered complete until a line had been built to serve Wallasey village. Replying, Dr. Napier confessed that elation was tinged with anxiety until the tramway had proved itself. He professed total confidence in the quality of workmanship and defended the Council's policy of supporting English firms even if they were a little more expensive than their foreign competitors. As for Wallasey Village, he assured Mr. Ellery that this would be attended to as soon as possible. Public service started immediately between Seacombe and New Brighton via Seabank Road, and the press were

King Street, Egremont

Car No. 20 at the King Street/Church Street junction in Egremont in 1902. Both of the single lines were originally used in both directions.
(*Moorhouse, Photographer, Egremont*)

fulsome in their praise — "a few mishaps, but they must inevitably be anticipated when first enslaving and domesticating such a fickle power as electricity."

In their first week of operation the trams carried 60,000 people, and in the first full month nearly 400,000, almost equally divided between the two routes. The single track and loops soon proved to be inadequate. As in Birkenhead, demand had been underestimated, and Wallasey had the additional problem of seasonal holiday traffic. As early as Easter 1902 the 17 available trams had failed to shift the crowds, and the third route — Warren Drive — was not yet in operation. It was inspected and opened on 17 May 1902, completing the initial programme, and was the third line to connect Seacombe with New Brighton.

The Manager recommended the purchase of five bogie single deck combination cars, for which Dick Kerr had quoted £585; however, the Tramways Committee overruled him and an order was placed for five more double deckers identical to Nos. 1-20, plus a multi-purpose works car. These became 21-25 and the works car 26.

Large crowds were carried during the 1902 holiday season — 125,000 in Whit week and 140,000 in early August, but these were exceeded by the 160,000 carried during the Coronation week of Edward VII. From September there was a seasonal downturn, with only 85,000 travelling during the week beginning 13 December. The electrification had stimulated social and economic change; building development increased, leading to a boom in land and property prices, the most sought after residences being those within easy reach of a tram stop. More people chose to live in Wallasey and work in Liverpool. Equally, many now found it cheaper to shop in Liverpool, which led to the slow decline of some of the older commercial thoroughfares such as Borough Road, Brighton Street and King Street.

Most of the traffic was towards the three ferries, with Seacombe capturing the lion's share. Patronage on the Egremont and New Brighton boats declined, to the chagrin of the Ferries Committee, who saw the trams as a potential threat to the future of the two northern stations. Both ferries were reached by long, exposed piers on which passengers could be soaked or buffeted by ferocious winds and although Egremont had its quota of regular commuters, it was not surprising that all but the hardiest opted for a tram journey to Seacombe with its short all-weather crossing.

In November 1902 it was agreed that the trams should carry flags tied to their trolley ropes to warn passengers when the northern boats had been suspended due to "stress of weather". One wit claimed that the Tramways Committee had only agreed so that they could demonstrate the superior service offered by their trams. A square blue flag meant "No boat from New Brighton" and a red swallow-tail "No boat from Egremont." Red metal discs were hoisted on various traction poles for the same purpose, at the top of Tobin Street, the top of Church Street, Grove Road/Warren Drive corner and at several points along Victoria Road. The Tramways Committee refused to allow ferry contract holders to travel free when the boats were suspended.

Relations between the Ferries and Tramways Committees in Wallasey were in sharp contrast to Birkenhead, where direct competition from the Mersey Railway had forced them to co-operate for their mutual protection. In Wallasey no combined bus/ferry fares were introduced until 1928. However, both committees accepted that the public expected regular and reliable service, and from 12 July 1902 timetables were adjusted to guarantee connections at Seacombe between the ten-minute boats and the ten-minute trams. This was to remain a guiding principle

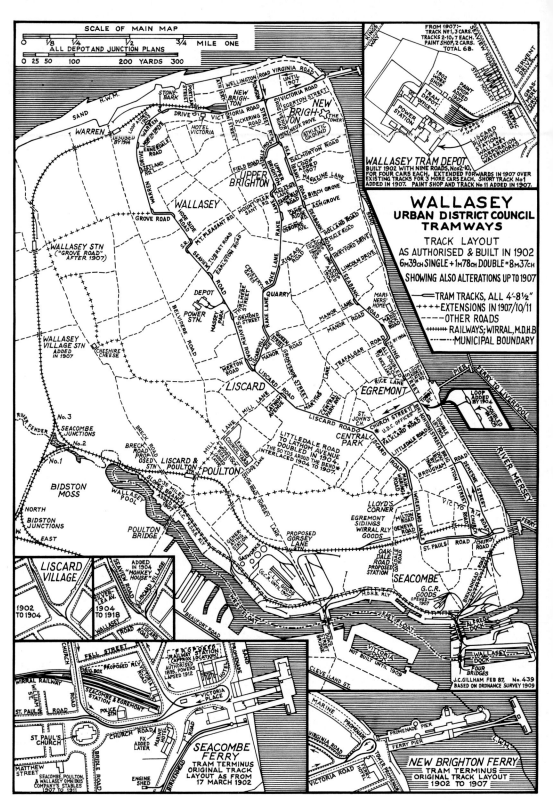

SCALE OF MAIN MAP

0 · 1/8 · 1/4 · 1/2 · 3/4 · MILE ONE

ALL DEPOT AND JUNCTION PLANS

0 · 25 · 50 · 100 · 200 YARDS · 300

WALLASEY TRAM DEPOT
BUILT 1902 WITH NINE ROADS, Nos 2-10,
FOR FOUR CARS EACH. EXTENDED FORWARDS IN 1907 OVER
EXISTING TRACKS FOR 3 MORE CARS EACH. SHORT TRACK No 1
ADDED IN 1907. PAINT SHOP AND TRACK No 11 ADDED IN 1907.

FROM 1907:-
TRACK No 1,3 CARS.
TRACKS 2-10, 7 EACH.
PAINT SHOP, 2 CARS.
TOTAL 68.

WALLASEY
URBAN DISTRICT COUNCIL
TRAMWAYS

TRACK LAYOUT
AS AUTHORISED & BUILT IN 1902
6M39CH SINGLE + 1M78CH DOUBLE = 8M37CH
SHOWING ALSO ALTERATIONS UP TO 1907

—— TRAM TRACKS, ALL 4'-8½"
+++ EXTENSIONS IN 1907/10/11
--- OTHER ROADS
++++ RAILWAYS; WIRRAL, M.D.H.B
---- MUNICIPAL BOUNDARY

LISCARD VILLAGE
1902 TO 1904
ADDED IN 1904 "MONKEY HOUSE"
SILVER LEA N. 1904 TO 1918

SEACOMBE FERRY
TRAM TERMINUS
ORIGINAL TRACK
LAYOUT AS FROM
17 MARCH 1902

NEW BRIGHTON FERRY
TRAM TERMINUS
ORIGINAL TRACK LAYOUT
1902 TO 1907

J.C.GILLHAM FEB 87. No 439
BASED ON ORDNANCE SURVEY 1909

Wallasey's Seabank Road route opened on 19 March 1902, two days after Rake Lane. Most of the route was single track, with local road-widening to provide space for passing loops like this one at Cambridge Road. Several sections were later doubled. *(Moorhouse, Photographer, Egremont)*

throughout the life of the tramways; everything was geared to meeting the boats on time. Late running was penalised and delays thoroughly investigated.

Stretches of single line, especially when shared by two services, worked against this and Greene lost no opportunity to argue the case for double track wherever possible. He presented several reports on the subject, advocating the use of parallel or neighbouring streets for one-way working as already adopted at both Seacombe and New Brighton. Plans for doubling virtually the entire network were prepared for inclusion in a new Tramways and Improvement Act to be presented to Parliament in 1904, but the Bill provoked such opposition from residents and householders that it proved impossible to acquire frontages for road widening, and was abandoned. Despite this, major track doubling was carried out during 1903-04 without specific Parliamentary sanction, increasing the total of double track to 3.38 miles by March 1905, and is best described by taking each route in turn.

Seabank Road Route (2.63 miles)

As the shortest route linking New Brighton and Seacombe, this always carried the heaviest traffic, serving all three ferry stations and the area of greatest residential density and commercial develop-

ment. Originally the journey time had been 20 minutes, but in the summer months it was extended to 23 minutes. The ten minute headway was found to be inadequate, especially in peak hours, and a five minute evening service was introduced on 12 July 1902 between Molyneux Drive and Seacombe, and was later extended to the morning peak, with a 7½ minute frequency between 10am and 1.30pm. Additional passing loops were put in at Rice Lane and Hale Road in the summer of 1902, and by 1904 the lines were doubled from Brougham Road to Falkland Road and from Rice Lane to Maddock Road. Some of the bracket poles were replaced by span wiring. A loop was laid at the top of Tobin Street, with an outbound-only connection into Church Street, and a crossover was installed at Trafalgar Road for part-way working. Other loops were added at Lincoln Drive (1904) and Magazine Lane (1907). At the same time, the main feeder from Manor Road to Holland Road was renewed. Greene also wanted to double the track in the narrowest part of King Street, but it proved impossible to acquire sufficient frontages.

Rake Lane route (3.25 miles)

This line picked up a certain amount of holiday overflow traffic from New Brighton but its main source of revenue was from the increasingly important shopping centre at Liscard together with passengers from Central Park and the Cemetery. Operationally the most difficult section was the length of

The tram terminus at New Brighton in 1902 *(above)* and 1905, showing trams negotiating the sharply curved anti-clockwise loop at the entrance to the twin ferry and promenade piers, in the roadway known as the Horse Shoe. In 1907 the loop was replaced by a 'grid iron' of four sidings.
(Priestley and Sons, Egremont and Rev. A. E. Parry)

Left: No. 10 in Hose Side Road on the Warren Drive service about 1906, flying a square blue flag tied to the trolley rope indicating that the New Brighton ferry had been suspended due to bad winter weather. Note the twin fleet numbers at the top corners of the dash. *(Courtesy M. Jenkins)*

Right: The short-lived section of interlaced track in Liscard Road, which existed only from 1903 to 1907. The only other interlaced track was at two railway bridges on the Poulton route. *(Commercial Postcard)*

Liscard Road from St John's Church to Liscard Village which it shared with the Warren Drive cars, as there were blind corners at either end and only one passing loop, at Martin's Lane. As early as September 1902, Greene advocated building a relief line for outbound Rake Lane cars along Manor Road and Grosvenor Street, but it was not adopted. During the winter of 1903-4 the double track on Liscard Road was extended to run from Littledale Road to Lathom Avenue which gave outbound drivers approaching Liscard a clear view of the narrow part of Liscard Road. A short length of interlaced track, the first in Wallasey, was laid between Church Street and Falkland Road being replaced by double lines when the gardens of houses were acquired in 1907. A single point allowed outbound Warren Drive cars to turn out from Church Street. Wooden blocks were laid outside the Central Hospital to reduce noise, and side brackets were replaced by span wires. Throughout its life, the Rake Lane route ran every ten minutes, and required six cars, supplemented at rush hours by three extras. The journey time was 26 minutes.

Warren Drive route (3.75 miles)

When first introduced, the Warren Drive cars operated only every fifteen minutes, with four cars and a journey time of 28 minutes. Loadings initially were light, producing 6.27d per car mile compared

with 8.71d on Rake Lane and 10d on Seabank Road, reflecting the fact that the Warren Drive cars operated through an area of low-density high-class residential property. However, Greene accurately predicted an increase in the summer when the line would offer unspoilt views of the whole Mersey Estuary and the Welsh hills. North of Liscard there were two loops on the way to the depot, and six more before the route rejoined the others at New Brighton. The three loops along Warren Drive itself at Ennerdale Road, Stonebark and near Atherton Street were all "blind", and a fourth loop was added at North Drive (Warren Point) in 1903. The service frequency was improved to ten minutes in May 1905.

Warren Drive cars left Seacombe via Demesne Street, sharing the track with the Seabank Road cars as far as Egremont and then traversing Church Street to reach Liscard Road. The two way single track along Church Street with its blind corners at either end proved a serious miscalculation. It was especially hazardous in fog, delays building up at the busy Tobin Street junction. Congestion also occurred every time a boat landed at Egremont, with people walking up the hill to wait for a tram. By December 1902, inbound Warren Drive cars were diverted to operate via Lloyd's Corner, leading to complaints from shopkeepers along Brighton Street. In 1904, as part of a plan to restore trams to Falkland Road (used by horse cars until September 1901) and to encourage greater use of Egremont ferry, it was proposed to lay two sidings in Tobin Street, with connecting tracks into Church Street, King Street and Falkland Road. The scheme was rejected, but demands continued to be made for a bus or tram route to serve Egremont ferry approach.

In May 1905 the last few yards of single track in Brighton Street (from Church Lane to Falkland Road) were doubled, and in July the Council approved the construction of a single track line along Falkland Road, at a cost of £2,050. They rejected an alternative scheme to widen Church Street. The 0.25 mile line was authorised in the Wallasey Tramways and Improvement Act 1906 and work began on 3 January 1907. The line was inspected and opened for use by Seacombe bound Warren Drive cars on 2 May 1907. The fourth tram route, to Poulton and Wallasey Village, did not materialise until 1910-11, and is described later.

Incidents and Accidents

The first 'fatality' occurred on 18 June 1902, when a sheep escaping from a butcher's shop in Liscard Road had been knocked down and killed, 10s. being paid in compensation. No human fatalities are reported until 17 October 1903, when a five year old boy named Cox had run from behind a stationary coal wagon on which he had been swinging, into the path of a tram travelling along Brighton Street. He had been caught under the lifeguard which had failed to operate correctly. The driver stopped with the emergency brake and "backed off the little fellow" who died from fractures of the skull in a nearby chemist shop. The accident prompted a spate of anti-tram feeling; drivers were accused of operating at dangerous speeds and people asked why the lifeguard had failed to function. The boy's grave still bears the inscription 'killed by electric tram.'

In 1902-3 free swinging trolley ropes with their tendency to coil out and strike people sitting on the open decks of cars travelling in the opposite direction gave cause for concern. The problem was partially associated with passing loops and several cases of laceration had been reported. Greene confided that 'a person might be strangled in this way' and the wires were restrung to follow the centre of the track, thus confining the lateral movement of the trolley pole within narrow limits and preventing the rope from swinging out at a sharp angle to the car. Pigtails (known locally as trolley governors) were fitted and conductors ordered to occupy the rear platform in order to guide the rope whilst negotiating a loop.

Thorough inspection of the overhead was ordered following two incidents in 1904 involving broken wires. On 26 July Councillor Barber was struck by a falling span wire, and one week later Mrs. Gattenby of Salford was hit whilst sitting on an open top car in Seaview Road. She was awarded compensation of £35 plus doctor's fees of two guineas. To reach

accidents more swiftly, the maintenance staff were given a bicycle. Gradually it was decided to replace existing overhead equipment with more modern anchor ears and outrigger spans from the poles to the wire either side of each section breaker.

Fog was an occupational hazard, frequently blanketing the whole of Merseyside for up to 72 hours. The northern ferries were usually suspended, putting extra pressure on the trams. In a real 'pea souper', the conductor often walked in front of the car carrying a storm lantern. At these times cars going towards Seacombe sounded two gongs whilst those travelling to New Brighton three in rapid succession. To assist single line working along Warren Drive, the Harrison system of coloured light signals was installed in October 1902; they proved invaluable in fog, but were never extended to the remainder of the system. Elsewhere, drivers relied upon a code of hand signals when cars were in adjacent loops:

'Waiting' — in daylight drivers would stand near the step and extend the right arm horizontally, at night they would cover the dashlight three times in rapid succession.

Reply 'Coming' — in daylight extend the right arm vertically above head, at night cover Pilot light for three seconds and proceed.

On 19 October 1906 Nos 18 and 19 collided head-on in Seabank Road, the Council agreeing to pay full compensation to the injured. Two weeks later a horse-drawn van owned by the Little Sisters of the Poor and driven by 'a deaf and aged man' banged into No 4 in Rowson Street, injuring his thumb and slightly shaking the nuns. Although the tram driver was blameless, the Council awarded the Sisters £5.

The first reported runaway occurred on 19 December 1903, when car 14 embedded itself in a pole outside the North and South Wales Bank on the corner of Rowson Street, New Brighton. As early as September Greene, alarmed at the prospect of a runaway down Rowson Street, had advocated the reversal of the one-way system so that a runaway car would continue across the junction on to the level section of Rowson Street north of Victoria Road, where it could more easily be brought under control, but no action had been taken.

A second more serious accident happened at the same spot on 13 May 1905 when a Seabank Road car ran out of control. The driver of car 4 had reported to an inspector that the brake handle had begun to slip and he could not get the proper leverage on the brake. Inspector Scott drove the car from Holland Road and found that there was a tendency for the ratchet to slip, but with careful handling the car could be kept under control. He told the driver to exercise great care down the hill and to change ends at New Brighton so as to use the other brake staff. Half way down the brake staff became locked in the ratchet; the electric brake was applied and the motors reversed but without effect, as the wheels

On 19 March 1907 car 36 jumped the rails in Seabank Road and damaged a garden wall; the Council paid £15 for the damage. The car was on a part-way duty to 'Molyneux Drive Only'. *(A. D. Packer)*

This time the manager's warning was heeded, and plans were prepared to reverse the one-way system; it was adopted from 29 March 1907. Guard posts were meanwhile placed around the Bank.

No further accidents as spectacular as this appear to have occurred in later years, but the minor accidents mentioned in the records are many and varied. Taking 1910 as an example, 30s. compensation was paid to Mr. Baryard for being jerked forward by a car at Quarry loop, £3 was paid to the owner of a furniture van demolished by No 50, 4s. was paid to Mrs. Hunt whose dust-coat had been smeared with grease from No 50's brake rigging and £5 was paid to an unfortunate woman who was dragged along by No 30 after the conductor had accidentally given a starting signal. In September a Mr. Ellis received 7s. 6d. for repairing his trousers, on 24 November two men were injured when Nos 39 and 47 collided in Wheatland Lane, and on New Years Eve an elderly lady fell off No 18 into Liscard Road. The Council also recovered sums from other parties, such as 10s. from Mr. Bryan for ripping seat coverings, 5s. from a Mr. Townsend whose float struck No 14, 1s. 6d. from Mr. Bradfield for breaking No 51's lifeguard, and £1 from Mr. Robertson who celebrated Christmas Eve by smashing a bottle of spirits on the side of No 4.

The records for 1912 reveal some more serious mishaps. On Easter Monday during a 'boisterous sandstorm' a young man was catapulted against the side of car 32 in Virginia Road, receiving serious injuries. Heavy compensation was paid to a Mrs. Kingham who sustained multiple fractures when cars 14 and 26 collided in Rake Lane on the same day. Children were particularly vulnerable, there being many instances of youngsters being knocked down. It should not be thought that Wallasey trams were more accident-prone than most, but they may have been more meticulous in keeping financial records.

were locked. The inspector used the rear brake handle, which tightened the brake, but the car jumped the track and collided with the Bank premises, the driver jumping off just in time. All seven passengers on the car complained of being shaken, but only one, Mrs. Rowbotham, was injured. George Fenny, the driver and J. Rawcliffe, the conductor were off work for 14 and 12 days respectively. Reporting the accident, Greene wrote:

"The primary cause of the accident was a defective brake handle, spring and ratchet, the teeth of the ratchet not properly engaging causing the brake staff to become locked and making it impossible to either tighten or release it. But for the fact that the brake became locked, there is a strong chance the car at the speed at which it was proceeding might not have left the track. The secondary cause was the non-use by the driver of the rear brake in lieu of the front brake as if he had known as he undoubtedly did, that the front brake might probably become inoperative he should have driven the car from the rear in descending the hill in order to obtain more effective braking power. The inspector too appears to have committed an error of judgement in not so directing the Driver, or ordering him to return the car to the Depot or to Seacombe in which latter case the defective brake would have been in front. The subsequent action of the Inspector in applying the rear brake as already detailed although it did not avert the accident was, however, commendable and probably reduced the force of the impact with the Bank premises."

Services, Fares and Profits

Greene's first Annual Report was presented in March 1903, and established several financial precedents. With an operating surplus of £12,000, the Council wisely agreed to the creation of a Sinking Fund and a Depreciation and Renewal Fund, into which a percentage of the profit was deposited annually. In the following year a sum was also transferred for relief of the rates. The life-blood of the system was the 1d fare, which encouraged ridership on a large scale. 70% of all tickets sold were 1d, 29.02% 2d and 0.08% 2d workmen's returns, with total receipts of £31,475. Expenditure amounted to £19,194 made up of wages £13,951, energy £6,630, maintenance £1,550, works staff wages

£1,276, and track repairs £76. The cars had run 654,742 miles, carried 5,685,182 passengers at an average fare of 1.3 pence. The construction costs to date including track, overhead, cars and buildings were £120,503 of which £109,000 had been raised by loans, repayments in the first year being £3,773.

On 5 April 1907 certain penny stages were extended; Seacombe to Manor Road (in lieu of Trafalgar Road), Falkland Road, and Egremont to Hose Side (in lieu of St. John's Church to Hose Side). In the following year 250,000 more penny tickets were sold on this route, but this was offset by a drop of 130,000 in 2d sales, a loss of £64. To handle the additional traffic extra mileage had cost £394, an overall loss of £458. Councillors frequently failed to acknowledge the financial consequences of their vote-catching exercises. In April 1908 the Council sanctioned a penny stage from Egremont to New Brighton (in lieu of Molyneux Drive) but postponed a decision on extending the Manor Road 1d stage to Holland Road when the Tramways Committee warned of a considerable "shrinkage in revenue"

Between 1903 and 1908 the fleet was augmented by the delivery of a further 14 cars. To carry the growing traffic, especially at peak hours, Wallasey expanded its use of part-way cars which, by 1905-6, accounted for a 5.2% increase in overall mileage. Each route had a number of intermediate termini, some more regularly used than others. Seabank Road usually had a 'part-way' following the through car as far as

Molyneux Drive, another to Holland Road and occasionally a third to Trafalgar Road. Rake Lane had no advertised 'part-ways' but cars were occasionally turned at Liscard Village, (known as Wallasey Road), at Earlston Road and at Mount Pleasant Road (Stroud's Corner); on Saturdays there were regular inbound part-way cars to Lloyd's Corner. Warren Drive had 'part-ways' to Grasmere Drive (the depot), Earlston Road, Hose Side (or 'Hoe Side') and Grove Road/Warren Drive junction. All these destinations other than Lloyd's Corner were followed by the suffix 'Only.' Originally wooden or brass part-way plates were hung on the bulkhead guard-rails but these were eventually replaced by small boards showing the part-way terminus attached to the rear dash by tiny brass chains.

Despite these arrangements, the manager was asked to refute an allegation made to the Board of Trade that cars were often overcrowded. He conceded that some overcrowding was inevitable at rush hours, in the high season and in wet weather, but maintained it was impossible to provide every passenger with a seat since many, despite the ample provision of part-ways, chose to travel on the leading car, leaving the duplicate half empty. Wallasey trams

Car No. 10 climbs up the 1 in 15 gradient of Rowson Street towards Molyneux Drive junction about 1924. The Seabank Road line is on the right, Rake Lane on the left. *(Valentine, Dundee)*

Car No. 4 ran away down Rowson Street on 13 May 1905, derailed on the curve into Victoria Road, and collided with the front of the North and South Wales Bank *(Left)*. After this incident guard posts were placed in front of the bank, and in March 1907 the direction of the one-way tram traffic was reversed so that Victoria Road was used only by ascending cars; those from Rowson Street now ran straight across the junction into Virginia Road. *(Moorhouse, Photographer, Egremont)*

carried 9.17 passengers per car mile, about the average for the whole country.

Unlike Birkenhead, Wallasey trams carried few industrial workers. Most of the passengers were white-collar employees travelling to and from Liverpool, with peaks between 8am and 9am and (the heaviest) between 5pm and 6pm. There was a third peak between 10pm and 11pm with people returning home from places of entertainment. However, from 24 March 1902 a half-hourly service for 'Artizans, mechanics or daily labourers' was operated to Seacombe from Molyneux Drive and Liscard Village (Wallasey Road), starting at 5.12am. Initially only a 2d workmen's return was sold on any car departing before 8am, but a 1d single ticket was introduced later. This enabled the unemployed who crossed to Liverpool in search of work but were unsuccessful to return home before the 2d ticket became valid at 4pm. From 13 May 1907 the Seabank Road departures were extended to Victoria Road/Rowson Street, operating every 15 minutes from 5.05am. Following a short-lived extension to Rake Lane (at Earlston Road) the other early morning cars were re-scheduled to start at the depot. They were supplemented by March 1908 (and probably from 18 December 1907) by a half-hourly service from Grove Road/Warren Drive, starting at 7.03am. Later, with the opening of the Poulton route cars left the same point travelling via Wallasey Village from 4.42am

(later 4.56am). This pattern continued virtually unchanged to abandonment. Although providing a necessary service, only an average of 1,100 per day used the early cars and of these 60% purchased the 1d single ticket.

The tramways augmented their ordinary revenue by hiring cars for use by private parties. The first known hire was on 15 October 1902 when the Committee agreed to convey 600 children free of charge from Seacombe to Clifton Hall on the occasion of a visit by Lord Strathcona of the Navy League. With the opening in 1911 of the tramway to Harrison Drive (described later) demand for hire cars increased and by the year ending 31 March 1912 7,660 passengers had been carried over 687 car miles for £64 at a rate of 22.36d per mile. The usual large load required five or six cars; however a Liverpool Sunday School outing required 12 cars to convey 793 children. From 1 April 1912 hire charges were revised to 10s per car for a return trip over a 1d stage and 15s over a 2d stage. There was a reduction for cars carrying 60 or over. The rates were again revised in July 1913 to 10s 6d per 1d stage, 15s 6d for a 2d stage and 21s for the new 3d stage.

Improving the Layout

The year 1907 saw major improvements to both the principal termini. As the loop at Seacombe was meant to handle three services it is surprising that it was designed with no sidings or loops; trams arrived at the ferry via Church Road, traversed the loop in a clockwise direction and left via Demesne Street (the reverse of the flow envisaged in the 1899 Act). Cars therefore had to depart in the order they arrived, and any breakdown there would cause major delays.

A siding, first used on 18 June 1902, was soon added on the south side of Victoria Place to enable the more frequent Seabank Road cars to overtake others, and in February/March 1907 the tracks on the north side were re-aligned to include a passing loop and a short dead-end stub for disabled cars. Inspectors could now regulate car movements before despatching them to the departure tracks. A facing crossover was laid at the foot of Church Road for emergency use, and a curve was built later linking Demesne Street to the north side of the loop, probably to provide for a suggested reversal of the flow into Seacombe urged in July 1911 by the Brighton Street traders. A six-month experiment was envisaged, but there is no evidence that it took place. No further alterations were necessary at Seacombe, despite the peak-hour provision from 1911 of some eleven cars to meet each 10-minute boat.

At New Brighton, the Tramways Department was faced by two problems, firstly the terminal loop and secondly the one-way system in and out of the resort. The anti-clockwise 'Horse-Shoe' (a name first given to the pier approaches in 1864) was inconvenient and inflexible, as cars were again obliged to leave in the order they arrived, and there was nowhere to park spare trams. From 29 March 1907 the loop was replaced by a grid-iron of four sidings each capable of accommodating two cars. A curve was also added from Virginia Road to Victoria Road allowing some cars to by-pass the grid-iron, especially on bank holidays. Two of the sidings incorporated parts of the old loop. Hitherto in the summer, drivers had experienced difficulty in edging round the loop when crowds thronged the ferry approaches; now conductors struggled to turn the trolleys as passengers clambered off one end whilst others pushed on board at the other. Point boys assisted car movements, temporary staff sold tickets to the waiting crowds and an inspector was always on duty in summer. In winter only the pair of sidings nearest the Ferry Hotel were used, but in summer the Seabank Road cars used the northern pair.

From the same date, 29 March 1907, the flow in and out of New Brighton was reversed, with inbound cars travelling via Virginia Road and outbound via Victoria Road, as a consequence of the May 1905 runaway. To counter local opposition to the reversed flow, Travers unsuccessfully explored the possibility of doubling the track in Victoria Road. The 1904 Bill, had it succeeded, would have provided a 90-yard storage siding in Virginia Road and a one-way avoiding line from Victoria Road via Grosvenor Road and Egerton Street to rejoin Rowson Street,

but Greene had opposed this, claiming that outbound cars would lose potential traffic by not passing through the main junction.

Further track improvements were made at the busy Rowson Street/Victoria Road junction in 1911. The single track at the foot of Rowson Street hill was doubled and a new crossover installed at Pickering Road. This was used by early morning cars which arrived from the depot via Warren Drive, reversed in the lower part of Rowson Street and then proceeded wrong track to the crossover. A Collins' automatic point controller was installed for outbound cars in Victoria Road for a three-month trial; if the driver wished to alter the setting, he went under the skate with the power on. Similar equipment was provided at Molyneux Drive, Brighton Street (Church Street) and Liscard Village in 1912 and in the following year at Seacombe Ferry and the top of Falkland Road. In February 1912 the track was doubled between St James' Vicarage and Atherton Street (Victoria Road), leaving a short length of single line immediately prior to the junction. The proximity of the Wirral Railway cutting at New Brighton station and the excessive camber of the road prevented any further extension of the double track.

A further improvement at New Brighton did not materialise. As part of a campaign to create a resort to rival Blackpool and Southport, the Council was determined to improve New Brighton's image. The 1906 Improvement Act had sanctioned a stretch of promenade linking the pier approach with a new Marine Park. In the process many old buildings near the ferry pier were swept away, including the notorious Ham and Egg Parade, a collection of seedy cafes and amusement arcades. The New Brighton Improvements Association recommended the construction of a double track tramway along the new promenade at a cost of £8,000, but due to the short distance and the seasonal nature of the traffic the Council refused. However, by 1913 they were again considering an application to Parliament for powers to build a line linking New Brighton with Harrison Drive/Grove Road, to be operated in the summer months by toastrack cars, partly on private track across the sand dunes. Unfortunately the war intervened and the idea was never revived.

By 7 February 1911 double track had also been laid in Wheatland Lane between Geneva Road and Milton Road, and in April 1912 along Warren Drive from a point north of Ennerdale Road down to Grove Road Junction. Attention then turned to the Seabank Road route. The most heavily used stretch of single track and loops on the system, from Molyneux Drive to Manor Road, was relaid in stages between March 1914 and March 1915, including some road widening and renewing the feeder cables and the overhead. A passenger shelter was also provided at Manor Road. A siding in either Manor Road or Trafalgar Road for cars awaiting cinema

Seacombe Ferry, the focal point of the Wallasey system, decorated for the Royal visit of March 1914. The terminus consisted originally of a single loop, but this was soon revised to include arrival and departure sidings for peak hour cars. Those visible include cars 55 and 58. The hydraulic accumulator tower on the right worked the vehicular lifts down to the landing stage. *(Wirral Borough Libraries)*

crowds was rejected, a second crossover being installed in King Street about 150 yards south of the existing one. To prevent wheel screech and reduce wear on sharp curves, track fountain hydrants were fitted in 1911 at Hose Side Road, Grove Road (Warren Drive) and Victoria Road (Rowson Street).

The Urban District of Wallasey became a Municipal Borough in 1910, and a County Borough three years later. The word "Council" was swiftly replaced by "Corporation" on the rocker panels of the cars, and the new coat of arms was applied, though some cars are thought to have retained the WCT monogram until after World War I. The population had risen rapidly by 25,000 to 78,000 during the ten years 1900-10 and by 1913 had reached 83,000, due in no small part to the joint role played by the trams and ferries.

Trams to Wallasey Village

By 1909, local agitation for a route to serve Poulton and Wallasey Village had been going on for seven years, but access to the area was bedevilled by steep inclines and extremely narrow roads which were unsuitable for trams. In late 1903 the Council rejected the idea of a line from Liscard down St Hilary Brow to The Cheshire Cheese, a pub on the outskirts of Wallasey Village, but asked Greene to prepare a report on the merits of using either trams or motor buses to connect Seacombe with Poulton and Wallasey Village (Harrison Drive), where the unspoilt beaches were already popular with railway travellers from Liverpool. The Wirral Railway had reached New Brighton in 1888 and had taken traffic from the New Brighton ferries, passengers being able to travel to the centre of Liverpool with one change at Birkenhead Park. However, the steam trains under the Mersey were particularly unpleasant, and following the opening of the Wirral branch to Seacombe in 1895 a local Seacombe-New Brighton service known as 'The Dodger' was introduced in 1896. It ran daily until some time in 1897 and at holiday peaks from 1899 onwards, but only on bank holidays in 1905, by which time the Mersey Railway had been electrified. 'The Dodger' was revived briefly in 1906 and a new station (Wallasey Village) was opened on 1 March 1907, but the service ran for the last time on August Bank Holiday 1907.

Greene reported that a quarter-hourly bus service from the ferry to Harrison Drive via Poulton Road would require six buses costing between £750 and £1,000 each and, with special depot facilities, the total capital outlay would be £8,000. Receipts were conservatively estimated at £7,772 per annum and specifications for buses were submitted by Milnes Daimler, Brush, Stirlings and Wolseley, the latter in association with Milnes, Voss. The cost of providing six cars and extra depot space for a tram service either to St Luke's Church or the Cheshire Cheese would be respectively £5,400 and £6,600, excluding track and overhead. Whilst favouring the use of trams, Greene recommended that the Council should seek statutory powers to operate motor buses.

Without waiting for this report, powers were sought in the abortive 1904 Improvement Bill for a primarily double track tramway 2.94 miles in length from Lloyd's Corner to Grove Road/Warren Drive via Poulton Road, Breck Road and Wallasey Village. Owing to the extreme narrowness of Breck Road and the demolition of property proposed in Wallasey Village, the Bill proved controversial and was thrown out. In November 1905 the Council deposited a further Bill seeking powers to build a line via Poulton Road and Breck Road but only as far as the Cheshire Cheese. Single track was included in two parts of Breck Road and over the railway bridge in Poulton Road.

The use of Breck Road was again opposed, and the route to Wallasey Village deferred. The bus powers were also defeated, although a rival Bill promoted by the Wirral Railway Company, who saw opportunities of operating feeder buses to their two stations at Wallasey and Liscard & Poulton, was successful but in such an emasculated form that it proved inoperable. A powerful municipal lobby in Parliament had inserted a clause precluding buses from operating in any city, borough or district already provided with a system of trams or buses without the prior consent of the local authority. The Wirral Railway never exercised its powers.

Perhaps to discourage further railway competition, the Council issued licences in 1907 to R & J Evans of 1 Matthew Street, Seacombe to operate a horse bus service between Seacombe and St. Luke's Church, Poulton on the understanding that they would cease trading as soon as electric trams were introduced. The Council had previously refused all requests from independent operators to serve the area, and in 1899 had forced Ellis Watson to cease running between Harrison Drive and Seacombe after one month. The Evans brothers were hauliers and team owners, with a large yard and stable in

Two ex-London horse buses of the Seacombe, Poulton & Wallasey Omnibus Company waiting at St. Luke's Church, Poulton in about 1909. They were replaced by a new electric tram route in 1910-11.
(Wirral Burrough Libraries)

Matthew Street. For the bus service they purchased four second-hand 26-seater double deckers from London which were sent by rail to Seacombe, and acquired 12-16 'vanners' — light horses capable of trotting. The buses were re-painted red, lined out in black and yellow and carried the name 'Seacombe, Poulton and Wallasey Omnibus Company' though no company was formed. A half-hourly service was run from 7am to 11pm, with peak hour extras. The route was originally along Borough Road and Poulton Road but following accusations of speeding and reckless driving, the buses were deliberately diverted to a slower route via Abbotsford Street, Belle Vue Road and Gladstone Road. The fares were 1d to Canterbury Road and 2d to St. Luke's Church. Bell punch tickets were issued. From 8 February 1908 the service was extended along Breck Road to Harrison Drive with a 3d through fare. Normally the buses met at St. Luke's Church where there was a water trough and time-table board. At rush hours, some buses terminated there. Tip horses were used at both Seacombe and Breck Road.

Meanwhile the District Engineer and Surveyor had been costing alternative tramway schemes. He estimated that to widen Breck Road for double track would cost £95,530 whereas if the trams followed a more circuitous route between St. Luke's Church and Wallasey Village it would be only £83,160. The route suggested was along Mill Lane, Marlowe Road (a specially made highway), Wallasey Road, Claremount Road, then by a new curving 'serpentine' roadway down to St. George's Road, Sandy Lane, Wallasey Village to Harrison Drive, then along Grove Road to link up with the Warren Drive route. The estimated cost included forming, making and sewering St. George's Road and Sandy Lane as well as constructing both Marlowe Road and the 'serpentine' roadway.

The Council abandoned plans for a line linking Liscard Village to Claremount Road via Wallasey Road. Costing £22,000, it would have provided depot access to and from the proposed new line and there were plans for a circular tram route between Liscard and Harrison Drive via either Wallasey Road and Sandy Lane or via Hose Side Road and Grove Road.

The circuitous route known locally as the "Switchback' was approved on 6 October 1908 and included in the 1909 Wallasey Tramways and Improvements Bill. However, not everyone was enthusiastic about Wallasey's fourth tram route; Canon Cogswell of St. Hilary's Church pleaded in vain that "The Mother Church should be spared the clang of the tramway bell and the drone of the electric motor." The controversial motor bus powers were not pursued, and the Council's 1909 Act authorised 3.25 miles of double track from Wheatland Lane along Poulton Road, Mill Lane, Marlowe Road, Wallasey Road, Claremount Road, "the new road authorised by this Act", St. Georges Road, Sandy Lane, Wallasey Village and Grove Road to a triangle junction with Warren Drive. The same act authorised three new sections of double track elsewhere on the system. In the event the 'serpentine' road was never built, the Council opting for the reconstruction of Folly Lane (later renamed Broadway), a steep footpath on the north side of St. Hilary's Church.

The first rails were laid by direct labour on Poulton Road railway bridge on 28 December 1909. Interlacing was chosen for both railway bridges in Poulton, and survived until abandonment. 100 lb/yd rail was used, and the first reinforced concrete tramway poles in the country. Span wires were employed throughout. There were crossovers in Mill Lane at St. Luke's Church, in Marlowe Road at Wallasey Road, at Harrison Drive and in Grove Road west of Warren Drive. The cost of the track, overhead and cabling amounted to £26,000.

The first section of line as far as St. Luke's Church, Poulton was inspected by Col. Von Donop on 8 July

An opening-day photograph of the Poulton route; No. 48 photographed near St. Lukes Church on 8 July 1910.
(Courtesy M. Jenkins)

The opening of the final extension in Wallasey on 7 February 1911 with the car standing at the top of Broadway. Note the fine array of hats, coats and beards and the ladies confined to the inside of the car.
(R. T. Ford, Photographer, Wallasey)

1910, using car 48. At 11.45am a decorated unvestibuled car driven by Alderman C. J. Woodroffe, Chairman of the Tramways Committee, headed a procession of three trams past the usual throng of cheering schoolchildren. Public service commenced at 12 noon. At the celebratory lunch Woodroffe speculated on possible future lines along Manor Road, along Wallasey Road, through the sandhills from Harrison Drive to New Brighton, as well as across Duke Street bridge to Birkenhead, but no formal proposals were prepared at this time.

The cars showed 'Poulton only', but later when the line opened throughout this part-way terminus was known as either 'St. Luke's Church only' or in a few cases 'Poulton Bridge Road only.' They all referred to the same location. The fare from Seacombe was 1d, and three cars provided a 15 minute service, with one extra at peak hours. Receipts were disappointing; 9.75p per car mile during the first nine days, and only 8.33p by the end of August. Greene reminded the Council that Warren Drive had begun in similar circumstances and that the real purpose of the new line was to encourage residential development of the countrified section to Harrison Drive. On 20 July the omnibus company was told of its obligation to cease running and the route was curtailed to provide a feeder connection from St. Luke's Church onward to Harrison Drive. On 14 September it was licensed to operate another route from Liscard Village to Wallasey Village Station via St. Hilary Brow, but only until the trams were extended; services finally ceased on 10 February 1911.

Wallasey's last section of new tram route, from St. Luke's Church through Wallasey Village to the junction of Grove Road and Warren Drive, was approved by Col. Von Donop on Tuesday morning 7 February 1911, particular attention being paid to the steep descent down Folly Lane (Broadway). A decorated car driven by Alderman Quinn and carrying the Mayors of Wallasey, Birkenhead and Bootle then left Seacombe at noon and covered the entire line, much of which passed through open fields along roads which had previously been little more than muddy tracks. Public service began immediately afterwards.

Except for about three hours on Sunday afternoons when cars regularly ran through to New Brighton, the terminus was Grove Road (Warren Drive), transfer tickets being issued to both New Brighton and Liscard Village. The penny stages were New Brighton to Harrison Drive, Grove Road to St. Luke's Church and Marlowe Road to Seacombe, 2d being charged for New Brighton to St. Luke's Church or Grove Road to Seacombe, and 3d for New Brighton to Seacombe. Part-way cars were operated from Seacombe to St. Luke's Church and Harrison Drive and later to Marlowe Road. Off-peak cars ran every 15 minutes, requiring five vehicles, and in peak hours every ten minutes with eight cars, plus part-ways. Journey times were 29 minutes to Grove Road and 35 minutes to New Brighton. Through cars ran according to demand, especially at weekends and bank holidays during the summer months

As anticipated, summer traffic to Harrison Drive was considerable. The wide expanses of beaches and sand-dunes attracted thousands of people from Liverpool, and it seems strange that no trams were operated to and from Harrison Drive via Liscard, but the existence of the single line in Liscard Road already used by two routes probably weighed against it. In 1912, a crossover was laid at Canterbury Road on Poulton Road for additional part-way cars to both Seacombe and Harrison Drive. At the height of the season, two cars provided a residents' service from Canterbury Road to Harrison Drive. Another crossover was installed at Perrin Road but was rarely used; one theory is that it was for use if Broadway should become ice-bound and inoperable.

Broadway was the most interesting feature of the new line, involving a gradient of 1 in 11.07. Owing to the steepness of the descent, the Board of Trade stipulated the fitting of slipper brakes, cars being required to halt outside St. Hilary's Church where a notice warned drivers to engage the slipper brake, whilst the conductor remained on the rear platform ready to apply the handbrake in case of emergency. Descending the hill the maximum permitted speed was 4 miles/h and ascending 8 miles/h. There was another compulsory Board of Trade stop at the foot of the hill where the slipper brake was disengaged. Cars 42-62 delivered by the Brush Electrical Engineering Co Ltd in 1910-13 were all equipped with slipper brakes. Eight unvestibuled cars were similarly equipped for holiday relief work, together with works car 26. Normal service requirements had now increased from 36 to 43 cars.

From 1 April 1913 identifying route letters and coloured lights were introduced. The codes were S for Seabank Road (purple light), RL for Rake Lane (amber), WD for Warren Drive (white) and P for Poulton (green). The coloured lights were fitted above the centre of the windscreen if one was fitted, and in the bulkhead of the unvestibuled cars.

The years before the war were marked by an acrimonious political controversy over the lengths of the penny stages. With gross profits amounting to £20,000 in the financial year 1912-13, the Council resolved to plough some of the money into longer penny stages. Greene estimated a potential loss of £1,200, though he thought some money might be recouped from people who had previously walked to Egremont ferry now riding the tram to Seacombe. The longer stages were introduced on 1 April 1912, radiating from Seacombe to Holland Road, Zig Zag Road, Earlston Road and Perrin Road. Greene was soon proved correct; despite nearly a million more passengers, overall profit in the following year was only £121, due to the number of extra cars provided which had operated an additional 34,000 miles. Receipts had dropped from 11.35d to 10.92d per car mile, and penny tickets had accounted for 82% of all sales, whilst the Ferries Committee had noted with alarm a considerable fall in revenue at both Egremont and New Brighton.

Fury erupted when on 1 April 1913 the stages on all routes except Seabank Road reverted to those in force a year earlier. Profits in the year ending 31 March 1914 recovered to £23,000, due almost entirely to the shortened stages. Faced with renewed demands for the stages to be re-extended, the Tramways Committee circulated tables showing the income for each route and the predicted income if the longer stages were re-introduced, which would leave a dangerously slender profit margin. The Council ratified their previous decision not to re-extend the stages, and rejected two alternative proposals, a penny return fare and a halfpenny stage (both thrown out before). The declaration of war cut short all further debate.

Broadway, Wallasey.

The steepest section of the Wallasey tramways was Broadway, built in 1910-11 to carry the trams down into Wallasey Village. Mechanical track brakes (slipper brakes) were required for all cars working on this route. The Wallasey gradients also prevented the use of trailers to supplement seasonal capacity, though they were considered. (Commercial postcard)

Miscellanea

In July 1904 the fleet was bedecked in flags to celebrate the holiday called in recognition of the King's visit to lay the foundation stone of the new Anglican Cathedral in Liverpool. In the early days, the trams frequently carried flags and bunting during the summer months as part of the general festivities associated with a major holiday resort.

An unusually shaped passenger shelter nicknamed the Monkey House was erected in the middle of Liscard Village in September 1904. Used by tram crews waiting to change duties and by the point boys who controlled movements through the junction, it was demolished in 1926 but the underground toilet retained the name for many years.

In 1905 a number of time-keepers were replaced by time-recording Bundy clocks costing £40 each. Each conductor was given a unique key which recorded his number and departure time on a paper roll inside the clock. These were eventually positioned at both termini and at Molyneux Drive, Grove Road (Warren Drive), Liscard Village, St. Luke's Church and Harrison Drive. In later years they were regulated by Inspector 'Big John the Watch' Nixon who would clamber on to a tram at New Brighton each day to watch for the flash of the one o'clock gun fired on the river wall at Birkenhead so that he could accurately check the exact time.

An oddly shaped passenger shelter known locally as the Monkey House stood in the middle of Liscard Village from 1904 to 1926. In this picture, taken about 1913 car 50 on route WD (Warren Drive) follows a car on route RL (Rake Lane) down the single line in the narrow part of Liscard Road. *Commercial postcard, courtesy A. K. Kirby)*

Power costs accounted for nearly 33% of working expenses, and specific instructions were included in the Rule Book relating to economic use of current. Meters were fitted to the cars in 1911 in an attempt to conserve power. Success with meters varied — Croydon claimed a 24% saving, Bradford only 5%. They must have proved sufficiently useful at Wallasey as they were retained until abandonment.

Short power failures were common, but a longer stoppage occurred in April 1908 when a power station breakdown halted cars on the Seabank Road and Rake Lane routes for 36 hours. The plant at Seaview Road was increasingly inadequate and plans existed for a new building on the Dock estate. After a series of coal strikes during the winter of 1911-12 a diesel generator was acquired to boost capacity. Matters had been made worse because the trams had to carry more people when the northern ferries were suspended due to coal shortage, though threats to suspend the Seacombe branch of the Wirral Railway did not materialise. Deep snow added to the general misery; over 50 tons of salt were distributed during one week in February 1912 and the cars were run all night to keep the tracks clear, crews working up to 18 hours.

Many towns had an Illuminated tram, and Wallasey was no exception. At first one of the 1-31 batch was used, followed later by one from Nos 32-36, finally No 54 was permanently adapted. Before any major civic event it was taken into the depot and fitted with up to 2,000 bulbs and other decorations. It made a regular annual outing during the Central

Liscard Village.

124

Brighton Street decorated for the Royal Visit of 25 March 1914, with car 47 heading towards Seacombe on route S. This was one of many sections laid with single track which had to be doubled within a few years to cope with the traffic. The photographer is standing at the corner of Brighton Street and Brougham Road, looking north. *(Wirral Borough Libraries)*

Park Carnival and was available for fund-raising activities by such bodies as the Lifeboat Institute. Many older residents still recall the thrill of watching the car proceed slowly along the dimly-lit streets filling the night with an impressive blaze of colour. It also ran during daylight but with the lights switched off. It was decorated to celebrate Wallasey's incorporation as a municipal borough on 13 July 1910 and again on 1 April 1913 when County Borough status was attained.

On 25 March 1914 King George V and Queen Mary visited the Borough to lay the foundation stone of the new Town Hall in Brighton Street. Their Majesties crossed from Liverpool to Seacombe on the ferry boat *Daffodil*. The town was festooned with decorations, the ferry fleet was dressed overall, Seacombe terminal had been repainted and the trams carried flags and bunting on the sides, balcony rails, trolley poles and ropes. On No 54 portraits of the royal couple flanked by the Lion and the Unicorn formed the main display. A large eight-point star was mounted at each end. Its last outing prior to World War I was in June 1914 when it paraded the streets to raise money for the Mayor's *Empress of Ireland* fund. It is thought to have been used on several occasions after the end of the war, and it is not known when it last appeared in public.

Wallasey in Wartime, 1914-18

The First World War, whilst interrupting and postponing many municipal projects, brought extra duties to the tramways. Declaration of war on 4 August 1914 led to the postponement of a proposed Parliamentary Bill seeking general omnibus powers as well as the New Brighton to Harrison Drive sea front tramway. Various improvements were shelved, including a plan to double the line from Liscard Village to the depot entrance and from Hose Side Road to Earlston Road, but work in hand was completed, comprising doubling the Seabank Road track between Sandfield Road and Onslow Road in the winter of 1914-15.

Within a few days of the outbreak of war, some late night cars were suspended and the Seabank Road service slightly reduced. Patriotic announcements appeared on the backs of tickets in September, and during one week in October collecting boxes on the cars raised £17 for the National Relief Fund. By the end of October, of a staff of 238, 94 had enlisted, the majority being conductors. The first fatality occurred on 6 November with the death of driver Doyle of the Irish Guards. In 1916 the tramways were declared vital to the war effort and drivers as being in a reserved occupation, but Greene nevertheless had to appeal against a move to enlist a further 26 men. By now he had lost 122 staff — over 50%. In addition to the use of the female staff (described in Appendix 4) some men had been retained well past retirement age — one cleaner although 'a little

125

Illuminated trams were a widespread symbol of civic pride. Wallasey at first used car 15 and later a car from the 32-36 class, seen here on the depot approach road swathed in bunting, flags and electric bulbs for the Coronation of King George V and Queen Mary in 1911. By 1914, car 54 had been fitted up on a semi-permanent basis to serve as Wallasey's illuminated tram, with over 2,300 bulbs and using the eight-pointed star and other decorations from the 1911 car, as shown in the lower photograph. The car consumed nine times the normal amount of electricity. After the war, No 54 re-appeared as part of the 1919 Peace Celebrations. *(Commercial postcards)*

infirm' was 78 — and retired drivers were re-engaged.

The generally healthy financial state of the undertaking allowed the Tramways Committee to continue to transfer money for relief of the rates as well as granting certain wartime concessions. From 1 November 1914 free travel was allowed for members of the armed forces, nurses and doctors. Within the first fortnight 17,277 were carried, an average of 1,234 per day, with a revenue loss of £36. By the end of the financial year the number was 286,172. In the following two years free riders rose to 626,464 and 684,603 respectively. Tempers frayed when fare-paying passengers were unable to board the reduced number of cars available and there were demands that the facility should be withdrawn. From 9 July 1917 the privilege was restricted to wounded men and nurses serving in local hospitals, though this was later changed to include all those involved in medical work. During the ensuing eight months, the cars still carried 400,000 free, many of whom were travelling to the new Town Hall which had become a temporary hospital.

In May 1915 the Corporation took delivery of six new cars built by Brush. Their numbers were 63-68, and one is portrayed on our cover in the livery which they carried when new. They worked mainly on the Seabank Road route, the older cars being transferred to the RL and WD. A new workshop facility was completed in 1916, but was immediately given over to the manufacture of armaments.

As the war continued, only one full time painter was still employed and the cars became decidedly shabby, the sea-green having faded to a washed-out white often caked in grime. Most of the luxury items such as curtains, seat carpets and cut glass lampshades were removed, although some were reinstated in 1919. Careful attention was paid to brakes, electrical equipment and trucks but general body and track maintenance virtually ceased. Some cars including No 16 appeared in an unattractive overall unvarnished green livery and for a brief spell 55 was painted in grey undercoat at one end only. As an air-raid precaution, criss-cross strips of green paper were affixed to the lower saloon windows, and some cars had blue bulbs. There was an acute shortage of spare parts, but some new machinery was purchased during 1917 including a crucible furnace and a shearing and punching machine. From 17 July 1918 Wallasey was classified as a No 1 system allowing it priority access to materials released under certificate by the Ministry of Munitions.

The only recorded death of a member of staff on duty occurred in 1917 when Joseph Sprackling, formerly a blacksmith with the United, alighted from car 18 to clean the points at Warren Point loop on the WD route and was struck and fatally injured by a motor car. On 20 February 1918 Jessie, the former tram horse, was humanely destroyed due to senile decay; the stable was converted for other uses and the horse-drawn lorry sold. A horse was hired to haul the tower wagon as required.

Wallasey suffered from a shortage of staff rather than of rolling stock. By summer 1917, with only 60 drivers and 70 conductresses available, only 80% of the fleet was in use. Peak-hour schedules were maintained at pre-war levels, but cuts were made at other times, including further curtailment of late evening cars. In July 1917 the cars operated 2,130 miles more than in the previous July, but carried an extra 250,000 people. Receipts soared to 17.9d per car mile in July and 18.97d in August, as thousands seeking relief from wartime austerity poured into New Brighton. In August 1918 the trams carried over 2,000,000. On one memorable day, due to an extremely low tide at New Brighton which prevented any steamers from berthing there, queues four deep stretched from Seacombe Ferry to the Town Hall along Demesne Street with packed cars still arriving from New Brighton every few minutes. The good-natured crowds had all been transported back to Liverpool by midnight.

Further service cuts became necessary from April 1918, when tramway operators in Board of Trade area 5 (Lancashire, Cheshire and North Wales) were ordered to make a 30% reduction in materials and power. Wallasey achieved this by reducing the number of part-way cars and by running the RL, P and WD every 15 minutes off-peak instead of 10 minutes, and the S every 10 minutes instead of every six. This and an early finish accounted for a 17% cut, the remainder being achieved by extending journey times and suspending all through Sunday operation to New Brighton on service P. Further savings were achieved by eliminating 49 stops, some of which had been less than 100 yards apart.

With coal in short supply, the Ferries Department was forced to withdraw peak hour sailings to New Brighton from 4 November 1918. Contract holders were accommodated on special replacement tram services running from New Brighton to Egremont via both Seabank Road and Warren Drive, requiring further cuts elsewhere. To avoid blocking the busy Egremont junction, a three-way point costing £250 was laid enabling cars to turn from King Street into Church Street; the WD cars returned to New Brighton via Seabank Road. During the first six days 9,705 contract holders were carried on the S and 2,028 on the WD; special tickets were issued, the ferries being debited with the costs. The Tramways Committee were angry when Commander Fry, the Ferry Manager, suddenly reinstated sailings to New Brighton on 1 December.

Two other junctions were modified in 1918, at a cost of £1,200. The New Brighton grid-iron was relaid with double-tongue Edgar Allen points (also used in all subsequent renewals throughout the system) and the layout at Liscard was altered so that inbound RL drivers could have a clear view down

Liscard Road; the new layout is shown on page 136. 14,000 fewer car miles were operated in November-December 1918 than in 1917, saving nearly 26,000 units of electricity, but 300,000 more people were carried. Wallasey trams continued to operate at a profit, the Department regularly contributing to the relief of rates, but some of the money accumulated because of the virtual cessation of capital projects and the decline in maintenance.

With severe overcrowding during the war, and inexperienced crews, accidents and claims were inevitable. Notices were posted reminding passengers not to alight from moving vehicles, that only the conductor could ring the bell to start, and that drivers must stop only at recognised places. On 16 May 1916 a private from the 3rd Cheshire Regiment died when he fell off No 9 whilst under the influence of drink, on 9 December 1916 No 21 jumped the points at Hale Road loop and demolished a wall (several passengers were injured) and four days later a lorry owned by the West Cheshire Brewery collided with two trams in succession. On 22 September 1917 the brakes on car 22 jammed whilst ascending Rowson Street and the car ran back, colliding with No 64.

The war ended at 11am on 11 November 1918. Ferry and tram crews deserted their posts and joined the thousands of people pouring on to the streets to celebrate. Stranded cars were rescued by office and works staff and those who had remained on duty were given double pay. The department's Roll of Honour included nine dead, most of whom had been killed in 1915-16.

WALLASEY

WALLASEY'S ILLUMINATED CAR PEACE CELEBRATIONS 1919

9 Wallasey 1919-1933

Wallasey tramways came through the 1914-18 war in better physical state than many others, and the principal worries as 1918 ended were financial. Greene, due to retire, was persuaded to remain in office to guide the department through its post-war recovery programme, and the Council approved a fares increase to take effect from Monday 16 December 1918. Gone were the days when managers vied with each other to offer the longest distance for one penny; now they were struggling to contain inflation, working expenses in Wallasey having risen by 3d per car mile in twelve months. All 1d stages were shortened, some new 1½d fares were introduced, and the Seacombe-New Brighton through fare was raised to 3d (4d via Poulton). The workmen's return was increased to 3d, with a 7am restriction, and prepaid scholars' tickets (introduced in 1910-11) became 1s. a dozen. By March 1920 only 44% of tickets sold were 1d, as against 82% in 1913.

Receipts rose, an extra £3,750 being taken in the first months of 1919. To offer some compensation to residents, the Corporation introduced a system of prepaid discount tickets at a rate of 13 × 1d for 1s.

and 13 × 1½d for 1s.6d. By March 1920 138,437 × 1d and 112,617 × 1½d had been purchased. Other seaside resorts had adopted the same policy, but with varying success. Southport allowed reductions of 1¾d in the shilling and Blackpool 2d in the shilling, but only on 2d stages. Wallasey withdrew the facility in July 1922.

Meanwhile, austerity was forgotten as thousands travelled to New Brighton for relaxation and enjoyment. Record business was reported and during the year to 31 March 1920 the cars carried the most passengers (21,435,873) and operated the highest mileage (1,465,595) in the history of the undertaking. In August 1919 passengers again topped two million, a figure almost reached in both July and September. New Brighton terminus was hardly able to cope, some cars being despatched direct from Virginia Road into Victoria Road, and schemes were considered for additional sidings; mobile queue

An immediate postwar view of New Brighton with cars 68 and 18 loading. In the foreground is the curve linking Virginia Road to Victoria Road. Note the Liverpool style blue request stop sign on the traction pole.
(Commercial postcard)

barriers were rejected as impracticable. A familiar sight to disappear was the New Brighton Tower, which had been declared unsafe and was dismantled for scrap between 1919 and 1921; cynics drew attention to the high price of scrap metal. A covered passenger shelter was erected on the north side of the sidings in September 1919.

Crowds were also carried during the Government-designated peace days — public holidays called to celebrate victory. Illuminated car 54 re-appeared, liberally festooned with flags and bunting, and all trams stopped at Central Park Gates to provide direct access to the revived carnival. Only a few of the 49 stopping places eliminated in 1917 were reinstated after the war. From the commencement of operations, Wallasey used metal stop signs generally similar to those in Liverpool. Red indicated a compulsory stop and blue a request stop, but in some cases red or blue on a white background was used instead of white on red or blue. The Sunday afternoon extension of service P to New Brighton operated only on fine days, and a passenger shelter was erected in 1919 at Grove Road where the cars normally terminated.

During August 1920 the cars earned a record 27.05 pence per mile, but for the six months to 30 September 1920 receipts at £55,228 were almost matched by working expenses at £55,210, a dangerously narrow margin. The manager recommended an immediate increase of ½d on all fares, bringing in a 1½d minimum, to avoid an estimated loss of £22,517 for the current financial year. Against considerable opposition the penny stages were discontinued from 6 December 1920, introducing 1½d stages from Seacombe to Trafalgar Road, St. John's Church and Canterbury Road (average distance 1⅓ miles), with 2½d stages to Molyneux Drive, Field Road and Earlston Road on the S, RL and WD routes. Through fares to New Brighton on the WD and P were raised to 4d and 5d respectively, but for the first time children aged 5-12 were offered a reduction, with a universal fare of 1½d. On 3 January 1921 two short-lived 3½d stages were introduced from Seacombe to Harrison Drive and from Marlowe Road to New Brighton. Receipts rose, but passenger figures fell and Greene stated that "the Revenue from the Undertaking has apparently reached its maximum under the present scale of fares."

However, the increases enabled the finances of the undertaking to regain their equilibrium, and the proportion of working expenses to revenue dropped from 83.6% in 1921-22 to 75% in 1922-23. This was lower than the 77.1% of 1919-20, the year which had seen the introduction of the 48-hour week. The Council reintroduced penny fares on 9 January 1922 but with shorter stages, e.g. Seacombe to the Town Hall (two-thirds of a mile) and New Brighton to Portland Street. The upper age limit for the child's

1½d fare was raised from 12 to 14, and a 1d child's ticket was subsequently introduced on 1½d and 2d stages. A campaign against fare-dodging was conducted during December 1922 and January 1923; 59 cars were checked, and 79 out of 1,214 people had not paid when approached. Greene urged the conductors to work faster.

The only other fare changes during the life of the tramways were made in 1923, when on 4 April the penny stages from Seacombe were extended, the new limits being Trafalgar Road (S), Central Park Avenue (RL, WD) and Clifford Road (P). Other stages were lengthened similarly, the 2½d and 3½d stages being abolished altogether, and the through 5d fare on service P reverted to 4d. Some further stages were extended on 5 July.

Greene always opposed the concept of contract or season tickets, declaring that it would be impossible to prevent abuses and that if a high percentage of regular passengers switched to this kind of ticket it would seriously affect the revenue. Only Aberdeen and Blackpool still used them, whilst Southport and Rochdale had discontinued them, leading in the latter case to an immediate increase in revenue of 13%. The free travel concession to military personnel was withdrawn in April 1921, but free travel continued to be granted to disabled ex-servicemen.

Track and Cars

It was often said of Wallasey in post-war years that the cars were excellent, the track deplorable. This was partly due to divided responsibilities, the track being under the control of the Borough Engineer, whose estimates for work were often considered excessive by the Tramways Committee. In 1919 the committee wanted to relay the remaining five sections of heavily-used single line on route S, but owing to financial restraints imposed on all municipal departments the Borough Engineer opposed this and recommended instead that the track should be treated by the Sandberg *in situ* hardening process and that the rail joints be electrically welded. In all, eight miles of track were dealt with by the National Welding Company over an 18-month period, starting in August 1920. The treatment offered a short-term solution, but was ultimately to lead to the abandonment of the tramway system when major track renewals could no longer be postponed some seven years later.

In one of his postwar reports Greene had advocated the elimination of single track in Liscard Road and Seabank Road by reducing pavement width, purchasing frontages, obtaining owners' agreement to reducing the 9ft 6in distance from the kerb, or, in the last resort, ignoring the statutory requirements. Two short lengths of single line were doubled in 1920 (costing £4,316), over the railway bridge in Wheatland Lane and from Maddock Road to Manor Lane. Unfortunately plans to double the

No. 58 rounding the corner at Harrison Drive, Wallasey Village in 1922. This was the nearest stop to the beaches and sand-dunes and required extra cars in summer. No. 58 is in the immediate postwar green livery with silver lining-out. *(F. B. Walton)*

length from Hertford Drive to Cambridge Road were frustrated by residents who still refused to sell their frontages. At a later date, the Highways Committee successfully resisted a move by Coun. Meggeson to have the second track between Maddock Road and Manor Lane lifted on the grounds that it contravened the statutory 9ft 6in distance between rail and kerb; instead, extra street lights were provided to reduce the risk of accidents.

No further track improvements were possible on the S, but in December 1923 the Council received a grant from the Unemployment Grants Committee to meet 50% of the interest charges on a £21,477 15 year loan for doubling two sections of track in Rake Lane, where the old quarry was to be filled in and the road widened. Early in 1924 the short length of single track opposite Princess Road was doubled, with a new crossover south of Sandfield Road. This enabled football cars to lie over on the southbound track during New Brighton football club's home games at Sandhey Park ground (opened in 1921) whilst service cars passed on the northbound track using the existing crossover at Earlston Road; New Brighton were then in the Football League and attracted sizeable crowds. An earlier proposal for a football siding on Seabank Road near Cambridge Road had been rejected. Next winter the very narrow portion of Rake Lane between Edinburgh Road and the Cemetery gates was widened to include double track, giving a continuous run from Liscard to Mount Pleasant Road. Falkland Road and parts of the New Brighton grid-iron were also relaid.

The tramcar works was handed back by the government in December 1918 and hurriedly equipped with new and secondhand machinery for use in overtaking the wartime arrears of maintenance. During 1919 the Council approved the purchase of 20 new cars similar to Nos 63-68, then in 1920 reduced the order to ten cars plus ten new bodies. This was then further amended in favour of an extensive rehabilitation programme, and selected cars from Nos 1-36 were stripped to their frames, some receiving new roofs, main pillars, waist and rocker panels. All had their upper decks strengthened; trucks, motors, controllers and brakes were thoroughly overhauled and worn parts replaced. The curtains and seat carpets were restored in some cars, but this was short lived.

When the first two of the ten new cars (Nos 69-70) were delivered in late July 1920 the cost had risen to £2,060 per car, and the final two delivered in October (77-78) cost £2,203. After assembly the average cost per car was £2,307 compared with £895 for similar cars 63-68 bought in 1915. They differed structurally only in having direct stairs, this at the insistence of the Board of Trade who had otherwise refused to sanction a £22,000 15-year loan. Car No 69 was pressed into service partially painted following a collision between Nos 17 and 34 on Warren Drive.

The state of the track in Liscard was the subject of many complaints, cars being described as swaying dangerously when crossing the junction. In July 1921 the committee rejected a claim for damage to a motor car caused allegedly by defective rails in Liscard Village, but they agreed to pay 8s 6d to a Mrs. Wells to clean her dress after the conductor of No 12 had spilt tea on it.

Council Motor Buses

In 1919 the manager proposed that the Council should apply for Parliamentary powers to run motor buses within the town. These were granted, and the Bidston and Birkenhead. This was agreed, and the first motor bus route opened on 3 April 1920. It followed the S tram route from Seacombe to Manor Road, then along Manor Road to Liscard Village, continuing via Wallasey Road, St. Hilary Brow and Wallasey Village to Harrison Drive; an earlier plan to run it purely as a feeder between Seabank Road (at Manor Road) and Harrison Drive was rejected. The

The last new trams bought by Wallasey Corporation were Nos. 69-78, built by the Brush Electrical Engineering Co. Ltd. in 1920 at a cost of £2,307 each. They differed from 1915 Brush cars 63-68 in having direct instead of reversed stairs. This March 1929 photograph of newly repainted car 74 was taken at the Grove Road/Warren Drive junction which served as the regular terminus of route P, through passengers for New Brighton transferring to route WD. On busy afternoons in summer the P cars ran through to New Brighton. *(Dr. Hugh Nicol)*

trams were protected over common sections by higher bus fares, and the through fare was sixpence for a journey of 20 minutes. The vehicles, six AEC "YC" 32-seaters with bodies by E & A Hora were noisy and uncomfortable, and represented no threat to the trams; Greene's successor described them as "vibrating monsters." In their first year the buses lost £9,000, but the Council was determined not to subsidise them from tramway profits.

The spare buses were used to assist the tramways when necessary, mainly during power shortages. In June and July 1920 they covered for part-way duties on the S between Seacombe and Holland Road, operating 983 miles and carrying 11,654 people. They also worked on the P from Seacombe to St. Luke's Church and Harrison Drive. During the three-week national coal strike from 23 October 1920 they were drafted on to Seabank Road to supplement the trams between New Brighton and Egremont when the New Brighton ferry was suspended (25-29 October); the service continued after the boats resumed, but was withdrawn a week later. A major power failure halted all trams at 8pm on 22 November 1920, one bus running on each of tram routes RL, WD and P and two on the S. Sufficient

power was restored by 2.30am for the trams to return to the depot, the crews, stranded for six hours in freezing weather, being sustained by food and drink provided by residents. Altogether the buses operated 1,914 miles on the S in October and November 1920 and carried 8,118 passengers. A second more damaging coal strike took place from 31 March to 4 July 1921, and after it was settled power costs rose to 1.94 pence per unit in 1922 compared with 1.4d in 1915.

After the 1920 power failures, the Council reluctantly agreed to allow private coach firms to provide temporary winter cover, but they were never used. However, the Council rejected an application by one operator to run a late-evening service for theatregoers between the Winter Gardens adjacent to New Brighton Station and Seacombe via Warren Drive. Instead, special P and WD trams were later provided to wait for theatre patrons.

With the availability of more reliable power, the trams were able to offer a full service, releasing the buses to develop more routes. On 19 March 1921 joint services were inaugurated with Birkenhead Corporation, and in 1922 four buses virtually identical with the first six were purchased from Liverpool Corporation. The ten solid-tyred AEC buses

remained in use until 1926 and were then replaced by ten Leyland Lion buses with pneumatic tyres and comfortable upholstered seats which were to play an important part in influencing local opinion in favour of the motor bus.

1923 saw the introduction of a circular boat-and-tram tour enabling passengers to travel for an inclusive one-shilling fare from New Brighton to Liverpool and back to Seacombe by boat and then by the P tram to New Brighton. 2,092 people were carried during the 1923 season from 14 May to 29 September, the ferries receiving 8d and the trams 4d. The tour was repeated each year until 1926. However, a suggestion that cars should run to meet the all-night boats was rejected in 1923 because the late cars run on election night had not justified the overtime paid to the crews. An experiment to hold outbound WD cars at Egremont after 7pm to wait for passengers off the ferries was short-lived, and a suggestion for express cars between Seacombe and New Brighton via Seabank Road was rejected as impracticable.

The proposals of 1922 to link the Wallasey and Birkenhead tramways by a line over Poulton Bridge connecting Wallasey's route P with Birkenhead's Line of Docks and Claughton routes have been described in an earlier chapter. Wallasey envisaged joint operation with Birkenhead and access to Woodside station, but the scheme failed and Wallasey turned to the motor bus, which could

Seacombe Ferry approach was built on reclaimed land in 1876-1880. The electric trams (from 1902) looped round Victoria Place in front of the ferry buildings and the hydraulic tower. The land behind the Ferry Hotel was intended for a railway station. (*Picton Library, Liverpool*)

negotiate the dock estate with far less potential disruption. Passenger shelters were provided in 1923 at Mill Lane and at Earlston Road/Seaview Road. One was proposed for Church Street/Liscard Road, but postponed until a tram body was eventually used about 1931.

Under New Management

During the early 1920s R. R. Greene was ageing and there is some evidence of inertia in the management of the Wallasey undertaking. Eventually he retired on 28 February 1923, aged 70, after 22 years' managerial service. He was awarded a pension of £268 per annum and a free pass for life. By 1923 most of the long-serving members of the Tramways Committee had also gone — Augustine Quinn, C. J. Woodroffe, F. E. Howse, W.S. Chanterell, A. H. Evans and J. Farley. During their stewardship from 1902 to 1924, the department had contributed £144,398 to the relief of rates, equal to almost 9½% of the gross revenues.

The new manager, selected from 52 applicants and a short list of ten, was Herbert Harold Lincoln ('Hell-fire Harry'), an engineer trained at Birmingham and Huddersfield with steam, cable, accumulator and electric trams. At his previous post in Sheffield he had been responsible for building new cars. His salary on appointment was £550 per year. After taking office on 1 March 1923, he soon clashed with some of the senior staff. The chief clerk, R. Samuel, who had held this post since 1901 asked for his job to be redesignated Assistant General Manager — he was moved to another corporation department. Doel, the car shed superintendent was placed on indefinite leave following a disagreement with Lincoln; his services were dispensed with on 31 December 1924. The newly appointed traffic superintendent, Mathews, was reprimanded for using disrespectful language to the manager, and on 17 December 1924 the senior wages clerk was suspended for irregularities and asked to resign. Trotter Brown, the Tramways Committee chairman, supported Lincoln throughout and was determined to establish an undisputed chain of command.

Lincoln wanted to involve himself in all aspects of the undertaking and influence decision-making, instead of relying on the advice of his departmental heads. He particularly wished to gain control over any track reconstruction programme. However, despite considerable pressure from Trotter Brown and deputy chairman Samuel Panter Brick, the bid failed and the Borough Engineer remained in control of permanent way.

H. H. Lincoln, General Manager at Wallasey from 1923 to 1943.

By the end of 1923 Lincoln had prepared a three-year programme aimed at overcoming the department's three main problems — track renewal, track doubling and car reconstruction. Meanwhile, the main feeder cables were renewed during the year and in some cases laid underground, £2,000 being spent on those linking Seaview Road substation with Mainwaring Road and Liscard. The substation at Seacombe was enlarged to cope with the increased demand. Steel tyred wheels became standard, replacing the last chilled-iron ones. During 1924 Lincoln was still attempting to alleviate the problems caused by the remaining lengths of single track, and one scheme envisaged a by-pass line in Liscard along Queen Street, Grosvenor Street and Martin's Lane to remove southbound RL and WD cars from the narrow stretch of Liscard Road. The plan would have cost £10,000, but met with opposition from traders and was dropped.

There had been several derailments on the worn-out track in Liscard, and the Council agreed to renew it. As part of the abortive scheme to re-route southbound cars via Grosvenor Street, the north side of Liscard junction was relaid in March 1926 to include a double turnout from Seaview Road into Liscard Village; the cost was £2,420, partly financed by an unemployment grant. The main renewal programme cost £21,862 (much over the £15,900 estimate) and provided a double track on the WD from Merton Road to Massey Park (but not as far as the depot) and from Earlston Road to Hose Side Road. A crossover for partway cars was added north of Earlston Road, and a passenger shelter was added in 1927. When this work was completed, the system comprised 8.42 miles of double track, 3.60 miles of single track and 0.9 track miles in the depot complex.

A major operation was mounted during the closure of Seacombe Ferry from noon on Saturday 2 May 1925 to 7am on Monday 4 May to facilitate the positioning of a new floating landing stage. Route S cars terminated at Egremont, where there was an increased ferry service; RL cars worked to Egremont via Seacombe but returned to Liscard via Church Street, whilst the P and WD routes were combined to form a circular route linking Egremont with Poulton, Liscard and Harrison Drive. Another disruption of the service pattern was caused by a major fire in 1927 at the Gandy Belt factory, when heat melted the overhead in Wheatland Lane; the RL cars were diverted via Church Street and Falkland Road, the P terminated at Lloyd's Corner, and a shuttle operated between Lloyd's Corner and Liscard.

The financial year 1924-25 proved to be a watershed for Wallasey trams, when two proposals for tramway extensions were rejected in favour of buses. Firstly, a double track line was envisaged along Leasowe Road towards Moreton, which was to be incorporated into Wallasey in 1928. Leasowe Road

Liscard junction was partially relaid in March 1926 to include a double turnout from Seaview Road to Liscard Village, used for depot journeys. During the relaying tram service WD operated in two halves. (*Wirral Borough Libraries*)

was being improved, but was already traversed (since July 1920) by Crosville buses running into Wallasey Village from West Kirby via Hoylake, Moreton and Leasowe, connecting for a while with the P at St. John's Road. With the collapse of the Moreton tramway proposal, agreement was reached for Crosville to extend their buses to Liscard (The Queen's Arms) as from 13 April 1925, but they never succeeded during the tramway era in serving the ferry stations. In April 1928 Wallasey Corporation buses began running to Moreton, from both Seacombe and Liscard.

The other proposal was for a double track to be laid from a point off Poulton Road along Gorsey Lane, a new highway under construction to link up with Duke Street Bridge and Birkenhead. This would have created a link between the Birkenhead and Wallasey tramways, but the Dock Board refused to consider a cross-docks tramway over Duke Street Bridge. Still hemmed in by the dock estate, Wallasey turned to the more flexible motor bus, which could negotiate the dock estate unhindered, and made no further attempt to expand its tram system.

In the year 1924-25 the Borough Engineer's office produced a detailed plan for relaying virtually the entire tramway system over an eight-year period from 1925 to 1933, at a cost of £194,850. The programme provoked considerable debate both in and outside the Council chamber on the long-term future of the trams, and Lincoln began work on a policy document detailing the alternative of tramway abandonment. Meanwhile some urgent track renewals were done, as already detailed. Most of the work done in 1926, which included repainting all the poles, was designed to relieve unemployment.

The last proposals for new tracks were contained in the Corporation's 1927 Act, which authorised two tram sidings, neither of which were built. The first, 96 yards of single track in Queens Road on the north side of the Town Hall, was intended for use in

The last section of the Wallasey tramways to be relaid was Demesne Street in 1927. Trams used a temporary track during the work. The trams ran up Demesne Street towards the Town Hall; when buses took over, the flow was reversed.
(*Wirral Borough Libraries*)

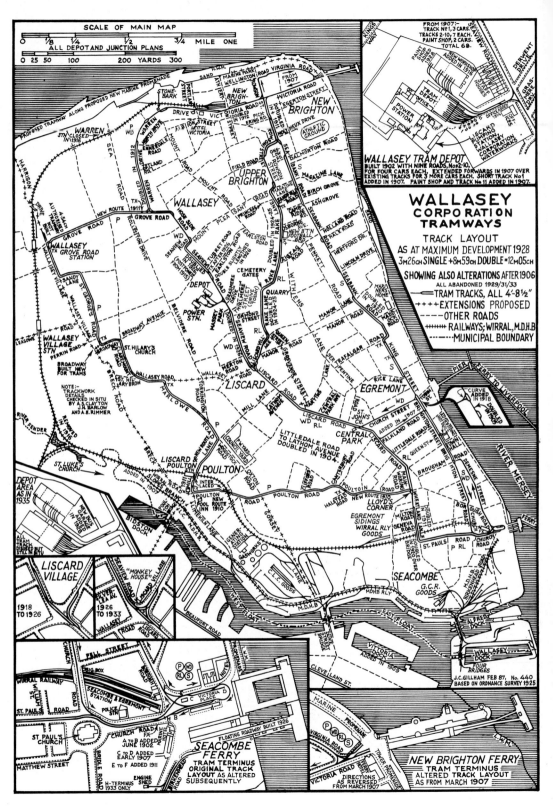

SCALE OF MAIN MAP
0 ⅛ ¼ ½ ¾ MILE ONE
ALL DEPOT AND JUNCTION PLANS
0 25 50 100 200 YARDS 300

FROM 1907:-
TRACK No 1, 3 CARS.
TRACKS 2-10, 7 EACH.
PAINT SHOP, 2 CARS.
TOTAL 68.

WALLASEY TRAM DEPOT
BUILT 1902 WITH NINE ROADS, Nos 2-10.
FOR FOUR CARS EACH. EXTENDED FORWARDS IN 1907 OVER
EXISTING TRACKS FOR 3 MORE CARS EACH. SHORT TRACK No 1
ADDED IN 1907. PAINT SHOP AND TRACK No 11 ADDED IN 1907.

WALLASEY CORPORATION TRAMWAYS

TRACK LAYOUT
AS AT MAXIMUM DEVELOPMENT 1928
3m 26ch SINGLE + 8m 59ch DOUBLE = 12m 05ch

SHOWING ALSO ALTERATIONS AFTER 1906
ALL ABANDONED 1929/31/33
TRAM TRACKS, ALL 4'-8½"
+ + + + EXTENSIONS PROPOSED
OTHER ROADS
RAILWAYS; WIRRAL, M.D.H.B
MUNICIPAL BOUNDARY

NOTE:-
TRACKWORK
DETAILS
CHECKED IN SITU
BY A.S. CLAYTON
J.N. BARLOW
AND A.E. RIMMER

BROADWAY
BUILT AS NEW
FOR TRAMS

LITTLEDALE ROAD
TO LATHOM AVENUE
DOUBLED IN 1904.

J.C. GILLHAM FEB 87, No. 440
BASED ON ORDNANCE SURVEY 1925

LISCARD VILLAGE
1918
TO 1926
1926
TO 1933

SEACOMBE FERRY
TRAM TERMINUS
ORIGINAL TRACK
LAYOUT AS ALTERED
SUBSEQUENTLY

A to B ADDED
JUNE 1902
C to D ADDED
EARLY 1907
E to F ADDED 1911
H-TERMINUS
1933 ONLY

NEW BRIGHTON FERRY
TRAM TERMINUS
ALTERED TRACK LAYOUT
AS FROM MARCH 1907
DIRECTIONS
AS REVERSED
FROM MARCH 1907

DEPOT
AREA
AS IN
1935

SUMMARY OF BOROUGH ENGINEER'S REPORT.

Priority	From	To	Via	Approximate financial year	Cost £
A	Liscard Village ....Mount Pleasant Road......Seaview Road			1925-26	15,900
B	Victoria Place ....Guinea Gap ....Demesne Street			1926-27	6,000
C	Seacombe Ferry ....Trafalgar Road ....Church Road, Brighton Street and King Street			1926-27	27,000
D	St. Paul's Church ....Liscard Road ....St. Paul's Road, Wheatland Lane, Mainwaring Road			1927-28	17,600
E	Trafalgar Road ....Virginia Road ....Seabank Road Rowson Street and Victoria Road			1927-28 1928-29	10,000 28,500
F	Mount Pleasant Road......Rowson Street ....Hose Side Road, Grove Road, Warren Drive and Victoria Road			1929-30 1930-31	28,000 4,000
G	Mainwaring Road ....Seabank Road ....Liscard Road, Liscard Village, Rake Lane and Rowson Street			1930-31 1931-32	24,000 24,600
H	Victoria Road ....Waterloo Road ....Rowson Street and Wellington Road			1931-32	2,200
I	Brighton Street ....Liscard Road ....Church Street			1932-33	4,600
J	Seacombe Ferry ....Birkenhead Road ....Victoria Place			1932-33	1,900
K	Rowson Street ....Victoria Road .... „ „			1932-33	550
	Total			8 years	194,850

connection with special functions. The second was for a 100-yard six-car siding in Harrison Drive to allow part-way and private hire cars to wait without obstructing other traffic; extra cars turning on the crossover were causing congestion. Some cars were sent up to Warren Drive to reverse. In the Parliamentary submission it was stated that 30,000 passengers were carried to Harrison Drive by trams and buses during the weekend of 10-11 July 1926 and at August Bank Holiday the figure was 100,000, the trams frequently carrying over 90 people. The duty inspector could only despatch a car every five minutes, to prevent two heavily-laden cars ascending Broadway in close proximity.

The last length of track to be relaid was Demesne Street during 1927, at a cost of £5,200. Completed in October, it incorporated a new junction at Brougham Road enabling southbound cars to reverse in Brighton Street, thus making the Town Hall siding unnecessary. The Ministry of Transport in 1927 sanctioned the borrowing of £16,000 to relay the Seabank Road line from Trafalgar Road through to New Brighton, including track-doubling, but the loan was never negotiated. Another proposal, to relay St. Paul's Road, Wheatland Lane and Mainwaring Road at a cost of £17,600, was postponed pending a decision on the future of the tramways. However, the worn-out curve from Wheatland Lane into St. Paul's Road was relaid for £180 in May 1929.

1927 was the year in which buses appeared on the tram routes on Sunday mornings. Demand for Sunday morning trams was small, and there were

Although Wallasey trams were profitable, it is unlikely that they could have recovered the cost of relaying the track, estimated in 1925 by the borough engineer at £194,850 spread over eight years. Wallasey opted for the cheaper solution of replacement by motor buses, starting in 1929.

also religious objections. An experimental Sunday morning bus service at 20 minute intervals was run in September 1925 between Lloyd's Corner and Harrison Drive via Poulton and Wallasey Village, but was withdrawn for lack of patronage. From 1 August to 21 October 1926 15-minute Sunday morning tram services were run on all four tram routes between Seacombe and New Brighton, and despite being unremunerative they were repeated from June to September in both 1927 and 1928. The buses were used in winter; from 27 October 1927 buses were run over tram route S to Molyneux Drive, WD to Hose Side Road (via Wheatland Lane) and P to Harrison Drive. From 4 March 1928 the Seabank Road journeys were extended to New Brighton (the first Corporation buses to reach the resort). The Poulton buses were discontinued with the opening of new bus routes to Moreton on 1 April 1928, and the Hose Side Road bus was not resumed in October 1928.

The buses continued to erode tramway traffic. From 12 September 1927 a peak hour limited stop bus service was started between Seacombe and Harrison Drive via Poulton Road and Breck Road, taking only 13 minutes compared with 18 minutes on the bus via Liscard and 23 minutes on the trams. The introduction of buses to Moreton on 1 April 1928 provided all-day competition for the Poulton trams.

One of the dummy clocks fitted to Wallasey trams after January 1929. Some of those plates were later transferred to buses. *(M. Jenkins collection)*

Bus fares were generally reduced from the same date and tram fares revised on 16 April to eliminate anomalies, two 2½d stages being reintroduced on route P. A month later the 1½d bus fare between Seacombe and Canterbury Road was discontinued, a 2d minimum fare being charged where buses duplicated trams. To revive Egremont Ferry's flagging fortunes, a new all-day bus service was started on 10 June 1928 between the ferry and Albion Street (Hotel Victoria) via Penkett Road and Mount Road; this extracted traffic from the WD and RL routes and to some extent from the S. Through bus and boat returns were introduced at 9d to encourage the further use of the ferry.

Trolleybuses

In July 1927 the first of several sub-Committees met under the chairmanship of Councillor Storey to consider the future of the trams and the respective merits and demerits of buses or trolleybuses. The manager had estimated in March that capital expenditure on the trams during the next five years would be £150,000 for new track and £24,000 for ten new cars. At this time the trolleybus was a serious contender for a prime role in local transport, and had the outspoken support of Councillor C. F. Rymer, an Independent member who was a motor dealer and held the agency for Tilling Stevens who had flirted briefly with the trolleybuses.

Rymer had tried to interest Wallasey previously in the trolleybus. He had set up a demonstration at Wigan in 1921, and arranged for the manager and members of the Committee to attend another at St. Helens on 26 November 1923. They were sufficiently impressed to ask him to organise a demonstration in Wallasey, and an AEC vehicle made a number of trips on 28 December 1923 along Brighton Street outside the Town Hall, with the positive boom on the tramway overhead and a negative skate trailing in the tram track.

Powers to operate trolleybuses as auxiliaries to the tramway system were included in the important Wallasey Corporation Act, 1927 which also authorised the annexure of Leasowe and Moreton and the construction of the new promenade between New Brighton and Harrison Drive. The trolleybus routes authorised were from New Brighton to Harrison Drive then via Wallasey Village, Perrin Road, Broadway, Broadway Avenue, Belvidere Road and Wallasey Road to Liscard Village, a branch along the eastern arm of Broadway Avenue into the depot, and a link along Belvidere Road, Rolleston Drive and Sea Road back to the promenade. The estimated cost for the five mile route was £32,000 including £11,200 for seven 36-seat vehicles, and fares were to be 1½d per mile. Only the Liscard-Harrison Drive section would have been operated throughout the

year, the remainder being seasonal, a highly unremunerative prospect.

No action was taken on this proposal, but in November 1929 Lincoln was asked to submit a report on the desirability of replacing the remaining trams and the Seabank Road buses with trolleybuses. He acknowledged that trolleybuses would continue to use municipally-produced electricity and their superior acceleration, silence and reliability, but condemned their inflexibility. He refuted arguments that the existing overhead poles could be re-used, and concluded by stating "In my opinion the Borough of Wallasey is not large enough for two distinct modes of transport and I would remind the Committee that we now have 56 motor buses." He added that to convert the S route to trolleybuses would have required 20 vehicles, plus special depot wiring, and there would have been limited use for surplus vehicle capacity ouside peak hours.

However, this was not the end of the matter as the Corporation decided in 1930 to apply for powers to operate trolleybuses in place of the trams. These were granted in the Wallasey Corporation Trolley Vehicles Order 1931, which authorised the use of trolleybuses on all the original tram routes and on a number of other roads which would have been useful as turning loops or alternative routes, viz. Borough Road, Oxton Road, Woodstock Road, Torrington Road and St. Hilary Brow. The appearance of the statutory notices on the traction poles created the impression that the trolleybuses might appear at any moment. This Order envisaged a trolleybus fleet equal in size to the tram fleet — 77 vehicles — and empowered the Corporation to borrow £154,000 for purchase of trolleybuses and £26,103 for overhead and other equipment.

Despite continued fact-finding expeditions to trolleybus systems such as Wolverhampton, the powers were never exercised. The success of the motor bus undertaking and the lack of interest in trolleybuses shown by neighbouring Birkenhead put an end to these schemes. The arrival in Wallasey of efficient and comfortable motor buses epitomised first by the Leyland Lion and then the Leyland Titan inevitably influenced the debate on the future of the trams, and in the year when the last tram ran the title of the undertaking was changed to Wallasey Corporation Motors.

Due to worn-out track the Seabank Road trams (route S) were replaced by buses from 20 January 1929. This photograph shows the poor condition of the recently abandoned track. The poles remained in use for street lighting and for possible trolleybus operation. *(Wirral Borough Libraries)*

The last innovation on the tramways was the provision in April 1927 of postal boxes on cars leaving New Brighton at about 9.30pm. They were attached to the front dash, and people would gather at stops to post their letters. They were a feature of Wallasey operation until about 1935.

The End of the Trams

On 11 July 1928 the Tramways Committee recommended that owing to the dangerous condition of the Seabank Road track, the S should be replaced by motor buses from 1 January 1929. The Seabank Road track had carried an intensive service of up to 36 cars on a 2.63 mile route. The Council ratified the decision, with little opposition. There can be relatively few other examples of an undertaking abandoning its heaviest line first, and within a year the trams, no longer sustained by route S, were said to be running at a loss, whilst bus passengers had increased by 300% since 1927. The trams were displaced by 18 lowbridge Leyland Titan buses, whose delivery was slightly delayed; the last tram ran on Saturday 19 January 1929, with departures from New Brighton at 11.27pm and from Seacombe to Victoria Road only (car 53) at 11.57pm. The poles and overhead were left intact with a view to future

trolleybus operation, but the track from Trafalgar Road to Molyneux Drive was lifted, starting in March 1930. Action was soon taken to widen parts of Seabank Road, as it was discovered that two buses had difficulty in passing each other at some points. On a number of occasions the buses had to be diverted to allow the disused track to be lifted.

The bus fares were again revised to coincide with the conversion of route S, penny stages being introduced on all bus routes except the express to Harrison Drive. Scholars tickets and parcel tickets were not continued on the buses, but after a series of complaints following their withdrawal, workmen's tickets were re-introduced at 2d single and 4d return if purchased before 7am. From 1 December 1930 the workmen's returns were issued at single fare, and by March 1931 their availability on both trams and buses was extended to vehicles leaving any terminus before 7.40am.

In the financial year 1927-28 the S cars had carried nearly 6,500,000 passengers; in the financial year 1929-30 the number using the replacing buses had dropped to 5,900,000. This was ascribed to changing travel patterns, the increased use of motor cars and the availability of combined bus/ferry fares at Egremont. The three remaining tram routes were the next highest carriers, with about four million each, followed by the Manor Road bus route at 2.5 million.

The track in Brighton Street, Falkland Road and along Warren Drive was now worn out and proposals were made during 1930 to curtail the tram service. The section of route P along Grove Road from Harrison Drive to Warren Drive was unremunerative, and might also have been abandoned but for its usefulness as a depot access line. The Corporation wished to serve Belvidere Road, the residents of which had been agitating for public transport since 1925, and curtailment of the WD tram route was delayed while Belvidere Road and Rolleston Drive were reconstructed for buses.

The date was set for 1 January 1931, but shortage of vehicles and non-completion of road works forced its postponement until 29 March 1931, when the WD and P routes were rearranged as a Circular between Seacombe and Grove Road via Wheatland Lane, Liscard Road, Seaview Road, Grove Road and along the P route back to Seacombe and vice versa. A ten minute service was provided in each direction with a circular fare of 5d. Outbound cars in both directions showed "Grove Road" with "Only" blanked out, except on Bank Holidays when they showed "Harrison Drive", also without the "Only." All cars working to and from Grove Road via Poulton showed P, and via Liscard WD. The route mileage had been reduced to just over eight miles, but officially there were still 58 trams in stock. In practice most of the unrebuilt non-vestibule cars had been stripped with a view to their sale as huts or sheds.

Route numbers were allocated to the bus services from 1 January 1931, the former S having become 1. A new bus route 6 ran between Seacombe and

New Brighton, covering the WD between Seacombe and Mill Lane and again between Grove Road and New Brighton. The buses used Church Street in both directions and one of the authors, then attending Church Street school, remembers the headmistress deploring the passing of the trams and exhorting the children to take care because of the higher speed of the buses and the fact that they ran both ways. At about this time, the remaining overhead along Seabank Road was removed, but many poles survived for street lighting until the 1960s. Track lifting after the 1931 abandonment cost £19,000, including the laying of plain track at the former Warren Drive/Grove Road junction. Cars damaged in collisions were now withdrawn and cannibalised for spare parts and those still running looked unkempt and neglected.

With the circular tram service now running via Wheatland Lane there were two routes running together every ten minutes between Seacombe and Liscard Village, but this rather wasteful arrangement was tolerated as a temporary measure. The replacement of the RL envisaged for late 1931 was delayed because of an accident in August 1931 involving one of the Corporation's six-wheel Karrier double deck buses in which a woman passenger fell through the floor trap on to the propeller shaft with fatal consequences. All eight six-wheel Karriers (six double deck and two single deck) were withdrawn from service and before they could be replaced the provisions of the Road Traffic Act 1930 took full effect and the backlog of applications for road service licences was such that the cars could not be withdrawn on the re-arranged date of 31 December 1932, as the licence for a bus service had not been granted by the Traffic Commissioners. In the event the last RL cars ran on Saturday 4 February 1933, leaving New Brighton at 11.15pm and Seacombe at 11.42pm.

With the abandonment of route RL, the remaining Circle trams terminated at the crossover in Church Road, and no longer used the track on the south side of Victoria Place leading to Seacombe ferry; the north side tracks had been discontinued in June 1932. The reason in both cases was the reconstruction of the ferry terminal. Responding to a Government circular asking Councils to submit estimates for major capital projects which could alleviate unemployment, Wallasey Council had responded with a plan to rebuild Victoria Place and Seacombe ferry terminal buildings for £107,000, towards which the Unemployment Grants Committee contributed £27,000. Started in 1930, the impressive terminal with its bus departure barriers on the south side towards which the vehicles reversed to stand in herringbone fashion was opened on 10 April 1933. It allowed passengers to transfer from boat to bus under cover.

The bus service (No 14) which replaced the RL tram at first ran to and from Seacombe only at peak hours; at other times passengers from Rake Lane changed at Liscard either to the WD car or the No 2 bus via Manor Road. Patronage along Rake Lane declined as dissatisfied passengers walked down to Seabank Road. Following complaints to the Traffic Commissioners, through running was introduced all day from 17 May 1933.

The tramway service now required twelve cars all day with six more at rush hours. All remaining unvestibuled cars were withdrawn, and while they were being dismantled in and around the depot an unusual 'collision' occurred on 23 May 1933 when bus 55 was reversed into the body of No 23. On another occasion a depot man breaking up a top deck inadvertently sawed through the piece that held up the canopy on which he was standing, and fell into the pit; fortunately he was not seriously injured.

Inevitably, the buses did not show up well in fog, and there were several tram/bus collisions. In February 1930 bus 36 struck car 63 in Church Street and car 70 was hit by bus 20 in Victoria Road. In December bus 59 was severely damaged by tram 59 in a crash at the Victoria Road junction (bus repairs £120, tram repairs 25s.) In the dense fog that blanketed the town on 12 November 1933 the trams again proved their superiority over the buses, losing only 5.17% of their daily mileage as against 23.69% for the buses. The last tram/bus collision happened on 4 October 1933, when car 60 damaged bus 76; both were returned to service.

The End of the Trams

Wallasey Corporation decided to operate its last trams on Thursday 30 November 1933. There was to be no ceremonial last car, and plans to revive the illuminated car were dropped. Throughout the last day, people made sentimental last journeys, keeping their tickets for posterity. 25 trams were available for use on the last day.

Four cars lined up at Church Road crossover, Seacombe for the final departure at 11.57pm. No 57 preceded by No 63 was to return to the depot via route WD, whilst 68 preceded by 67 was to travel via route P. No 68 would therefore be the last car to enter the depot, and became the official Last Car. The rostered driver was J. M. McElroy, a former horse car driver, but for the last trip he handed over to E T

No. 37 on the south side of Victoria Place, Seacombe in the summer of 1932. By this time the north side tracks had been abandoned and the RL was the only tram route still serving New Brighton. Former radial-truck 'long car' 37 was retrucked in 1925 on a Smith pendulum truck.
(M. J. O'Connor)

WALLASEY'S LAST TRAM ROUTE

After route RL closed on 4 February 1933, the only remaining tram service was the Liscard and Poulton Circle. In these July 1933 photographs, No. 52 is shown passing No. 66 in Liscard Village (No. 66's destination indicator shows 'Grove Road'), No. 78 passes the former junction with Warren Drive, and car 52 is about to pass 51 at the foot of Broadway near St. Hilary's Church in Wallasey Village. The tower on the right dates from 1530.
(H. Hughes)

(Courtesy J. B. Horne)

Davies who had driven the first electric tram 31 years earlier.

Watched by a small crowd, Nos 57, 63 and 67 pulled away at 11.57pm, but No 68 blew her circuit breaker, delaying her departure until the ferry clock struck midnight. Aboard were some 60 passengers including a handful of local enthusiasts together with the Mayor, H T Hall, the Chairman of the Motor Bus Committee (redesignated thus in April 1933), Alderman Storey, Alderman Panter Brick, the Town Clerk and the General Manager. The car wound its way through Poulton and Wallasey Village, passing small knots of people en route, and at Grove Road a score of employees boarded the car for the last half mile to the depot. A noisy well-behaved crowd surrounded the car at the depot entrance as photographs were taken, and finally No 68 disappeared into the depot for the last time. It was 12.40am on 1 December 1933.

The Circular service had been only a temporary measure, and was not perpetuated by the replacing buses, which reverted to much the same route as the original WD and P trams between Seacombe and New Brighton, route 16 via Church Street, Seaview Road and Warren Drive and route 17 via Poulton and Wallasey Village. There was some duplication with existing bus services, and several changes were made to these during 1934 to improve results.

For the next few months, the cars continued to move under their own power in the depot. The remaining trams including the works car were offered for sale and were eventually acquired for scrap by Grahamsleys of Newcastle-upon-Tyne in March 1934. The Council refused to allow the firm to sell any of the bodies locally, which delayed their removal. The depot was finally cleared on 3 December 1934 after the bulk of the bodies had been sold to a dealer in North Wales who then resold them individually at £5 a saloon, many still surviving today. Some bodies from cars 1-40 were retained by the Corporation for conversion to bus shelters.

Some poles were uplifted and sold for £2 each, but many were retained to carry street lighting. Some track was lifted, and £600 worth of track, crossings and junction material was sold to Blackburn Corporation. However, the high cost of removal and road reinstatement persuaded the Council to leave much of the track *in situ* and covered over, to re-emerge subsequently during road resurfacing as reminders of the long-abandoned tramways.

The trams had carried a total of 430,724,689 people, earning £2,432,918 and operating 35,552,632 miles. Capital expenditure had totalled £331,151, comprising trams £69,610, permanent way £169,302, overhead and electrical equipment £40,580, build-

ings and fixtures £23,242; the discrepancy between these totals presumably represents sale of assets. The Council resolved that the tramway liabilities should be transferred to the bus account and that the cost of removing rails and the unproductive debt on the track and electrical equipment would be paid out of the bus reserve fund. Total liabilities met from motor bus profits amounted to £111,000.

With the growth in motor car traffic and the opening of the Mersey road tunnel in July 1934, which included a dock branch close to the Wallasey boundary, the northern ferries suffered an irreversible loss of traffic in the winter months. Both closed down in October 1936, not re-opening until Easter, a pattern which continued until the outbreak of war in 1939 when Egremont was closed altogether as a 'temporary' measure; the pier was severely damaged in 1941 and it was never reopened. New Brighton soldiered on during the season and after the war it enjoyed a considerable revival, with boats operating every few minutes on fine days in the late 1940s and early 1950s.

Faced by dwindling traffic and increasing problems with drifting sandbanks, the New Brighton ferry closed for good in September 1971, the pier being subsequently dismantled together with the amusement pier. The cross-river luggage boats from Seacombe to Liverpool, reprieved because of the war, last operated on 31 March 1947, leaving only the passenger ferry. Wallasey Corporation's compact network of bus routes was absorbed into the Merseyside Passenger Transport Executive on 1 December 1969, the familiar Wallasey primrose and cream giving way to a livery combining Wallasey's cream with Birkenhead's blue. Prior to handover bus route 17 (ex tram P) was withdrawn in 1965 largely without replacement, due to lack of patronage. Routes 14 and 16 (ex-RL and WD) survived virtually unaltered until 1986, still linking Seacombe ferry to New Brighton, though at lower frequencies. Route 1 (ex tram S) has been combined to form a through route to Birkenhead. The MPTE successfully introduced greater through working between Wallasey, Birkenhead and Moreton, with former Wallasey routes being extended to serve Hoylake and West Kirby, thus fulfilling the early ambitions of the old Corporation.

Postscript

A Wallasey Tramcar Preservation Group was formed in 1970 to restore one of the Brush built cars, using the lower saloon of car 52 and parts from several others and adding new platforms, stairs and upper deck. A truck was acquired from Brussels in 1973. Tragically the restored lower deck of 52 was destroyed by fire at Leasowe Castle on 5 November 1978, probably a malicious act. The truck was sold to the Black Country Museum where it has subsequently been shortened and regauged for use under a Dudley & Stourbridge single-decker. More recently the Merseyside Tramway Preservation Society have secured the lower saloon of Wallasey's highest-numbered tram, No 78, with a view to long-term restoration as the last Bellamy-roof tram ever built in Britain; it is safely stored in Liverpool Museum's large exhibits store at Prince's dock.

Newly-delivered cars of series 1-20 await the start of electric service in Seaview Road depot early in 1902. The first 30 passenger cars were standard Dick, Kerr products mounted on Brill 21E trucks.
(Wallasey Council Tramways)

Restored crown board from Wallasey car No. 52 *(Courtesy M. Jenkins)*

10 The Wallasey Tram Fleet

Although smaller in both area and population than its neighbour, Wallasey eventually boasted a bigger tram fleet than Birkenhead — 77 passenger cars, compared with 65. Unlike those in Birkenhead, all the Wallasey cars had a strong family resemblance, differences being confined to matters of detail. The first 30 cars were delivered in 1902-03 with open top decks, but one of them was given a top cover in 1903 before entering service. Impressed by the increased revenue from this car, the Council approved the covering of the whole fleet, which was completed by May 1905 making Wallasey one of the first systems to eliminate open top cars. All the top covers were of the 'Bellamy' type with unroofed open end sections to the upper deck, and the appearance and appointments of the cars thereafter changed very little over the years. Wallasey was the last tramway to place new cars of this type in service (in 1920) and probably the last to operate a tram fleet made up entirely of Bellamy-roof tramcars. Lt-Col Greene was accused of perpetuating an outmoded design, but said that the public preferred open balcony cars in the summer. The traffic figures to and from New Brighton suggest that he was right.

Nos. 1-25 E R & T C W Ltd, Preston
Four-wheel double deck open top 1902

Wallasey's first electric trams were double deck open top four wheel cars with three windows per side, built by the Electric Railway & Tramway Carriage Works Ltd. at Preston to that firm's standard design, known then as the Liverpool type.

In Wallasey they were latterly referred to as the "Little Cars" or "Dick Kerrs." Nos. 1-20 were delivered between January and May 1902, Nos. 21-25 in October 1902. They were 27ft 5in long over fenders, with saloons 16ft 0in long over corner pillars and 5ft 0in platforms, and weighed 7 tons 17 cwt. Other dimensions were width 7ft 1in, interior height 6ft 9in, height to trolley plank 9ft 9½in, wheelbase 6ft 0in, wheel diameter 30in. The electrical equipment was supplied by Dick, Kerr & Co Ltd., Preston and comprised two DK25A 25hp motors, and two Dick Kerr DE1 Form B controllers with electric short-circuit emergency brake; normal braking was by hand. The trucks were of the Brill 21E type made in the USA and had chilled iron wheels.

The car bodies were constructed of oak and ash, the ceiling having three white panels with oak surrounds lined out in gold and brown. The stairs were of the Bellamy 90-degree reversed type, rising clockwise from near the bulkhead to the outer end of the balcony. This design was disliked by the Board of Trade as it severely restricted the driver's left hand view, but it had the advantage that any passenger falling downstairs merely struck the bulkhead rather than falling in the road. The cars seated 22 inside on oak-ribbed longitudinal seats, and 34 upstairs on transverse reversible garden seats. All interior wood was highly polished, with some ornamental features; there were green curtains with stitched gold tassels, and green patterned Wilton seat carpets interwoven with the monogram "W. C. T." The WCT emblem was also engraved into the glass of both lower saloon

No. 22, one of the second delivery, passing Wallasey Central Hospital in Liscard Road displaying "Via Rake Lane." Unlike most tramways, the indicator boxes on Wallasey trams from 1902 to the early 1920s showed the route instead of the destination. *(Commercial postcard)*

Wallasey Corporation Electric Tramcar Fleet

Car Numbers	Type (as built)	Year built	Builder	Seats	Truck	Motors	Controllers
1-25	Open top (note a)	1902	ER & TCW	22/34 (a)	Brill 21E	DK 25A 2 × 25hp	DK DE1 Form B
26	Works car, ex-water car	1902 (rebt. 1905)	ER & TCW	—	Brill 21E	DK 25A 2 × 25hp	DK DE1 Form B
27-31	Open top (note b)	1903	ER & TCW	22/34 (a)	Brill 21E	DK 25A 2 × 25hp	DK DE1 Form B
32-36	Top covered, Bellamy roof	1905	UEC	22/38	Brill 21E	DK 3A (d) 2 × 35hp	DK DB1 Form C
37-41	Top Covered, Bellamy roof	1907	UEC	24/38	M & G Radial (note c)	DK 3A (d) 2 × 35hp	DK DB1 Form C
42-51	Top covered, Bellamy roof	1910	Brush	22/38	Brush flexible	Brush 1204E 2 × 40hp	Brush 8B
52-56	Top covered, Bellamy roof	1911	Brush	22/38	Brush flexible	Brush 1204E 2 × 40hp	Brush 8B
57-62	Top covered, Bellamy roof	1913	Brush	22/38	Brush flexible	Brush 1204E 2 × 40hp	Brush 8B
63-68	Top covered, Bellamy roof	1915	Brush	26/40	Peckham Pendulum P22	Brush 1210J 2 × 45hp	Brush 8B
69-78	Top covered, Bellamy roof	1920	Brush	26/42?	Peckham Pendulum P22	Brush 1210J 2 × 45hp	Brush 8B

Seating figures shown thus: 22/34 are for lower and upper decks respectively.

Notes
(a) Cars 1-25 top-covered by Milnes Voss 1903-1905, seating increased to 22/38
(b) No 27 top-covered by Milnes Voss before entering service, 28-31 top-covered later in 1903. Seating increased to 22/38.
(c) No 41 retrucked with UEC Flexible Axle truck 1911: 37 with Smith pendulum truck 1925; 38-40 with Peckham P22 type 1925/26.
(d) The DK 3A motors appear in Wallasey's own records as DK 35A.

Key to Manufacturers
Brill - The J G Brill Co, Philadelphia, USA.
BTH - The British Thomson-Houston Co Ltd, Rugby.
Brush - The Brush Electrical Engineering Co Ltd, Loughborough.
DK - Dick, Kerr & Co Ltd, Preston.
ER & TCW - The Electric Railway & Tramway Carriage Works Ltd, Preston.
GE - The General Electric Company, Schenectady, USA.
Hurst Nelson - Hurst Nelson & Co Ltd, Motherwell, Scotland.
McGuire - The McGuire Manufacturing Co Ltd, Bury, Lancs.
Milnes - George F. Milnes & Co Ltd, Birkenhead and Hadley.
Milnes Voss - G C Milnes, Voss & Co Ltd, Birkenhead.
M & G - Mountain & Gibson Ltd, Bury, Lancs.
Peckham - Peckham Truck & Engineering Co Ltd.
Siemens - Siemens Brothers Dynamo Works Ltd, Stafford
UEC - United Electric Car Co Ltd, Preston.

doors. Bell cords ran the length of the lower saloon and there were 16 straps for standing passengers. There were three lighting circuits with six pale blue lamps downstairs, and two oyster lamps on the top deck. Originally some cars had insubstantial two-bar lifeguards but these were quickly replaced by Tidswell lifeguards, though Wilson and Bennett lifeguards were also tried on some cars during 1902.

The R. W. Blackwell trolley standard was slightly off-set from the top deck centre-line and contained an internal spring. The upper deck was surrounded by two guard rails intermeshed with wire netting. In September 1902 five cars were fitted with Brawn's patent 'dry seats' as used at Birkenhead, and in October the others were provided with canvas knee-aprons, the invention of Captain C. H. Kemp of Falkland Road. These tarpaulin covers hung from the rear of the seat when not in use, and were rolled up neatly in summer. Unfortunately, they were prone to vandalism and the Tramways Committee expressed concern at the fact that several had been "wantonly damaged."

Capt. Kemp had also designed a collapsible top deck cover, which was fitted experimentally to a car in December 1902, being erected within the existing upper deck railings. It had a flat roof, outside slung saloon door and no glass, the window spaces being protected by canvas blinds which could be lowered in wind and rain. As in the case of a similar experiment in Liverpool, the blinds proved incapable of withstanding the ravages of a Mersey gale and the cover was soon dismantled.

Nos 27-31 E R & T C W Ltd. Preston
Four wheel double deck open top 1903

To carry the growing traffic, five more cars identical with Nos 1-25 were ordered from the same manufacturer in March 1903. The Tramways Committee considered the provision of 'a light adjustable cover for the upper deck' but accepted the quotation of Dick Kerr to build the cars with open tops at a cost of £580 per car. They declined Dick Kerr's offer to provide "Bellamy round-roof canopies" as used in Liverpool for an additional £85, preferring instead the Milnes, Voss top cover which cost only £56, including dismantling if unsatisfactory. The Board of Trade requested that the new cars should be built with the safer 180-degree reversed stairs, folding steps and trigger lifeguards. The Council acceded only to the latter request, specifying the successful Tidswell lifeguard. Nos 28-31 entered service in June in their open top condition, whilst Milnes, Voss workmen converted No 27 into Wallasey's first permanently top covered tram.

After considering the enclosed-end type of top cover used in Sheffield, the Committee opted for open balconies, a solid Bellamy style roof (without the sliding panels chosen in Liverpool), outside slung doors, a roof-mounted trolley base and the Magrini arrangement whereby the window frames could be wound down simultaneously to simulate an open car in warm weather. The final price including two Eros ventilators for extracting tobacco smoke was £57.6s. It was agreed that the cover would be placed on the first new car to arrive.

After a three day trial with the cover in place, No 27 entered revenue service on 11 August 1903 and six weeks later Greene advised that its earning capacity was 1.9 pence per car mile more than the rest of the fleet. His 1903-04 report described Wallasey's version of the Bellamy top cover in some detail. "The cover is constructed to give the greatest possible headroom and also ventilation and has the advantage of being the lightest arrangement of roof covering of a permanent type yet produced. The inside of the roof is boarded with pitch pine boards, handsomely varnished and in order to keep the top clear of smoke when the cover is closed, two Eros ventilators are fitted. The ends which are oak and ash, handsomely panelled, are fitted with sliding doors similar to those on the saloons. The sides which are of mahogany are fitted with three windows to harmonise with those in the car body and operated in one length by the conductor by means of racks, pinion wheels and spindles. This method has proved entirely satisfactory as it does away with disputes which so constantly occur between passengers when windows work independently."

Nos 28-31, the rest of the 1903 batch, were top-covered by October at £64 per car, giving an overall height of 16ft 2½in. The seating was increased to 60 (lower saloon 22, upper saloon 32, plus six on balconies). Ten of the earlier cars were fitted similarly during the winter at £62 each, the first conversions being Nos 16-20, and by the end of the year the use of top-covered cars had increased overall earning capacity by 0.6 pence per car mile. By 31 March 1905 26 cars had been top-covered, and the remaining four were completed shortly afterwards, the last being No 15. The total programme cost just under £2,500, bringing the expenditure on Nos 1-25 and 27-31 to £683 per car. All thirty original cars were now top-covered, and formed a single class. Nos 27-31 had slightly flatter roofs than Nos 1-25.

In 1906 Nos 2, 10, 12, 17, and 25 were damaged by fire at Seaview Road depot and repaired, as were 4 and 14 after their runaway accidents. In 1907-08 additional spiral springs were fitted between body and truck to carry the extra weight of the top covers. The car frames were also strengthened to prevent platform sag. Other modifications carried out over the years included the fitting of five-bar balcony rails, and (in postwar rehabilitation) some cars received new roofs and one-piece waist and rocker panels; in thirteen cars wood was substituted for the quarter lights above the upper deck bulkhead windows. No 23 is reported to have been mounted at some time on a different type of Dick, Kerr truck.

In 1924 seven cars of this class were withdrawn, including 1, 7, 8, 21 and 31, of which three including 31 were later returned to service. In 1924/5 Nos 3, 5, 11, 13 and 31's trucks were lengthened to 7ft or 7ft 6in wheelbase. Nos 9, 12, 15, 16, 19 and 20 were withdrawn in 1929 and Nos 4, 6, 14, 17, 18, 22, 24, 25, 27, 28, 29 and 30 in financial year 1930/31, leaving Nos 2, 3, 5, 10, 11, 13, 23 and 31 in stock until 1933. The bodies were dismantled and sold, including six lower and six upper saloons to the West Cheshire Golf Club. Some were used by the Corporation as

bus shelters, of which No 18 survived at the top of Church Street until 1983, and No 24 was used as a cricket pavilion at Oldershaw School; the dismantled parts have been kept.

Nos 32-36 United Electric Car Co Ltd, Preston
Four-wheel double deck, short top cover 1905

These top covered cars with three windows per side and open balconies were completed and delivered in December 1905 and entered service in February 1906. They were built by the United Electric Car Co Ltd (successors to the E R & T C W), a subsidiary of Dick, Kerr by which name the cars were known in Wallasey. They were similar in most respects to their (modified) predecessors, but had slightly longer platforms (5ft 3in), bringing their overall length to 27ft 8in. The top covers were fitted with inside slung doors; there were four scoop ventilators above the lower saloon windows, and no Eros ventilators. The total cost was £3,000 or £600 per car.

These cars were more powerful than Nos 1-31, having Dick, Kerr DK3A 35hp motors, again in Brill 21E 6ft wheelbase trucks. They were equipped with the more modern DK DB1 Form C controllers which included five notches of rheostatic braking. They had 180 degree reversed stairs, and Hudson Bowring lifeguards. Seat carpets and curtains were again provided in the lower saloon, and elongated

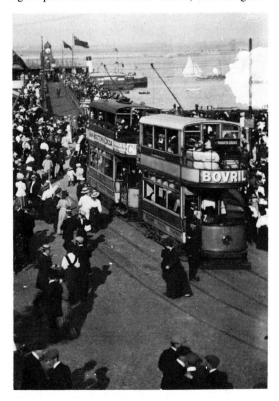

Wallasey 32-36 were built with top covers fairly similar to those added to the original cars but more strongly built, with shallower roofs and inside-hung doors. This 1907-8 view at New Brighton also shows other detail differencies between the two batches of Dick, Kerr cars including variations in the livery. (Wallasey Council Tramways)

tong gates fitted on each platform as on the earlier cars; these were removed by 1914. At least one of the class had ornate wrought iron balcony rails. Slipper brakes worked from a hand-wheel concentric with the handbrake staff were fitted to 32, 35 and 36 in 1911 for relief work on the Poulton route and probably also to 33-34, since these cars were occasionally used as snowploughs and had to cover all parts of the system.

32 and 36 were included in the 1924-25 rehabilitation programme and lasted until February 1933, but 33, 34, and 35 were withdrawn from passenger service in 1929 and possibly retained as snowploughs. Some bodies were used as bus shelters, but no survivors are known.

Nos 37-41 United Electric Car Co Ltd, Preston
Four-wheel double deck, short top cover 1907

These cars were longer than the previous batches, with four window saloons measuring 17ft 2in over corner pillars and an overall length over fenders of 28ft 10in, with 5ft 3in platforms; other dimensions were as for 32-36. They seated 24 downstairs, 32 upstairs plus six on balconies, a total of 62, and had two DK3A 35hp motors and two Dick Kerr DB1

Car 37 of series 37-41 was built by UEC in 1907 on a Mountain & Gibson 8 ft 6 in radial truck. The trucks were unsuccessful and all five cars were eventually retrucked. The Wallasey UDC crest and title were applied to all cars delivered up to the time when Wallasey became a Burrough in 1910. *(Wallasey Council Tramways)*

Form C controllers. The stairs were again 180-degree reversed, and they were the last cars to be delivered with open platforms; ornate wrought iron grilles linked the bulkhead with the dashplate. Four scoop ventilators per side were provided, and hinged half-lights above the lower saloon windows. The cars had the usual seat carpets and tong gates, but differed from all other batches in having brown leather window blinds, cut-glass lampshades (with ordinary, not blue bulbs) and had a ventilation panel in the upper portion of the saloon doors. They were built in 1907 and entered service in February 1908, costing £3,281.15s., or £656.7s. per car.

Nos 37-41 had Mountain and Gibson 8ft 6in wheelbase radial trucks, chosen no doubt to give better support to the long body than the short wheelbase trucks of the older cars. The M & G Radial was a design which allowed the axles a certain amount of play, in theory easing cornering and reducing oscillation, noise and wear and tear. In practice, unless the track was in excellent condition both axles had a tendency not to revert to the parallel position, which shortened the life of both wheels and track. To the Wallasey staff the cars were known as "Long Toms" or "Bogie Cars." Despite the problems involved in fitting track brakes to radial trucks, slipper brakes were added to all five in 1911.

In the same year, the UEC Co were asked for their advice on the radial trucks, as the axle boxes were causing constant problems. They recommended

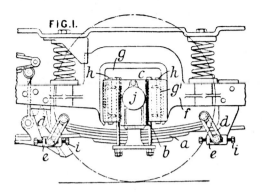
Below: Axlebox suspension of the 1910 Brush Long base truck (also known as Brush Flexible) fitted to Wallasey 42-62. The wheelbase was 7 ft 6 in.

FIG.1.

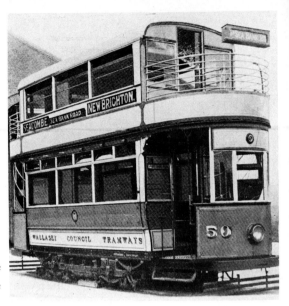

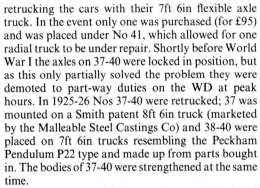
Right: Nos. 42-51, built by Brush in 1910, were the first Wallasey trams to be fitted with partial driver's windscreens. They were built to work the Poulton route, for which track brakes were required, and Spencer slipper brakes were fitted to their Brush trucks. No. 50's livery when new was apple green and cream. *(Wallasey Council Tramways)*

retrucking the cars with their 7ft 6in flexible axle truck. In the event only one was purchased (for £95) and was placed under No 41, which allowed for one radial truck to be under repair. Shortly before World War I the axles on 37-40 were locked in position, but as this only partially solved the problem they were demoted to part-way duties on the WD at peak hours. In 1925-26 Nos 37-40 were retrucked; 37 was mounted on a Smith patent 8ft 6in truck (marketed by the Malleable Steel Castings Co) and 38-40 were placed on 7ft 6in trucks resembling the Peckham Pendulum P22 type and made up from parts bought in. The bodies of 37-40 were strengthened at the same time.

Cars 37-41 were withdrawn when route RL closed in February 1933. The lower saloons of 37-39 became bus shelters and the others were sold. The lower saloon of 40 survives in North Wales, its upper deck having been dismantled on a Wirral farm and the parts stored for possible use in preservation schemes.

Nos 42-51 Brush Electrical Engineering Co Ltd
Four-wheel double deck, short top cover 1910

Additional cars would be required in 1910 to work the Poulton route, and an order for ten was placed in October 1909 with the Brush Electrical Engineering Co Ltd of Loughborough at £592 each; the final cost including extras was £648.8s.3d. per car. They were three-window cars with 16ft bodies, 28ft 4in long over fenders, with 5ft 6in platforms. Interior saloon height was 6ft 7in, overall height 16ft 1in, width 7ft 2in and weight 10 tons 17 cwt. Seating was for 22 downstairs and 32 upstairs, plus six on balconies. The corner seats upstairs were fixed, backing on to the bulkheads. Known to the staff as "Glass-Enders"

150

these were the first to be fitted with partial weather-screens, 42-51 having a three-paned version which led to complaints from drivers of draughts whistling round their necks. The open balconies were enclosed by six parallel guard rails, and the stairs were again of the 180 degree reversed type. The cars were delivered in March and April 1910.

The Brush company also supplied the electrical equipment, consisting of two Brush 1204E motors of 40 horsepower, and two Brush 8B controllers. The truck was the Brush 7ft 6in wheelbase flexible type with semi-elliptical leaf springs under the axle-boxes; these were later removed, the trucks becoming rigid-type. In addition to the usual hand and rheostatic braking, Spencer slipper brakes were fitted at £10.15s. a pair, and worked from a wheel on the platform; the brake blocks were usually oak, and were often renewed daily. As a further precaution for operating down Broadway, "automatic run-back preventers" were fitted at £6.10s. per car; details of this equipment have not survived.

Few changes were made to these cars during their lives and all ten lasted until 1933, 42, 43, 45 and 51 being withdrawn in February, the rest in November. All were sold in 1934 to Messrs Grahamsleys, who dismantled them and sold the saloons for further use. The lower saloon of 45 was dismantled in 1972 for spares for use in preservation schemes.

Nos 52-56 Brush Electrical Engineering Co Ltd
Four-wheel double deck, short top cover 1911

More cars were found necessary after the February 1911 opening of the extension to Warren Drive and an order for five was placed in March with the Brush Company at Loughborough. They were similar to 42-51 except for having four-paned ves-

Two batches of Wallasey trams had five-window top covers with Laycocks' individually-opening frameless windows, Nos. 52-56 of 1911 and Nos. 57-62 of 1913. They had Brush bodies and Brush Flexible trucks. By March 1929, when this view of No. 61 was taken at Seacombe Ferry, the flexible axlebox gear had been removed. (*Dr. Hugh Nicol*)

tibules, but the price had risen to £753.12s. per car, the batch costing £3,768.4s.2d. £16 per car of this was accounted for by fitting five independently operated self-balancing frameless windows patented by Laycocks instead of the usual Magrini geared equipment. 54 was permanently wired as the illuminated car, described on page 125. At 11 tons 8 cwt they were slightly heavier than 42-51.

Nos 52-56 remained in stock until closure in November 1933 and were then sold to Messrs Grahamsleys, who sold the saloons for further use. That of 52 was rescued for preservation in 1971 (plus parts from 53's upper saloons) but after being partially restored it was destroyed by fire at Leasowe.

Nos 57-62 Brush Electrical Engineering Co Ltd
Four-wheel double deck, short top cover 1913

These six cars were ordered in October 1912 to cope with the increasing traffic and were delivered in January 1913. Their cost was lower at £688.9s.2d. yet they were identical in all respects with 52-56. They lasted until 1933 and were then sold to Messrs

Grahamsleys. The lower saloons of Nos 56 and 57 survived in North Wales until the 1970s.

Nos 63-68 Brush Electrical Engineering Co Ltd
Four-wheel double deck, short top cover 1915

The original specification for these six cars, issued in 1914, was for short bodies similar to those of 52-62 and mounted on 7ft 0in trucks. The design was then changed to provide longer four-window bodies on Peckham Pendulum 7ft 6in wheelbase trucks, increasing the length to 17ft 2in over corner pillars (29ft 6in over fenders) and seating 26 inside, 32 upstairs and eight on balconies, a total of 66. This increased the cost by £234 per car to £895. In this revised form the order was placed with Brush in July 1914, but due to the war the first car did not arrive until May 1915. No 63 of this class is portrayed on the cover of this book.

The electrical equipment was by the Brush company and comprised two Brush 1210J 45hp interpole motors and two Brush 8B controllers. Braking was hand, rheostatic and hand-operated slipper brake. The width and height were as for cars 42-62, and there were eight scoop ventilators along the cantrail. Despite wartime conditions, they were delivered with curtains, seat carpets and cut glass lampshades. They carried side guards below the offside of each plat-

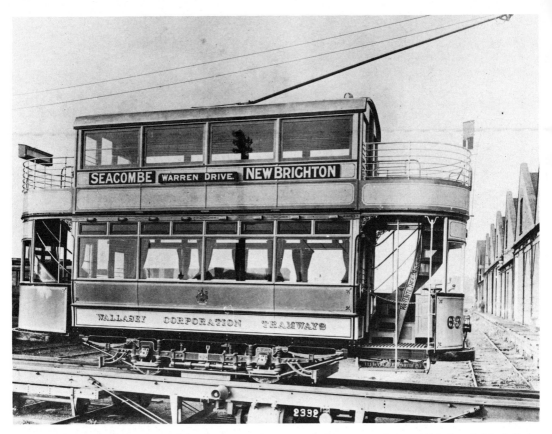

No. 63, the Wallasey tram on the cover of this book, was built by the Brush Electrical Engineering Co Ltd at Loughborough, where this picture was taken in 1915. These cars (63-68) had Peckham Pendulum P22 trucks. (*British Electrical Engineering Co Ltd*)

form, but these were later removed despite a request from the Board of Trade that all cars should be fitted. This followed the death of an infant girl who had been crushed beneath the tray on No 29 in Demesne Street.

The six cars remained in use until 1933, when 65 was withdrawn in February, 64 and 66 in June and 63, 67 and 68 in November. 68 was the official Last Tram; its controller handle and reversing key have been chromium plated and preserved. The cars were sold to Grahamsleys in 1934 and dismantled at Seaview Road. The body of 63 survived in North Wales until the 1970s, and the two decks of 65 are still in use on an industrial site in mid-Wales.

Nos 69-78 Brush Electrical Engineering Co Ltd
Four-wheel double deck, short top cover 1920

At the end of the war, the Council approved the purchase of 20 new Brush double deck cars similar to Nos 63-68, but in April 1919 they reduced the order to ten cars. The contract price was £20,600 (£2,060 per car), but inflation was constantly pushing up costs and after assembly the average cost per car was £2,307. A further decision to rebody ten cars produced tenders in February 1920 for car bodies from English Electric (£1,230), Brush (£1,385, plus £100 if using teak) and Hurst Nelson (£1,600),

whereupon the Council decided instead to reconstruct some of the original Dick Kerr cars, as already described.

Nos 69-78 arrived between July and October 1920. They were very similar to 63-68, differing only in having illuminated route letter panels and 180 degree direct stairs (instead of reversed). They were the last Bellamy-roof cars to be built in the United Kingdom, but this somewhat outmoded design was considered the most suitable for Wallasey traffic requirements. In official records these cars like 63-68 are shown as seating 66, but in practice the direct stairs permitted the balcony seating to be extended and accommodate ten persons rather than eight.

It has been stated elsewhere that Nos 69-78 were withdrawn following the closure of Seabank Road in January 1929. If so, these relatively new cars were presumably offered for sale to other tramways, but no buyer being found they were returned to service. They lasted until 1933, when 69, 70 and 74 were withdrawn in February, 71 in July and the remainder in November. They were sold to Messrs Grahamsley and dismantled in 1934; the lower deck of No 78 has been acquired for preservation.

No 26 E R & T C W Ltd, Preston
Four-wheel works car 1902

The only powered non-passenger car in the Wallasey fleet was a water car and track cleaner built in 1902 by the Electric Railway & Tramway Carriage Works Ltd, with truck and equipment identical to those of Nos 1-25. It was originally fitted with water tanks and brushes, and was employed to spray water along the tracks and clean the rail grooves. In 1905 it was decided to rebuild No 26 by removing her water tanks and brushes and fitting a van body for storing tools and towing gear for use at breakdowns. The platform ends were left open, but the roof extended the full 22ft 6in. Rail grinding equipment was fitted, with snowploughs in winter. In summer, No 26 was also used to transfer takings from Seacombe and New Brighton to the depot. Slipper brakes were fitted in 1911, with separate wheel and track brake columns. No 26 was withdrawn in November 1933 and the body is reported to have been used on a farm in Neston. At the time of withdrawal the car was painted in an overall dark green. There was also a horse car used as a works trailer, described on page 105.

Wallasey 71 of the 1920 batch of cars (69-78) at Seacombe Ferry in 1928, painted in the livery adopted in 1924. (*B. R. Miller*)

Salt and Stores Wagon

This railway type wagon was built by the United Electric Car Company for £76 and delivered in February 1911; it was fitted with a hopper for salting the track, and was usually towed by No 26 and occasionally by Nos 33-35. It was 15ft 1in long, 6ft 0in high, with a wheelbase of 5ft 6in. The internal dimensions were 12ft 10in long, 5ft 7in wide and 3ft 4in deep. It was withdrawn in November 1933.

Wallasey's salt trailer, built by UEC in 1911 and photographed here in 1934. (*Wallasey Corporation Tramways, courtesy A. E. Rimmer*)

Battery Tower Wagon (HF 3283)

This was built by Electromobiles Ltd for £1,076 and delivered in January 1925. It was fitted with a Rawlinson patent tower, mounted on a 5hp two-ton

Wallasey works car 26 at Seaview Road after abandonment. This car was rebuilt from a water car in 1905 with a van body and used as a snowplough and breakdown car. During the summer, takings from New Brighton were transferred in the locked central portion.
(*Wallasey Corporation Tramways*)

153

Wallasey's Electromobiles Tower Wagon of 1925, fitted with Rawlinson's
patent tower. It replaced a horse-drawn tower wagon.
(Wallasey Courtesy Tramways, courtesy T. B. Maund)

chassis and had solid tyres. It was capable of a top
speed of 13 miles/h.

Livery

One of the most enduring legends surrounds the
Wallasey colour sea-green. It was said that on a visit
to Seaview Road one of the officials from Preston
asked what colour the new trams should be painted.
He was told 'Oh, see Greene', a colour which the
Preston paint-shop men successfully invented. When
the first batch of cars were being off-loaded at
Wallasey station, a reporter from *The Wallasey News*
recorded that they were painted "green, with a red,
white and gold mystic monogram W. C. T. on the
side." Officially, the livery was described as sea-
green and cream outlined in gold. It was an attractive
eye-catching scheme, but subjected to sustained
sunlight and sea air it faded rapidly.

Initially, the green was very pale and the lining out
relatively simple. The green was applied to the waist
panel, dashes and stair stringers; the trucks were in
brown oxide and the fleet numbers and the inscription Wallasey Council Tramways in gold, blue and
ultramarine, the title being on the cream rocker
panel. Railings and other metal parts were either
brown or black, and the words "WAIT UNTIL THE
CAR STOPS" appeared on the inner stair stringer in
black capital letters. This was the livery applied to
cars 1-25 and 27-31.

Perhaps because the pale green faded quickly or
showed the dirt, the next deliveries had their waist
panels and dashes painted in a darker shade of green,
while apparently retaining the original pale green
around the upper deck. 37-41 had more elaborate
lining out, including trefoils in the corners of the
dashes, and their waist panels were divided into three
unequal sections; ornamental patterns were displayed between the ventilator scoops. The Brush cars
of 1910-13 mostly had their dashes and waist panels
painted in a dark apple green with double gold leaf
lining and acanthus motifs in the corners of the waist
panel, which was designed to appear as one continuous length. 45, 47 and 49-51 are known to have
entered service in this livery, but 42-44, 46 and 48
started life in the sea-green, but with the new style of
lining-out. Gradually, the darker green was applied
to some cars of series 1-36, though other shades of
green were tried, including a golden russet green and
a dark olive.

Cars 63-68, delivered in 1915, were painted in a
brighter mid-green (or leaf green) half way between
the original sea-green and the dark apple green
applied to car 45, but still apparently retained the
sea-green around the upper deck; the difference in
tone between the two decks is evident in the Brush
works photograph. Paint samples taken from a

recently-surviving lower deck have been used in
trying to re-create this 1915 livery for the drawing on
our cover. Despite the war, 63-68 were attractively
lined out with double black beading and ornamental
patterns on the main pillars. As the war proceeded
and fewer painters were employed, some cars were
hastily painted in overall unlined green whilst others
were only partially painted, e.g. 55 which ran with
one end in battleship grey. After the war, the overall
green livery (now described as blue-green) continued, but with some lining-out in silver, and no
motifs. Car roofs were generally brown or grey,
though 31-36 had started life with white roofs, and
certain earlier cars were painted similarly when first
top-covered. A few cars, including 9 and 37-40, are
remembered as still displaying the Wallasey UDC
crest after the war.

New cars 69-78 of 1920 appear to have entered
service in the same two-tone livery as 63-68, but as
the older cars were repainted they were gradually
returned to a sea-green livery. Recollections vary as
to how closely it matched the original, and several
observers state that it now had a yellowish tinge, due
perhaps to repeated coats of varnish or possibly to a
change from lead-oxide to zinc-oxide based paints.
When the new manager H H Lincoln arrived in 1923
he found four different basic liveries in the Wallasey
tram fleet, though there were probably many
differences of shade and tone. Engineer Arthur
Cocker, who joined in the same year, kept a list of the

The pre-1910 Wallasey crest and title on a car of series 1-20. *(T. M. S.)*

cars and when this was checked against paint samples from surviving car bodies there was only one discrepancy.

'Original Sea-Green': 2-6, 9, 11-16, 21, 23, 24, 27-36, 41-46, 55, 57, 59 (34 cars): Dark apple green: 10, 20, 22, 25, 47-54, 56, 58, 60-62 (17 cars): Russet green: 1, 7, 8, 17-19, 37-40 (10 cars): Midway green: 63-78 (16 cars)

Lincoln introduced a completely new livery in 1924, applying it first to car 77. The main colour became "Wallasey Yellow" (a greenish-yellow with the trade name Primrose Green), with cream rocker panels, red oxide trucks, silver-grey roofs, and brown and orange lining-out. This livery was used in all repaints from 1924 onwards, except for a short time in 1927 when a handful of cars including 6 and 71 reverted to the 'original sea-green' (to use up paint stocks ?) but with maroon oxide trucks, slate grey roofs and gold and black lining-out. A few cars, including 9 and 12, had still probably not been repainted since before 1914. Towards the end, a few cars were painted in the yellow livery with no lining-out, and in some cases the rocker panels were not repainted, to avoid using new transfers. Repainting of trams ceased in 1929 or early 1930 and many cars began to look neglected.

Anyone attempting to identify accurately the exact colours used on Wallasey trams is faced by insurmountable problems, and eye-witnesses have frequently failed to agree on an exact colour description. Perhaps the problem can best be illustrated by listing the four different liveries discovered by Mr. H. G. Dibdin when he stripped a bulkhead panel from car 45, namely (1) a top coat of final 'Wallasey yellow' with no lining-out and little varnish; (2) a very pale yellow-green fully lined out with gold leaf acanthus motifs in all corners and double orange lining out (believed to be the postwar version of 'original sea-green'); (3) after a layer of undercoat, a

much bluer green apparently without motifs but with a single lining of silver, probably the immediate postwar livery, and (4) under a thick layer of white undercoat, the original dark apple green with double gold lining out and corner motifs identical with those on preserved Leicester car 76.

Internally, all timber was french polished and then varnished. Downstairs all cars had white ceilings with ornamental borders and corner motifs, except for cars 32-41 which had brown and yellow ceiling panels with triangular patterns. The base for each light fitting was in polished oak. Upstairs, ceilings were boarded overall with narrow V-joint secret-tongued pitch pine with dark oak beading.

The following notes on tram painting were left by Arthur Cocker who joined the Corporation in 1923 and became General Foreman in 1928: 'Three coats of priming — should be white lead; then two or three coats of filling after which the surface should be smoothed out. As many coats of finish paint as the job specifies (16 coats is not too many in some jobs). Finish by varnishing two or three times. Cars should be run into the paint shop every six months and platforms, canopy tops and staircases should be dried off then painted.

Cars 1-41 originally had the fleet number painted above the headlamps. The numerals on 1-31 were similar to those used in Liverpool at the same period while 32-41 had smaller, neater numbers. The 1910 Brush cars introduced the BET practice of having fleet numbers on both sides of the headlamp; they were larger, heavily outlined and shaded. This style was subsequently adopted for the older cars, though 37-40 were not altered until 1925-26. Even the works car was given dual numbers. When the Corporation repainted the cars they placed the offside fleet numbers too far round the dash, giving the cars an unbalanced appearance; some even had the dual

155

numbers in the extreme upper corners of the dash. Starting with No 6 in 1927 the cars reverted to a single number above the headlamp but with small numbers added in the bottom left hand corner of the rocker panel. Those which still had dual numbers when withdrawn included 26, 31, 40, 41, 74, 75 and 78. Interior fleet numbers were carried on the crown boards on both decks; the Dick Kerr emblem was carried above the fleet number, but the Brush motif appeared on the upper part of the saloon doors.

Advertisements

Wallasey cars displayed a variety of advertisements virtually from their inception, the first three-year contract being awarded to A. C. Burnley in March 1902. Various-sized metal advertising plates were fixed on the upper deck sides and ends of the cars, though photographs show that many spaces were often left untenanted and they were never carried on cars 69-78. A new advertising contract for 67 cars was signed on 30 June 1923 for £1,172 per year, but with the closure of route S early in 1929 the next advertising contract was limited to 38 cars only at £25 per year each. As abandonment drew nearer the contracts were allowed to lapse and no adverts at all were carried at the end. Wallasey buses did not carry advertisements until 1952.

Destination Equipment

When the first Wallasey tram routes were opened in 1902 it was not thought necessary to provide destination indicators, since all cars going north ran to New Brighton and all cars going south ran to Seacombe Ferry. The only indication provided during the first weeks was a cardboard notice hung in the nearside window stating 'via Rake Lane' or 'via Sea Bank Road.'

Shortly after operation began, route and destination boards began to be carried, slung along the upper deck railings. At first there were five on each side, the outer two being larger and always showing 'Seacombe' and 'New Brighton' whilst the three middle ones covered intermediate streets, e.g. 'Brighton Street, King Street, Sea Bank Road'. Within a year the centre trio had been displaced by a single board, e.g. 'Warren Drive'. Sea Bank Road was later spelt as Seabank Road, and the boards remained in use until 1931.

Meanwhile, in June 1902 the cards at each end of the car were replaced by 'BEC' internally-illuminated metal destination boxes carried on the upper deck canopy railings. These boxes cost £13.10s. per pair and each one had two rear dioptric lenses to provide some top deck illumination. The apertures measured 30in by 3½in and the display showed the main thoroughfare traversed (Via Rake Lane, Via Seabank Road, or Via Warren Drive). The lettering was white on black, except for a period around 1910-14 when the colours on some blinds were reversed.

When part-way cars were introduced on a wider scale in 1905-6, small boards showing the part-way terminus were attached first to the bulkhead window rails and later to the rear dash by small brass chains, and the short-working destinations were added to the indicator blinds, all except Lloyd's Corner being followed by the word 'Only.'

Cars delivered from 1905 onwards had wooden indicator boxes, those on cars 32-40 having sloping fronts, after which they were straight-fronted. Cars 42-51 arrived fitted with four additional small roller-blind indicator boxes fitted in the nearside upper and lower deck bulkhead windows to show the route traversed; the upper deck ones were later removed, and the lower deck boxes were re-positioned in the saloon window nearest to the platform. Similar boxes were subsequently fitted to the earlier cars.

When route letters were introduced on 1 April 1913 they were painted on black enamel plates slotted into wooden holders mounted on the balcony rails, and coloured lights were fitted above the centre

Cars 52, 65 and 45 at Seaview Road in the summer of 1933, after the advertising contracts had been allowed to lapse in view of the forthcoming abandonment. The last day of tramway operation was 30 November 1933. *(R. Crafter)*

156

of the windscreens and, later, in the bulkhead of the unvestibuled cars. The codes were S for Seabank Road (purple light), RL for Rake Lane (amber light), WD for Warren Drive (white light) and P for Poulton (green light). The alternatives of W (Wallasey), WV for (Wallasey Village) and HD (Harrison Drive)had been considered for the Poulton route but rejected. Henceforth the letters were used in all departmental publicity and by local shopkeepers and landladies. In 1931 the route letter holders were moved from the balcony rails of cars 42-68 to the nearside of the vestibules where they were more accessible, and similar holders were fitted to cars 69-78, but shortly after this these cars reverted to using their illuminated route letter stencils.

After the war the destination blinds were altered to show 'New Brighton' and 'Seacombe' for the first time, and some cars of series 42-62 were fitted with large 'via' indicators in the upper part of the saloon window nearest the platform. They were made of transparent cloth tightly stretched in a wooden frame clipped to the window frame.

A further type of indicator was introduced early in 1929 above the nearside lower saloon bulkhead windows of cars 42-78 in the shape of enamel plates with two dummy clocks and adjustable hands to indicate the departure times of the ferries from Egremont and Seacombe with which the car was scheduled to connect; total cost £45. This brought the number of indicators possible on each car to a maximum of 19, though it is extremely unlikely that this number were ever used simultaneously on any car. The total is made up of two roller-blind destination indicator boxes, four small route indicator blinds at the saloon ends, the route indicator blinds in the side windows, route boards on each side of the upper deck, route letter(s) at each end, the front-end coloured light, the ferry clocks, part-way boards attached to each dash, and flags displayed when bad weather interrupted the northern ferries.

The route boards on the car sides were discontinued at the end of 1930. During the final three years, shorn of advertising material and with no route boards the cars looked increasingly unkempt and neglected.

Two different types of Wallasey ticket punch. The round one was made by the Prescott Patent Ticket Punch Co. about 1910, the other type was hired from the Bell Punch Co at £1 each per year, an arrangement also adopted by Birkenhead. (*Wallasey Tramcar Preservation Group*)

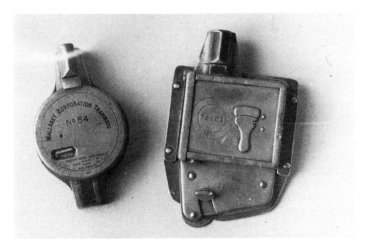

Three Birkenhead tram tickets printed by the local firm of Auto-Tickets Ltd.; 1½d (white) and ½d child (pink) of the final tram-only series, and a yellow and green through return to Liverpool by tram (or bus) and ferry, circa 1930.

157

11 Fares and Tickets

After reliability, the aspect of public transport which interests the user most is that of cost and, at a time when public transport fares have risen rapidly, it is of interest to examine the fare structures of earlier years and analyse the objectives of those who devised them. The impact of lower fares after electrification has been mentioned earlier and the underestimation of the demand which was stimulated by the lower charges created great difficulties in the first few years. When the economics of electric tramway operation were better understood, thoughts were turned towards the maximisation of returns and the filling of as many empty off-peak seats as possible. Municipal trading was a new phenomenon in most towns in the early years but not so in Birkenhead which had been operating ferries since 1842. However, whilst trading surpluses were a useful source of revenue for the Rate Fund, it was generally accepted that the duty of a municipal trading concern was to provide the best possible service at the lowest possible cost.

Electric tramway undertakings, being statutory concerns, inherited some of the obligations which had been thrust upon railway companies in earlier years. Thus all operators had maximum charging powers defined in their original Acts though these were often far in excess of what was required for many years. The spirit of the Cheap Trains Act 1883 was also applied to tramway undertakings, obliging them to provide cheap facilities for 'artisans, mechanics and daily labourers'. These concessions and the extended operating hours of municipal tramways brought mass tramway travel to the working classes for the first time.

Fare increases during the 1914-18 war were introduced as much to discourage travel as to raise additional revenue but the steep increases after the war were inevitable to meet rising costs. The deflationary measures of the early 'twenties (which included wage reductions) resulted in fares coming down and tramway fares remained stable throughout the remaining years of both undertakings. By comparison, bus fares in both towns were high — there was originally a 2d minimum — and a high differential in favour of the trams was always maintained where buses and trams shared a section of route. As bus operation became more extensive and technical improvements reduced costs, fares were progressively reduced after which they were unchanged for several years.

The information surviving in the available records differs somewhat between Birkenhead and Wallasey,

the Wallasey records being more detailed in regard to the ticket forms. This difference will be reflected in the following sections.

Birkenhead Fares Policy

Through tram and ferry tickets had been suggested by G. F. Train in 1860 and rejected by the Birkenhead Town Commissioners but social policies and support for the ferries undertaking were important facets of fare-fixing at Birkenhead from early times. The use of tapering scales whereby the rate per mile decreased with the distance travelled ensured that would-be passengers in the more distant suburbs were not priced out and this helped to alleviate overcrowding in the older parts of the town and indirectly contributed to better housing conditions for many Birkonians. Concessionary fares were aimed at first at providing cheap fares for workpeople and, second, at encouraging recreational travel, particularly to Bidston Hill.

The existence of the competitive Mersey Railway led Birkenhead Corporation to adopt a policy of through booking by tram (and later bus) and ferry. The publicity line was that ferries were healthy and (by inference) underground railways were not, but the railway had many adherents who found it more convenient to be taken to the heart of Liverpool's shopping district rather than be decanted on to a windswept landing stage. The railway company was equally alive to the attractions of cheap fares and from time to time devised many alluring offers. One of these, a 3d return between any two stations in Birkenhead (including Rock Ferry and Park), seems to have caused the Corporation less loss of traffic than might at first have been expected.

When the tramways were first electrified, through fares were generally 2d with 1d intermediate stages. The first 1½d fare was between Woodside and Palm Grove via Claughton Road and the through fare to Higher Tranmere was later reduced to 1½d. In 1903 a number of other 2d fares were reduced to 1½d and the fare for a trip round the circular route became 2d instead of 3d. Four ½d stages were introduced between Conway Street (Argyle Street) and Woodside; Market Place South (Chester Street) and Woodside; Park Street (Cleveland Street) and Woodside and Whitfield Street and Bebington Road. The first two were available in the inward direction only but the others were available both ways. Later a ½d stage was introduced between Argyle Street and Park Entrance.

On 1 July 1905 through tram and ferry return

SECTIONAL FARES.

WOODSIDE FERRY ^{TO AND}_{FROM} PALM GROVE	· ·	**3**d.
WOODSIDE FERRY ^{TO AND}_{FROM} ARGYLE STREET	· ·	**1**d.
ARGYLE STREET ^{TO AND}_{FROM} Top of PARK ROAD EAST,		**1**d.
Top of PARK ROAD EAST ^{TO AND}_{FROM} PALM GROVE	·	**1**d.

SEPTEMBER, 1890.   BY ORDER.

A Birkenhead United fare card of 1890. Similar fares (with three end-to-end penny stages) applied on the Prenton route, but the Docks route had only two 1d stages, meeting at Duke Street. *(Courtesy T. G. Turner)*

tickets were issued for the first time from Bebington Road (4d), Whitfield Street (3d) and Upton Road (4d). The latter point was the nearest stop on the tramways to Bidston Hill and right up to the end of tramway days there was a board reading 'Alight here for Bidston Hill' above the shelter there. To encourage the use of trams by picnic parties, etc. special cheap bulk-travel tickets were issued at the ferry turnstiles to parties of 20 or more at any time and to smaller parties after 1.00pm on Saturdays and Sundays at the rate of 4d per person, from June 1906. Eventually tram and ferry tickets were issued in weekly booklet form at the rate of 3s. per book of 12 for any 1d stage and 3s.6d. and 4s.6d. for 1½d and 2d stages respectively.

From 1 July 1911, workmen's mealtime 1d returns were issued between Green Lane and St. Pauls Road, available between 8.15 and 9.00am and 1.00 and 2.00pm. For the 1911-12 football season 3d Saturday afternoon excursion return tickets were introduced to Liverpool from any 1d stage and these were followed on 13 March 1912 by 2d football excursion return tickets between Central Station and Prenton Park. From 31 March 1912, 4d day excursion tickets were issued to Bidston Hill from New Ferry, changing cars at Market Place South or Woodside; from Higher Tranmere, changing at Central Station and from Prenton, changing at Balls Road East. The short-lived introduction of Laird Street-Green Lane transfer tickets in 1910-11 has been mentioned on page 53.

A timetable issued in 1910 shows through return tickets from any Liverpool Overhead Railway station to Upton Road or the Docks terminus (for Bidston Hill) at the rate of 8d (first class rail) or 6d (third class rail). "Work singles" issued up to 8.00am from a terminus cost 1d. There was also a "1d stage return" for 1½d and books of scholars' tickets available between 8.00am and 5.30pm at 18 for 1s. Another facility which was offered was for storage of bicycles, push-chairs and parcels at New Ferry

depot. A bicycle storage contract cost 2s.6d. per quarter in 1910. This, of course, was to encourage people to cycle from outlying districts and continue their journeys by tram.

During 1916, partly to discourage pleasure travel and partly to increase revenue, the majority of the concessionary fares were withdrawn. These included the Bidston Hill and football excursions, tram and ferry weekly books and the ½d stage between Argyle Street and Park Entrance. On 11 June 1917 all remaining ½d stages were withdrawn except for children under 12. Various 1d stages were shortened in length and the through fares on the Tranmere, Claughton Road and Docks routes were increased from 1½d to 2d, all intermediate 1½d fares being withdrawn at the same time.

Proposals for sharp increases in April 1919 were not fully implemented but the deteriorating finances of the undertaking necessitated a much more drastic increase when from 13 August 1921, a 1½d minimum fare came into operation, except on the first short stage from Woodside, where the fare was 1d. These 1d stages extended to Park Street (Cleveland Street), Central Station, Argyle Street (Conway Street) and Market Place South (Chester Street) and conformed approximately to the pre-1917 ½d stages. The through fares became 3½d to New Ferry, 3d to Prenton, 2½d to Tranmere, Docks and Egerton Road and 4d round the circle. Workmen's tickets were issued for 1½d single or 3d return (2d and 4d to New Ferry) and the mealtimes returns (now 2d) were issued between Market Place South and Seabank Road and Green Lane and St. Paul's Road. Certain reductions were made on 1 June 1922 and the 1d stages to and from Woodside were extended from 13 December 1923, 1d fares being reintroduced throughout the system on 1 April 1924.

Bidston Hill tram and ferry tickets reappeared at 8d, double their pre-war level, on 7 July 1922, being reduced to 6d from 18 January 1924 and a through 3d tram and ferry single between New Ferry and Liverpool, via the Rock Ferry was issued between 24 March 1924 and 31 May 1929 to silence opponents of the abandonment of the New Ferry following the accidental demolition of the pier in 1922. Stages were lengthened on the town routes from 9 February 1925. During this period there was no overall policy of through fares to Liverpool and there were many opponents who felt that such facilities would encourage Birkenhead people to shop in Liverpool.

Through 6d return tickets to Port Sunlight via the Rock Ferry and bus appeared in March 1925 but a general scale for all routes did not come into force until 1 April 1928 on the basis of 5d for 1d and 1½d stages, 6d for 2d, 2½d and 3d stages, 8d for the first 4d stages and 10d for other 4d and 5d stages. Only the 5d and 6d tickets were applicable to trams. The ferries received 2½d from each ticket. The special Bidston Hill tickets were absorbed into the new

A green card ticket to New Ferry issued at Liverpool Landing Stage, probably in 1926. A sixpenny tramway issue (KO 8617) is reproduced on page 157, punched for day of issue and clipped twice at the ferry turnstiles and once on the final tram. *(Courtesy R. Atkinson)*

scheme. Tickets were made available for return on the day of issue or the following day; later Saturday's tickets were available for return on Monday. The protagonists of road and ferry were able to point out that thousands of day trippers from Liverpool were attracted to the Corporation's services by these facilities and the benefits accruing to Birkenhead far exceeded the loss of trade which might arise from tickets issued in the other direction. Bell Punch tickets were issued on the trams but special railway type Edmondson card tickets were issued at the ferry.

Workmen's return tickets were first introduced on buses, on selected stages only, in 1925 and were gradually extended until a new scale of workmen's return fares for both trams and buses was brought into operation in 1930. This was based approximately on single fare for the return journey (minimum 2d) available up to 8.00am on weekdays and all other forms of workmen's tickets were withdrawn. New scales of children's fares were introduced in May 1929. These extended the age for reduced fares from 12 to 14 and gave a ½d fare for 1d stages on trams only and 1d fare for any greater distance. Halfpenny fares were not issued on buses until 1936.

Conversions from tram to bus almost always involved a fare increase as the bus stages were shorter. When the Claughton Road trams were replaced by buses there was a 1½d minimum over the former track and a 2d minimum on the extended section to St. James' Church but 1d fares on buses had appeared on some stages in 1924 and were in general use before the end of 1925. On later conversions there was in most cases a bus route over most of the tram route and the bus scale was adopted on the replacement service.

Birkenhead Tokens

Birkenhead seems, by British standards, to have been a major user of tokens in the nineteenth century. The adoption of tokens on trams and omnibuses was more widespread in the U. S. A. than anywhere else and it is tempting to attribute it to the American influence of G. F. Train.

It is not definitely known how tokens were used. Klapper in *The Golden Age of Tramways (Routledge & Kegan Paul, 1961)* records that on Trains's Surrey Side Street Railway in London "...the fare was 2d or eight tickets for one shilling. The advance booking tickets were oval brass tokens about 1in long with a tramcar depicted on one side". Probably the Birkenhead tokens were used in a similar manner, being sold only at the company's offices but this is not certain. A Birkenhead token in the Williamson Art Gallery and Museum, Birkenhead also depicts a tramcar and an edifice which may be meant to represent the Marble Arch or Birkenhead Park Entrance (see page 6). Possibly a common reverse was used on the tokens of all Train's lines.

As noted on page 16 books of 25 3d tickets were obtainable for five shillings. This was announced in an advertisement in the *Advertiser* of 20 May 1865. Despite the reference to "books" one can speculate that these "tickets" were actually tokens. If they were indeed tickets these may well have been the earliest British tram tickets on record.

Tokens were widely used in Birkenhead and examples are known from the Birkenhead and District Omnibus and Carriage Co. (1884-9), Theobald's Dock Omnibus (1864 -c1873), James Evans Omnibus Hero and most usefully historically from "B. T. and O. Co. Ltd.". If it can be accepted that these initials were an abbreviation for the Birkenhead United company the method of fare collection can be deduced. There are three known variants, all of which show 'CHECK WORKMANS' and the following:—

(a) Top Compartment Only — To be Placed in Box

(b) To be Placed in the Box — To be Used after 5pm Only

(c) To be Placed in the Box — To be Used after 6pm Only

These would have been used in connection with fare boxes, sealed metal boxes carried by conductors. These tokens must have been issued on the morning workmen's cars as Workmen's Checks to be surrendered in lieu of payment of fare on the return journey in the evening. These particular tokens were not pre-purchased at an office but were issued by conductors.

Whilst the above points to the use of fare boxes in the 1890s, there is strong evidence in 1879 of the use of bell punches and tickets rather than fare boxes. An advertisement in the 1879 edition of

Duncan's Manual by the Bell Punch Co. Ltd. claimed that the Registering Bell Punch was in use by a number of listed tramway companies including "Birkenhead". However, this may have referred to the Wirral Co. of whose fare collection system no evidence has survived.

Birkenhead Corporation Tickets

Tickets were used from the start; the manager, A R. Fearnley, bought the first three tickets issued on the first New Ferry car. An arrangement was made with the Bell Punch Co. Ltd. to hire punches at £1 per punch per year and for at least the first ten years tickets were printed by Bell Punch. The tickets were typical geographical issues and there were probably different sets for various routes. A through 2d ticket for the Prenton route, Storeton Road-Woodside Ferry is illustrated below.

Thereafter Birkenhead's ticket printer was Auto-Tickets Ltd. who from 1912 to about 1922 traded in Liverpool so that "L'pool" generally appeared after the printer's name in the imprint at the foot of the ticket. The company then moved to new premises in Laird Street, Birkenhead almost opposite the depot.

The tramway tickets remained geographical up to the end of World War I. During the post-war period of fare fluctuations many operators, including Birkenhead, went over to numerical stage tickets which could normally continue in use when fares and stages had changed.

From the late 'twenties separate series of tickets were issued for "Birkenhead Corporation Tramways" and "Birkenhead Corporation Motors". The tramways issue, requiring fewer stages, was shorter than the equivalent bus tickets. The tram tickets had the stage numbers arranged horizontally 1 to 10 and "Destination of Car". Above these was "Inward and Circle via Conway Street" on one side and "Outward and Circle via Borough Road" on the other. The final set comprised ½d salmon, 1d orange, 1½d white, 2d pink, 2½d dark brown and 2d workmen's return blue. The ½d was overprinted "½" in blue and the workmen's "2d W". There was also a green unpriced "Special Ticket" overprinted "L" in red which was issued by Lever Bros. to their employees.

In the mid-thirties the "Motors" series was retitled "Transport" and it is possible that these may have been issued on trams in the very last days.

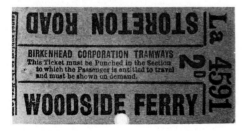

A 2d red Birkenhead Corporation ticket issued prior to 1912 on the Prenton route.

Bus/Tram and Ferry Through Returns

The 5d and 6d through tickets to Liverpool were originally titled "Tramways and Motors" and the conditions carefully reflected their dual use viz. "Issued on all trams and buses running through to Woodside and on buses running through to Rock Ferry Pier ...." During the 1930s the words "Available on one tram or bus only each way" were added to the conditions on the through returns. The subsequent "Transport" issue was used on trams and buses and both were mentioned in the conditions until 1937.

These tickets were issued in both directions and passengers originating in Liverpool bought them at the ferry terminals. Throughout the life of the tramways (and later) they were Edmondson cards. The special single to New Ferry illustrated on page 160 was also of this type.

The tickets issued on the trams and buses were punched on issue in the day of the week, clipped at the ferry and finally cancelled with nippers on the final tram or bus. All had a coloured stripe, the fare and "Adult" and a box of vertical and horizontal lines overprinted. The 5d was purple and blue and the 6d yellow and green. There were no children's through returns.

Wallasey Corporation Tickets

The general trend of tramway fares in Wallasey from 1902 to 1933 mirrored that in Birkenhead, but the fare structure was simpler as there were no halfpenny fares (adult or child) and no through bookings between trams and ferries. At the time of electrification there were only three tickets on issue on each route, viz. 1d single, 2d single, and 2d workmen's return. At first each of the three routes had its own geographical tickets, but combined three-route tickets were introduced about 1904, the 1d ticket listing the stages in groups for each route (separated by thick black lines) and the 2d divided into sections marked 'Via Warren Drive', 'Via Rake Lane' and 'Via Sea Bank Road.' The 1d tickets were green, as were most 1d issues until 1933; the 2d ticket was orange. The various alterations in fare stages between 1907 and 1913 described in Chapter 8 required some adjustment to the wording on the 1d tickets.

A higher value ticket appeared in 1911 when a 'Through Fare 3d' facility (brown ticket) was introduced with the extension of the Poulton route to Grove Road (Warren Drive). It applied to through journeys between New Brighton and Seacombe via Poulton, with or without change of car at Grove Road, and a transfer at this point was also allowed on 1d and 2d stages. Greene opposed the general concept of transfer tickets as being open to abuse, but defended their adoption on route P as "practically the only alternative to, and a minor evil compared with, the through running of cars to New

Geographical tickets of Wallasey Corporation issued before and after the Harrison Drive route opened in 1911. *(C. Kidd)*

1902, as had the horse cars before them. This revision introduced 1½d and 4d tickets, and those which followed added 2½d, 3½d and 5d values, 3d workmen's returns, and resident's prepaid discount tickets. The use of these tickets and the circumstances of their introduction have been described in Chapter 8 and the full range of colours was 1d green, 1½d magenta, 2d orange, 2½d yellow, 3d brown, 3½d pale green (or blue), 4d mauve and 5d dark olive, though at one period there were 2d light blue, 3d orange and 4d brown tickets.

A change to numerical tickets took place with the fare revision of 6 December 1920, using the wording '1st stage', '2nd stage' etc., with eight stages on the 1½d and 2d tickets and four stages on the 4d and 5d. With the re-introduction of penny stages on 9 January 1922 a further new range of tickets was introduced with plain stage numbers 1-8. 1922 also saw the withdrawal of the resident's prepaid tickets, which had been 1d (or 1½d) buff, 2d pink or 3d orange.

Some further changes occurred in the last years of the trams. Workmen's fares were temporarily discontinued with the abandonment of route S in 1929, but were re-introduced on buses and trams in 1930.

Brighton during certain hours of the day, which would have involved ruinous expense in traversing that part of the route already served by ample service."

Child tickets (1d violet; 1½d dull primrose) were introduced in 1910/11, with an age limit of 12, later raised to 14. At the same time a buff Scholars Through Ticket was introduced, prepaid and sold in packs of twelve at reduced rates. They had to be dated (in writing) by the user before handing to the Conductor, who then issued an Exchange Ticket. The same white Exchange Ticket was issued in exchange for Workmen's returns, transfers, or Post Office tickets and was originally geographical, in two versions (routes WD/WV, and routes SB/RL) and was boldly worded No Charge For This Ticket. A different yellow Transfer Exchange Ticket divided by the days of the week was issued if the homeward journey involved a change at Warren Drive/Grove Road.

When New Brighton ferry was suspended due to bad weather but Egremont was still running, New Brighton contract holders could by producing their contracts obtain a free ticket either on the tram or at the ferry toll booth; in the latter case, the conductor took it and issued an exchange ticket. The Ferry department then re-imbursed the Tramways Department. There was no such cover if Egremont was also suspended. In November 1918 New Brighton ferry was closed at peak hours due to coal shortage and special pale green tickets overprinted with a red skeleton F were issued to New Brighton contract holders giving free transport to or from Egremont.

The last batch of geographical tickets was that used from 16 December 1918 to 5 December 1920; with these, 'Parcel' was added at the foot of each column, though the trams had carried parcels since

A Wallasey fare sheet dated April 1928 as displayed in the inside bulkhead to the left of the saloon door. *(M. Jenkins Collection)*

The introduction of short-working cars to Canterbury Road (Poulton Road) in the summer was accompanied by the introduction of a further transfer (3d, red) allowing passengers to take another car on to Seacombe, and a 5d sage green ticket was introduced on 1 April 1931 for a complete journey round the Circle. A buff 2½d ticket was reintroduced on 1 April 1928. The final numerical issues showed eleven stages to cover the extended bus routes, but were also issued on trams; by this time the department's title was Wallasey Corporation Tramways and Motors.

Wallasey's tickets were supplied by two ticket printing firms at different dates. The first contract was awarded in April 1901 to J. R. Williams and Company (Liverpool) Ltd and the same firm continued to supply Wallasey until 1933, except for a change to the Bell Punch company from June 1904 to June 1908. After liquidation in 1913 Williams' firm became The Auto-Ticket Printing Co Ltd, and later Auto-Tickets Ltd when it moved to Laird St., Birkenhead. In 1918 the tickets were costing 10½d per thousand and advertising revenue from the backs was £3 per million. Punches, plates and straps were

hired from the Bell Punch Co Ltd and from Alfred Williamson of Ashton under Lyne, but in 1910-11 the Corporation bought 75 punches from The Prescott Patent Ticket Punch Company at 30s. each.

Free passes had been issued by Greene in relatively large numbers in pre-war years, as a form of extended patronage, though some were suspended during the war. The new manager H. Lincoln reduced the number, and the writer's grandfather complained bitterly when his pass was withdrawn in 1923; he had formerly been Acting Chief Librarian. The Town Clerk still issued medallion passes (56 of them) to Aldermen and Councillors, but Lincoln reduced the other passes to 129, including 85 limbless ex-servicemen, 7 totally blind residents, 4 nurses, 10 Poor Law Guardians and the editor of the *Liverpool Courier*. Free travel was also granted to uniformed Police Inspectors on duty, and to ex-soldiers and sailors attending hospital if they produced their hospital treatment card. All passes were numbered, and only holders of passes 6 to 29 (and medallion passes) were invited to ride the last car, No 68, on the night of 30 November 1933. The last waybill and a set of tickets were framed and preserved.

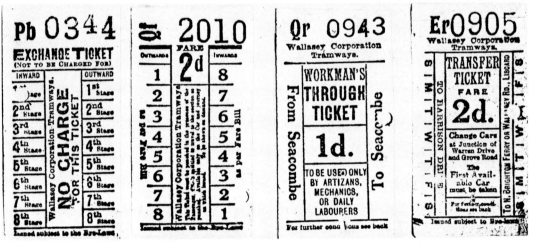

In 1920 Wallasey discontinued geographical-stage tickets and adopted the designation '1st Stage', '2nd Stage' etc. Plain stage numbers (1-8) were adopted in 1922.

Appendix 1 — Depots

Palm Grove, Birkenhead

A depot on this site was originally erected by the Birkenhead Street Railway Company 1861, but the building now occupying the site is that of 1879 and bears a stone 'Birkenhead Tramways Company 1879.' There is evidence of demolition at the rear in modern times, but the remains are insufficient to determine the track layout. Palm Grove was a large depot by 19th century standards and must have required considerable stabling, possibly on two levels. The office and omnibus stabling was at 2-4 Devonshire Road nearby, and the gable of 2 Devonshire Road still bears a stone "T. E. 1863" as evidence of Thomas Evans' occupation.

Borough Road, Birkenhead

When the Borough Road horse tramway opened in 1878, a separate depot and stables was provided. Individual stables for each route reduced the risk of equine diseases spreading throughout the system. The building was situated on the east side of Borough Road near Elmswood Road; it had two tracks and normally eight or nine cars were stationed there. Offices and a waiting room for passengers were also provided, and stabling would have been required for about 80 horses. The depot was brought into use on 11 July 1878 and it continued to serve the Borough Road route until electric cars took over on 27 September 1901.

New Ferry, Birkenhead (Bebington)

This depot and stables, built for the Wirral Tramway Co. in 1876-7, was on the east side of New Chester Road a few yards north of New Ferry Toll Bar. In later years the site was awkwardly shaped but it is possible that the rear section was added later when the fleet expanded. In its final horse days the main section, situated obliquely behind, was stabling. 90 to 100 horses would have been needed for the New Ferry route.

The electric car shed was converted in 1900-01 from the horse car shed and stables. The awkwardly shaped site measured 1,987 square yards of which the buildings occupied 1,850. 330 yards of single track was laid in two separate buildings, connected by a single line. It was necessary to widen the entrance, raise the roof and excavate pits for nine cars. Workshops, messrooms, sand drier and stores replaced the stables, and both gas and electric lighting was installed. The nominal capacity of the depot was 14 cars, but it seems likely that 17 were stationed there from 1903 and potentially 19 after 1913, less any cars away at Laird Street for maintenance or repair.

When motor buses were first operated in 1919 they were somehow squeezed into New Ferry depot. As their numbers increased the buildings were adapted, about £1,500 being spent in 1920-21 on alterations, inspection pits and the installation of a petrol tank. After abandonment of the New Ferry tram route in 1931 the buses were moved to Laird Street and the premises were demolished. A new building was erected on the site which acted both as a bus depot and bus station, and this continued to be used until closed by Merseyside PTE in 1973.

Laird Street depot, Birkenhead had nine shed tracks in three groups of three. By 25 May 1936, when this photograph was taken, most of the depot had been taken over by buses. The cars visible (left to right) are 18, 14 and works car 60. *(H. B. Priestley)*

Laird Street, Birkenhead

The main car shed for Birkenhead's electric tramways was built on the north side of Laird Street west of Brassey Street in 1900-01 and is still in use as a bus depot. The main section measured 213ft by 98ft and had accommodation for 42 cars on seven roads but a three-road extension 34ft wide was built almost immediately and the capacity increased to 60 cars. The ground sloped away to the north-east and the depot was, in effect, built on stilts, the track being supported on 18in thick concrete walls placed 10ft apart centre to centre. Advantage was taken of the topography to create storage space with headroom of 7ft below the main shed. An electric traverser was installed at the back of the shed connecting the first four roads.

The adjacent workshops were equipped with a hydraulic wheel press, a surface and screw-cutting lathe, radial drills, shaping machine, cold saw and grindstone. These and a Root blower in the smithy and a woodworking machine were powered by a 15hp electric motor. Two overhead cranes ran the full length of the shops.

In the post-1918 period various schemes were proposed to extend the depot to provide additional accommodation for trams and for the new buses which were increasing in numbers. These were deferred and the initial plan which would have cost £20,000 was replaced by one to cost £48,000. Neither was proceeded with and eventually the extensions made in 1927-8 were to provide for the needs of buses only, a separate entrance being provided in nearby Plumer Street, though after a time this was little used. As the tramways ran down sections of the depot were adapted to accommodate buses and by the last few months of operation in 1937 only four roads were available to trams.

The staff usually referred to Laird Street as North End depot, and to New Ferry as South End depot.

Field Road, Wallasey

Robert A. Busby, engineer and architect of Liverpool, a member of the well-known tramway family had produced a basic design for a combined stables and yard which could be adapted to individual sites and after approval by the Local Board in January 1879 such a building was erected on the north side of Field Road, Upper Brighton by a local contractor, Mr. Ridehalgh. The glass and zinc roofing was supplied by Busby & Co. The building comprised a central yard 124ft by 40ft with two tracks branching from just inside a 12ft wide door. Four stables each of ten stalls ran the length of the east wall except at the road end where there was a two-storey house for the Manager. On the west side was another stable for ten horses, a smithy, two loose horse boxes for isolation purposes, an engine room with a 40ft chimney, a mess room and a small office. Separate at the rear was a manure pit. On either side were

storage areas for lamps, oil and tallow whilst above there was a hay and corn loft with a cutting room. The brick-built gabled building occupied an area 136ft by 88ft.

In 1884 another stable for 20 horses was added with a large open sided wooden shed to provide accommodation for the bus fleet. A new and larger smithy was built in 1888 by W. & I. Varty. In 1890-1 a 136ft by 30ft gable-roofed extension designed by Robert Busby was built to handle the expanding bus operations; it was similar in outline but smaller than the original and it occupied the site of the open-sided shed which was demolished. It provided accommodation for 50 horses and above was a storage loft with cutting machines and a hoist. A side entrance gave access from Busby Cottages, which were built by the Company for staff employed at the depot. When the Council vacated the premises in March 1902, the former tramway buildings were sold for £1,450 to a funeral director, J. McKenna, who occupied them for many years. Remains of the track were visible until about 1960, and specimens were kept. During excavation work it was reported that workmen had uncovered a turntable at the rear of the yard. The depot buildings and Busby Cottages still survive.

Seaview Road, Wallasey

The depot for Wallasey's electric trams was erected on the east side of the municipal generating station off Seaview Road, and was built by J. H. Vickers of Nottingham to designs by the District Surveyor. It was a simple square building of 14,400 sq.ft. with accommodation for 36 cars on nine equal roads (or lyes as Wallasey called them). The three-gabled roof incorporated Heywood's patent glass panelling. In addition to overhead electric lighting a few gas street lamps were placed inside the building. The gable fronts were of wood with steel columns between each road, and steel shutters. Inspection pits ran the length of each road, and a small repair area on the north-east side was equipped with heavy lifting machinery, a wheel press, lathes and other equipment. Another section also on the north-east side acted as a paint shop. A sand drying kiln was soon purchased and an area set aside for storing sand and salt. The forecourt was unpaved until 1906 when setts were laid extending 3ft from the outer rails.

Within the depot building were a smithy, storerooms and a stable; offices and a mess room occupied the east wing. Initially the manager had a small office there until the two-storey administrative block facing Seaview Road was completed in September 1902. At the same time the depot superintendent was allocated a council owned cottage at 5s. per week. Eventually the Corporation owned several houses on Seaview Road which were rented to senior staff especially those involved in night work. The office block was extended in 1914.

Fire was an occupational hazard feared by all tramway managements. By 1905 Wallasey had only just finalised comprehensive insurance cover for all its capital equipment when late on Friday evening 23 November 1906 fire destroyed the roof of the paint shop area, damaging a number of cars and causing the loss of valuable spares. Fortunately, the fire brigade and the night staff contained the blaze within an hour. Damage amounted to £757 of which £177 was spent on repairing the scorched cars. Structural repairs to the depot were carried out by James Mills & Sons and were incorporated into existing plans for extending the building.

An extension built on the front of the depot building was completed in December 1907 at a cost of £5,416 and accommodation was increased to 68 cars. A red brick facade of ten narrow arches was added, with Kinnear roller shutters. A twin-gabled roof spanned the original nine roads and a new short three-car road on the west side. On the east, a new wing housed a separate paint and varnish shop. Road 1 held three cars, 2-10 seven cars each and road 11 (the paint shop) two cars. The total floor space was now 33,000 sq.ft. and included an electrical store, traffic office and social club with billiard tables and reading material. Commemorative stone tablets marking the original opening and the extension are still to be seen.

After World War I each route was allocated individual depot roads, which are believed to have been road 1 reserved for works car 26, the salt wagon and the former horse car; roads 2-3 route S, 4-6 WD, 7 RL and 8-9 P. Road 10 was used for storing disabled or withdrawn cars. Route letters were painted on the arches and a faint WD can still be seen.

By 1912 the cramped works area inside the depot building was inadequate and it was decided to build a separate works building east of the depot at a cost of £8,639. Work started in 1914, but due to wartime shortages was not completed until 16 June 1916 when it was immediately requisitioned for the manufacture of 18 lb shells. It was handed back for tramway use in December 1918, and was hurriedly re-equipped with new and secondhand machinery. The general repair shop had five single-car tracks, and there was a separate two-track joiners' and woodwork shop; there were also blacksmith's and armature shops, a mess room and small offices. A record survives of the kinds of wood used in the body shop — English oak for pillars, rails, waist rails and canopy bends, oak for solebars and platform bearers, spruce for platform floorings, mahogany for panels, pitch pine for platform headers and walking boards.

In a surprisingly late move, a two-track paint shop, designed for eventual use by buses, was added to the north of the works building in 1928, and the last tramcar repaints were carried out here in 1929-30. This brought the total workshop area to 5,700 sq. ft. Two tramcar controllers from cars 30 and 31 were used to drive certain DC machinery, and both were acquired many years later for the Seaton narrow gauge tramway, where one at least is still used on car 2. The works building still stands today, virtually unaltered and complete with track.

A completely separate bus garage was built on adjoining land in 1928, and following the closure of route S in 1929, road 11 was closed and converted into a traffic office. During 1931-32 part of the original depot was closed to trams and converted into a bus garage; protective gratings were placed over the tram pits. In 1935 the building was altered by knocking pairs of adjacent arches into one to allow easier access for the buses. The depot is still recognisable today, and includes some track; the office block eventually became the Wirral divisional office of the Merseyside PTE. The depot was closed on 26 October 1986 and the buses transferred to Laird Street, Birkenhead.

Wallasey's electric tram depot at Seaview Road opened in 1902 and was enlarged to the form shown here in 1907. The capacity was then 68 cars including two in the separate paint and varnish shop on the right. The cars visible are (left to right) Nos. 34, 32, 41, 7 and 37. (Courtesy M. Jenkins)

Appendix 2
Power Supply

___

Birkenhead

Birkenhead Corporation first supplied electricity in September from a plant in Bentinck Street, off Claughton Road but the Tramways department built an independent station on an adjoining site in Craven Street. With buildings covering an area of 1535 sq.yd, the station was dominated by a 128ft high chimney seven feet in internal diameter while alongside, a reservoir 28ft by 26ft by 9ft deep provided cold water for condensing purposes. Five 30ft by 8ft Lancashire boilers supplied steam to drive four Willans vertical compound condensing engines three of which were coupled to compound-wound six-pole 225kW Siemens generators and the fourth to a 500kW generator. The high pressure cylinders were 14in in diameter and the low pressure 23in; the stroke was 6¼in. The usual economiser, condensers and cooling tower were installed. Adjacent to the main switchboard there was a 'throw-over' board connecting the Craven Street plant with the Bentinck Street lighting plant so that each station could assist the other if the need arose. A separate generating plant was built at the Refuse Destructor in New Chester Road, Lower Tranmere to supply the New Ferry tram route and some lighting demand. It was similarly equipped but on a smaller scale, the total output being 450kW.

The Craven Street power station had a long life despite its obsolete plant and lack of a rail connection. Five Willans reciprocating engines and two small turbines were still available for generating 2mW in the late 1930s though since 1923 the bulk of Birkenhead's electricity had been purchased from other towns. From that year a 33kW supply came from Wallasey and in December 1931 a cable through the Mersey Railway tunnel brought Liverpool power so that by the time the Birkenhead tramways closed nearly all the supply was imported.

Both stations were handed over to the Electricity department in 1910, when the increased use of electricity for domestic purposes made the more general distribution of their output an economic proposition.

Wallasey

In Wallasey, plenty of space was available for the power station, the tram depot and administrative offices near the Council's water pumping station at Seaview Road. A small a.c. lighting station had opened in February 1897 and provision had been left for a second bay to house further machines dedicated to the traction supply. These machines were high-speed vertical compound steam engines of the all-enclosed type, directly coupled to six-pole 500V dynamos. Two sets were installed for the opening, each of 500ihp/300kW nominal capacity but capable of considerably greater output for short periods. The engines had cylinder diameters of 18in and 30in by 12in stroke.

The original boilers had been of the Lancashire type; the boiler house was common to the lighting and traction stations but was extended with more modern plant for the added load so that when the tramways opened there were four Lancashire boilers with Meldrum furnaces and one Babcock & Wilcox water-tube boiler. There were the usual economiser, condensers and cooling tower.

The main contractor for the power station plant was the Lancashire Dynamo & Motor Co. Ltd. of Trafford Park, Manchester. Although they made the two dynamos they sub-contracted the boilers, engines and other steam plant to Galloways Ltd. of Manchester and the switchboards to Ferranti of Hollinwood. The buildings themselves were erected by the Nottingham firm of J. H. Vickers (as were the tram shed and offices) but even in the power station the Council elected to do some of the work with their own men and installed the steam pipework to the new plant in a residential area. Although admirable for tramway purposes the Seaview Road site was remote from a railway. Coal was transported by convoys of horse-drawn carts, one of the contractors being R. & J. Evans, operators of the Poulton horse bus service from 1907 to 1911.

Work on a new generating station on the Dock Road near Limekiln Lane with direct access to the Seacombe branch of the Wirral railway started in 1913 and in August 1915 a 700kW turbo-generator was commissioned. Further expansion was delayed by wartime shortages. Power was increasingly in short supply and as early as 1912 a 750 bhp diesel generator had been used at Seaview Road. This was a very early application of diesel power and most unusual in these circumstances. In August 1922, a second turbo-generator was installed bringing the capacity at Dock Road to 12,000kW, sufficient to handle the town's domestic and industrial demand. By 1930-1 it was generating 60 million units of which the trams used only 1.3 million. Half the output was sold to Birkenhead where some was used to power their trams. The three 500kW rotary convertors at Seaview Road continued to supply the traction and waterworks load. There was one sub-station at Seacombe, and another at the power station.

Appendix 3
Tramways Committee Chairmen and Managers

BIRKENHEAD

Chairmen of Tramways Committee

1901 — 06	Counc. Dr. H. Laird Pearson
1906 — 07	Counc. W. G. Wall
1907 — 12	Counc. G. Proudman
1912 — 26	Ald. H. Halsall J. P.
1926 — 32	Ald. S. Vaughan J. P.
1932 — 35	Ald. H. Halsall J. P.
1935 — 38	Counc. J. Coulthard

Managers
Managers of Birkenhead United Co. and predecessors (exact dates unknown)

1864	T. M. Wiswell
1874 — 76	Robt. J. Vanderkiste
1876 — 83	Geo. Lloyd
1884 — 93	Wm. Bulmer
1894 — 97	James Murphy
1899 — 01	Fredk. Tidswell

Wirral Tramway Co. Ltd.

1877— ?	Wm. H. Stark
1896(?) — 1900	Jas. Duddleston

Corporation General Managers

1901 — 04	A. R. Fearnley
1904 — 13	W. Wyld
1913 — 42	Cyril Clarke

WALLASEY

Chairmen of Tramways Committee

1898 — 1901	Counc. W. G. Ellery
1901 — 04	Counc. Dr. T. W. A. Napier M. D., J. P.
1904 — 05	Counc. J. Braithwaite
1905 — 07	Counc. Dr. T. W. A. Napier M. D., J. P.
1907 — 08	Counc. E. G. Parkinson
1908 — 10	Counc. A. Quinn
1910 — 11	Ald. C. J. Woodroffe
1911 — 13	Counc. J. Farley
1913 — 14	Ald. J. Farley
1914 — 21	Counc. F. E. Howse
1921 — 22	Counc. S. H. Roberts
1922 — 26	Counc. W. H. T. Brown LL. B.
1926 — 29	Counc. J. G. Storey
1929 — 32	Counc. S. Panter Brick
1932 — 33	Ald. S. Panter Brick
1933 — 37	Ald. J. G. Storey J. P.

Managers of Wallasey Tramways Company/ Wallasey United Tramways and Omnibus Company

1879 — 86	Henry Busby
1886 — 1891	Robert Craig
1891 — ?	Bryan
? — 1901	Tom Hale

Council/Corporation General Managers

1901 — 23	Lt. Col. R. R. Greene T. D.
1923 — 43	H. H. Lincoln A. M. I. Mech. E., A. M. Inst. T.

Appendix 4
Staff Working Conditions (Wallasey)

Whilst the main outlines of both Birkenhead and Wallasey tramway history can be elicited from Council minutes and references in the local press, the fortunate survival of departmental correspondence and staff records for the Wallasey tramways (but not for those of Birkenhead) allows a fairly complete picture to be given of the staff side of tramway operation in Wallasey. This is therefore included as the example, and the reader is asked to bear in mind that a generally similar pattern would emerge from Birkenhead had similar details survived.

On taking over the horse tramways on 31 March 1901, Wallasey Council reduced the hours of work to an average of 62 hours per week at between 4½d and 6d per hour depending on the type of work. A contributory Benefit Society was established in July 1902 to provide sickness and death benefits. The Council made their first sick payments in May 1902 and employees were entitled to one week's annual holiday after a year's satisfactory service. At first no uniforms were issued, only cap badges, but during 1902 military style clothing with high collars and

Wallasey manager R. R. Greene (sitting centre) poses with his staff outside the 1902 depot building at the time of opening. The depot was extended forward in 1907 and given a brick-arched facade. *(S. Barton, Photographer, Wallasey)*

peaked pill-box caps was issued to platform staff together with heavy overcoats and waterproof clothing. Drivers were given gloves and conductors received whistles, cash bags and wallets. Metal 'Driver' or 'Conductor' badges and staff numbers were worn on the coat, though in everyday speech the conductors were referred to as guards. The following year light weight summer uniforms were provided including white tops for caps, a feature of the Wallasey men for years.

Discipline was strict. Greene, dressed in frock coat, bowler, wing collar and white kid gloves, would sometimes emerge from his house on the corner of Seabank Road and Rowson Street and inspect the uniforms of the early morning crews, who were expected to salute him before speaking. In 1903 a conductor who had made a waybill error accused a passenger of not paying her fare; when she complained, the Council, anxious to avoid litigation, offered her £2 which was deducted from the conductor's wages. Drivers committing misdemeanours were demoted to the back platform. Crews were also expected to prevent breaches of the bye-laws relating to spitting and drunkenness, and they were urged by the Chief Constable to admonish the many small boys who would cling to the rear dashes of moving cars.

In December 1903 the platform staff petitioned for standard rates of pay, overtime at time-and-a-quarter, promotion by seniority and and a two-shift system with alternate early and late weeks. Because the cost of living in Wallasey was considered to be high the Council agreed to increase hourly rates for drivers to 5½d on engagement, 6d after six months and 6½d after 12 months, conductor's rates being 1d

per hour less. At the time, the highest hourly rate was paid at Manchester (7d) and the lowest at Great Yarmouth (4½d). On average the men gained 1s.4d. per week. In 1905 drivers were granted bonuses paid on good conduct, freedom from accidents and power conservation at the rate of 1s per week after four consecutive six-month periods of good behaviour. In 1906 they were provided with a fully-equipped social club above the depot.

From summer 1904 the Council employed conductors seasonally. They were guaranteed a three day week (four days from 1912) and their main duties were to sell tickets to the waiting crowds at New Brighton and to work extra cars including private hire. The wage of ticket inspectors and time keepers prior to 1910 is not recorded, but in May 1910 they received a 1s. increase to a maximum of 37s. per week.

In November 1908 Greene was involved in an unusual confrontation with the staff. The dispute revolved around the speed limits imposed by the Inspecting Officers of the Board of Trade and set out in the Rule Book. Many of these limits were unrealistically low, as demonstrated by what occurred on 14 November. Driver Jackson was dismissed for 'capricious behaviour which culminated in disorganising the Seabank Road route'; what he had done was to observe strictly all the speed limits set out in the Rule Book, in protest against a new 50 minute round-trip time. He claimed to have been unfairly dismissed, and his case was referred by his union to the Board of Trade. Greene stated that the 50-minute timing had been in force since 1902 and that the 55 minute turnround last used on 8 November only applied in the summer months; he quoted distances

Wallasey driver Edwin Thomas Davies wearing the 1926-style uniform cap. He began his career with the Liverpool tramways, joined Wallasey in 1902 and drove trams until 1933. *(Courtesy Mrs. E. Mitchell)*

received full pay less their army separation allowance, whilst single men had full pay less army pay. From 18 November all serving men were paid one-third of their former salary. The bonus became 2s. to those earning from £1 to £2.5s. per week and 1s. to those earning under £1. The allowances and bonuses cost the undertaking £1,859 in the 1914-15 financial year and were later increased in line with inflation.

By November 1914, with 94 men having joined the forces, Greene advocated the employment of female platform staff. He cited those systems already employing women — Glasgow 800, Birmingham and Sheffield 300, Newcastle 200, Salford 70, and smaller numbers at Birkenhead, Oldham and Wigan. The first conductresses were recruited in early November and after a brief training assumed their duties on 15 November 1915 at a fixed rate of 5¾d per hour. Stylishly dressed in high-necked tunics, ankle length skirts and Australian-type bush hats, they were immediately popular with the public but not with their male colleagues. Each one was issued with a thermos flask, and separate toilet facilities were rented from the Ferries Department at Seacombe for £1.1s. per year.

In March 1916 the men demanded an extra ½d per hour, alleging that their earnings had been reduced since the employment of the conductresses. Greene refuted the allegation and produced figures to show that there had been little change in take-home pay. Wages at this time were 34s. to 49s. per week for drivers, 30s. to 44s. for conductors. The Council already incurred a wage bill of 2.37 pence per car mile, well in excess of Southport's 1.96d and Birkenhead's 2.10d. Angry at the Council's refusal to meet their demand, the men threatened to strike on 15 July 1916, but the threat was withdrawn.

Concluding his 1916-17 report, Greene praised the dedication and professionalism of his staff who had "rendered useful and valuable service in maintaining efficiency and smooth working." In fact the generally good staff relations had deteriorated, due in part to difficult duty rosters. The Council, aware of unrest in Liverpool, had hitherto bought peace by improved wages and bonus payments; fringe benefits included a bonus paid immediately before the annual holiday, an extra day's pay for working on public holidays, full pay for sick leave due to injury or accident whilst on duty, and one-third pay for illness for those contributing to the Superannuation Fund. Average war bonuses were now 6s.6d. per week. However, this did not prevent a threat of strike action in September 1917 when the men protested against a decision by the Council to employ female drivers; the first women were being recruited, and the first trial trips had taken place on 8 September.

On 11 September 1917, Driver Creer, Secretary of the Wallasey Tramway Workers' Union and acting independently of the Amalgamated Association of Tramway and Vehicle Workers, notified Greene that

and schedule speeds to show that the system average was 6.58 mile/h, well below the national average. With the 50 minute turnround it rose to 6.66 mile/h. The union maintained that the journey time should be 35½ minutes, an average of 4.8 miles/h and well below that achieved by the horse buses.

The Board of Trade calculated a speed of 5.05 miles/h if all stops were observed, and at the Council's request the entire system was re-appraised by Col von Donop on 17 February 1909. New limits of 12 mile/h were agreed for Church Road, Wheatland Lane, most of Liscard Road and the whole of Warren Drive as far as Portland Street, and the number of compulsory stops was reduced to nine, all at dangerous junctions or the top of gradients. Little alteration was made to the Seabank Road restrictions, and drivers continued to break the speed limits to maintain the schedules, though the low powered trams of the period were incapable of high speeds. When the Poulton route opened in 1910-11 there was a general limit of 12 mile/h, increased to 16 mile/h on parts of Grove Road, Sandy Lane, St George's Road and from St. Hilary's Church to Mill Lane (Marlowe Road). This was the highest speed allowed for hand-braked trams.

From the outbreak of war in August 1914, allowances were paid to dependents of men in the Forces and a war bonus to those still employed. From 3 August to 17 November 1914 married men unless the tuition was stopped, the men would strike the next day. Greene met a delegation of 20 men who expressed fears that the employment of women drivers would adversely affect men returning from the forces and that it was simply a way of obtaining cheap labour. Greene denied this, and warned that strike action would be illegal if the men failed to inform their union headquarters in Manchester.

By midnight Creer had galvanised sufficient support to stop any cars leaving the depot the following morning. By 7.30am only a handful had left, manned by office staff. Following telephone calls to the union in Manchester, the men presented Greene with a list of their grievances at 3pm and undertook to return to work next day. The driver training programme for women was suspended, but the Council refused to entertain the idea of equal pay for men and women, stating that 5¾d per hour for women had been fixed for the duration of the war.

The records of this incident include a complete list of the 189 staff at 30 November 1917 with their hours of work, weekly wages, and war bonus. The 63 drivers (all male) worked 60 hours for £2.2s. to £2.8s.3d. per week, the five male conductors worked 60 hours for £2.0s.9d. to £2.5s.9d., the 76 conductresses worked 54 hours for £1.14s.11d., and the supervisory staff (3 ticket inspectors, 4 timekeepers, 1 depot inspector and 1 assistant depot inspector) received between £2.12. and £2.15s. for 58 or 60 hours; the chief inspector was paid £3.12s.6d., 1s. more than the depot and works foreman. The engineering staff worked a 53-hour week at rates of £1.17s. to £2.18s., the lowest rate applying to track cleaners, labourers and truckmen, the higher rates being those paid to the joiners (3), turner, painter, blacksmith, fitter and electrician; there were also three apprentice fitters at 12s.9d. per week including 4s.9d. war bonus. The maintenance staff worked 57 hours and comprised a night foreman, a brakesman, two controller cleaners and a greaser, plus an assistant night foreman working a 66-hour week.

The end of the war found a rapidly changing situation, of which a portent was the failure of crews to report for duty on Christmas day 1918, it being union policy that there should be no service on that day. The Tramways Committee was forced to spend increasing time on industrial relations matters. In 1918 they joined the recently constituted Lancashire and Cheshire Tramways Authorities Council, whose aim was to present a united front on questions of pay, conditions, overtime, piece work and demarcation. A national agreement between employers and unions in 1919 established the principle of the eight hour day and the 48 hour week, and codified overtime and holiday entitlement. As a result of the reduction in working hours, the number of employees rose from 265 to 337.

Controversy surrounded moves by the tramway crews to persuade inspectors to join their union, and some inspectors complained of intimidation. The Tramways Committee refused to entertain the idea of inspectors belonging to the same union as the men they were meant to discipline. The matter was settled under the threat of strike action with inspectors being given the option of joining a different union if they wished.

Meanwhile, the vestiges of the wartime emergency were being swept away. The last conductresses left on 23 September 1919. After a somewhat stormy introduction, they had given excellent and popular service, in recognition of which the Council organised a social evening for all 76 ladies, together with the lady cleaners who had left in April. The war bonus payments to staff continued, costing £27,805 in 1920 and £36,119 in 1921.

On 22 April 1922 Greene concluded a local labour agreement which confirmed the 1919 national agreement but with certain amendments. A working week was defined as 48 hours with a minimum duty of 44 hours and a maximum of 52. The management was allowed to allocate temporary work if regular work was not available. In the event of a partial stoppage in the service work was to be equitably divided. Overtime rates were simplified and certain misunderstandings eliminated.

1926 was the year of the General Strike, and also the year in which Wallasey tramwaymen received new-style uniforms. The coincidence was rather unfortunate for the management. On Sunday morning 2 May the men paraded in new uniforms of dark blue serge with silver buttons and flat topped peak caps (contrasting strongly with the old uniforms with peaked pill-box caps) and before the inspection a message was read from Ernest Bevin calling on them to stop work at midnight next day. The town council, except Labour members, went to the depot at midnight to meet the men and appeal for volunteers to maintain a skeleton service, but came away empty-handed.

No attempt was made to run trams, but some buses went out, manned by volunteer crews and protected by wire netting; they were quickly immobilized in violent confrontations with the strikers. A number of employees were convicted in the magistrates' court on 14 May, two being imprisoned. A few men reported for work on 13 May and trams were run on Seabank Road with policemen or special constables riding on the platforms. Meanwhile the strikers had been dismissed and told to re-apply for employment.

On 14 May there were nine buses and eight trams on the road, and the service gradually improved until a virtually normal situation was reached on 19 May. The jailed employees were released on 17 May, but attempts by the strikers to negotiate terms of reinstatement with the Corporation failed; many volunteers were kept on, and the *Wallasey News* of 22 May said 'the service is now normal but new faces are to be

Two Wallasey tramwaymen and a non-tramway colleague standing alongside car 65 at Seacombe in 1923. This view shows the old style uniforms replaced in 1926. Note the jaunty angle of the cap worn by the tram guard (never "Conductor" in Wallasey).
(Courtesy M. Jenkins)

(Courtesy T. A. Packwood)

seen amongst both drivers and conductors.' For a primarily residential town, the strike was marked by considerable violence and the men were among some of the last tramway workers to return to work in the country.

During the conversion to buses, 125 tramway platform staff became bus drivers, five tram drivers were retrained as bus conductors, and 88 permanent and 32 temporary tram conductors became bus conductors. The other 17 tram drivers did not transfer to the buses, the Committee being told that they were 'too short in the leg' to reach the motor bus pedals.

Appendix 5 – Opening Dates of Routes

BIRKENHEAD

Route	Inspection Date	Public Opening
New Ferry (to Brandon St)	31 Jan 1901	4 Feb 1901
New Ferry (to Woodside)	27 June 1901	6 June 1901
Laird Street	13 Aug 1901	14 Aug 1901
Claughton Road	13 Aug 1901	14 Aug 1901
Higher Tranmere	13 Aug 1901	14 Aug 1901
Prenton	27 Sep 1901	27 Sep 1901
Shrewsbury Road	27 Sep 1901	27 Sep 1901
Line of Docks	24 Dec 1901	24 Dec 1901
Oxton and Claughton Circle	17 Feb 1902	2 Mar 1902

WALLASEY

Route	Inspection Date	Public Opening
Rake Lane	14 Mar 1902	17 Mar 1902
Seabank Road	14 Mar 1902	19 Mar 1902
Warren Drive	17 May 1902	17 May 1902
Poulton (to St. Lukes Church)	8 July 1910	8 July 1910
Poulton (to Grove Road)	7 Feb 1911	7 Feb 1911

Appendix 6 — Statistical Tables

BIRKENHEAD CORPORATION TRAMWAYS

Year Ending 31 March	Revenue £	Passengers Carried	Miles Run	Passengers Per Car Mile	Average Fare Per Passenger d
1901	2,143	182,903	16,434	11.13	2.82
1902	31,594	6,456,361	718,726	8.98	1.18
1903	52,876	10,535,765	1,279,087	8.24	1.21
1904	56,074	11,598,980	1,349,702	8.60	1.16
1905	55,026	11,400,334	1,309,903	8.71	1.16
1906	54,595	11,354,283	1,319,079	8.61	1.16
1907	55,408	11,696,691	1,324,743	8.83	1.14
1908	55,937	11,932,895	1,299,776	9.18	1.13
1909	56,112	12,124,297	1,278,015	9.49	1.11
1910	57,597	12,283,344	1,201,476	10.23	1.13
1911	59,024	12,640,261	1,207,761	10.47	1.12
1912	63,651	13,273,858	1,225,544	10.83	1.15
1913	65,653	13,622,361	1,235,277	11.03	1.16
1914	72,108	15,167,958	1,300,717	11.67	1.14
1915	65,785	14,822,697	1,209,117	12.26	1.07
1916	72,821	16,676,022	1,176,951	14.17	1.05
1917	80,748	17,950,433	1,186,186	15.14	1.08
1918	97,838	20,538,476	1,219,250	16.85	1.15
1919	114,974	23,942,837	1,229,610	19.48	1.16
1920	148,179	22,836,034	1,275,022	17.91	1.56
1921	152,304	21,182,390	1,286,921	16.46	1.73
1922	137,845	17,966,065	1,150,558	15.62	1.85
1923	126,300	17,117,170	1,149,424	14.90	1.77
1924	125,565	17,617,852	1,171,453	15.04	1.71
1925	123,322	20,341,820	1,207,506	16.85	1.46
1926	122,305	20,832,164	1,245,353	16.73	1.41
1927	111,577	19,092,982	1,223,980	15.60	1.41
1928	113,634	19,607,155	1,257,571	15.60	1.39
1929	98,764	17,340,618	1,215,790	14.27	1.37
1930	88,707	16,683,135	1,185,685	14.07	1.28
1931	78,621	16,558,542	1,177,314	14.07	1.14
1932	66,742	13,982,124	1,073,222	13.03	1.15
1933	52,535	11,003,409	870,056	12.65	1.15
1934	51,500	10,771,572	867,574	12.42	1.15
1935	41,853	8,750,905	727,635	12.03	1.15
1936	28,942	5,939,560	501,449	11.85	1.17
1937	27,731	5,597,747	501,832	11.16	1.19
* 1938	8,182	1,661,693	149,404	11.13	1.19

* 3½ months only

WALLASEY CORPORATION TRAMWAYS

Year Ending 31 March	Revenue £	Passengers Carried	Miles Run	Passengers Per Car Mile	Average Fare Per Passenger d
1903	31,475	5,685,182	654,742	8.68	1.33
1904	35,873	6,564,493	757,688	8.66	1.31
1905	38,768	7,142,881	778,851	9.17	1.30
1906	40,571	7,528,337	819,216	9.19	1.29
1907	43,608	7,995,451	862,123	9.27	1.31
1908	43,824	8,331,038	891,540	9.34	1.26
1909	46,372	8,977,726	932,001	9.63	1.24
1910	47,640	9,387,665	945,948	9.92	1.22
1911	50,418	9,990,653	1,059,629	9.43	1.21
1912	58,107	11,459,807	1,227,935	9.33	1.22
1913	58,022	12,352,006	1,261,855	9.79	1.13
1914	63,713	13,105,204	1,291,046	10.15	1.17
1915	64,505	13,555,876	1,284,938	10.55	1.14
1916	66,321	14,306,621	1,231,469	11.62	1.11
1917	70,756	15,125,641	1,249,809	12.10	1.12
1918	82,562	17,111,453	1,284,647	13.32	1.16
1919	100,078	19,354,654	1,273,333	15.20	1.24
1920	130,239	21,435,873	1,465,595	14.63	1.46
1921	138,204	20,806,448	1,398,436	14.88	1.59
1922	144,927	17,773,244	1,379,739	12.88	1.96
1923	135,964	17,745,218	1,329,953	13.34	1.84
1924	122,963	19,918,359	1,414,855	14.08	1.48
1925	128,134	21,009,303	1,402,848	14.98	1.46
1926	129,641	21,292,638	1,414,768	15.05	1.46
1927	118,848	19,729,922	1,392,855	14.17	1.45
1928	122,531	20,441,380	1,421,140	14.38	1.44
1929	105,242	17,981,159	1,309,014	13.74	1.40
1930	68,240	12,142,667	931,355	13.04	1.35
1931	61,832	11,352,416	909,549	12.48	1.31
1932	46,602	8,734,638	761,983	11.46	1.28
1933	40,503	7,617,852	708,282	10.76	1.28
* 1934	17,756	3,356,089	335,768	10.00	1.27

* 8 months only

Acknowledgements

The authors acknowledge with gratitude the valuable assistance of the following:—
J. N. Barlow, W. H. Bett†, R. G. Brown†, A. Cocker†, M. Colebourne, R. Crafter, D. S. Deacon, H. G. Dibdin, H. Evans, R. Evans, N. N. Forbes†, S. Forrester, J. C. Gillham, W. Gratwicke†, R. S. Griffiths, J. B. Horne, Mrs Jean Jenkins†, R. S. Jones, C. Kidd, A. K. Kirby, K. P. Lewis, R. T. McMahon, E. Nicolson, G. Parry, E. R. Pollard, N. Porter†, J. H. Price, H. B. Priestley, D. Randall†, D. Redmond, A. E. Rimmer, C. Rycroft, E. V. Shaw, V. A. Shaw, K. W. Swallow, T. G. Turner.

The Staff of:—Beaulieu Motor Museum, The House of Lords Record Office, Merseyside P.T.E., Public Record Office, Wirral Borough Libraries, especially David Thompson, the Archivist.

The authors have received especial help from the late Jerome McWatt and A. D. Packer in providing many previously unpublished photographs.

T. A. Packwood has kindly made available his original and detailed research into the early history of both undertakings and carried out valuable further research at a late stage to resolve some outstanding queries, whilst A. S. Clayton has provided much detail relating to the Wallasey system, particularly the tram fleet. R. Atkinson kindly supplied certain tickets and the accompanying text which has been incorporated in Chapter 11.

The authors wish to express particular gratitude to John C. Gillham for his work in preparing the maps. His expertise in this field is well known and the authors were fortunate to secure his services.

The authors have consulted the following publications and other documents:—
Birkenhead and Cheshire Advertiser
Birkenhead News
Bus and Coach
Gore's Directories
Light Railway and Tramway Journal
Liverpool Courier
Liverpool Daily Post
Liverpool Echo
Liverpool Mercury
Modern Tramway
Modern Transport
Motor Transport
The Journal of Transport History
Tramway and Railway World
Tramway Review No. 9
Wallasey News
Wallasey and Wirral Chronicle
Local Transport in Birkenhead and District, 1959 (T. B. Maund)
Local Transport in Wallasey, 1969 (T. B. Maund)
West Coast Steamers (Duckworth and Langmuir)
Wirral Railway (C. Highet)
Various Minute and Report Books of the constituent undertakings including the Wallasey Tramways Manager's Report Books
Reports of the Inspecting Officers of the Board of Trade
Birkenhead Corporation Transport Department, 50 years of Municipal Transport 1901-1951

The authors wish to thank past members of the former Wallasey Tramcar Preservation Group as well as present members of The Friends of Birkenhead 20 and those members of the Merseyside Preservation Society involved in restoring Wallasey 78. This work is dedicated to their skill and determination.

With a view to publishing an Addendum in *Tramway Review* the authors and publishers would welcome any additional information on either system, especially the horse tramways, and any previously unpublished photographs.

The Last Car for New Brighton

This postcard by the Cynicus company of Tayport, Fife appeared in many towns, bearing a local place-name. It started at New Brighton, and the tram was always shown in Wallasey's pale green livery. *(Courtesy J. J. Herd)*

Index